REVOLUTION

Volume 14

HUNGARY 1956
REVISITED

HUNGARY 1956 REVISITED

The Message of a Revolution – A Quarter of a Century After

FERENC FEHÉR
and
AGNES HELLER

LONDON AND NEW YORK

First published in 1983 by George Allen & Unwin Ltd

This edition first published in 2022
by Routledge
4 Park Square, Milton Park, Abingdon, Oxon OX14 4RN

and by Routledge
605 Third Avenue, New York, NY 10158

Routledge is an imprint of the Taylor & Francis Group, an informa business

© 1983 Ferenc Fehér and Agnes Heller

All rights reserved. No part of this book may be reprinted or reproduced or utilised in any form or by any electronic, mechanical, or other means, now known or hereafter invented, including photocopying and recording, or in any information storage or retrieval system, without permission in writing from the publishers.

Trademark notice: Product or corporate names may be trademarks or registered trademarks, and are used only for identification and explanation without intent to infringe.

British Library Cataloguing in Publication Data
A catalogue record for this book is available from the British Library

ISBN: 978-1-032-12623-4 (Set)
ISBN: 978-1-003-26095-0 (Set) (ebk)
ISBN: 978-1-032-14698-0 (Volume 14) (hbk)
ISBN: 978-1-032-14701-7 (Volume 14) (pbk)
ISBN: 978-1-003-24061-7 (Volume 14) (ebk)

DOI: 10.4324/9781003240617

Publisher's Note
The publisher has gone to great lengths to ensure the quality of this reprint but points out that some imperfections in the original copies may be apparent.

Disclaimer
The publisher has made every effort to trace copyright holders and would welcome correspondence from those they have been unable to trace.

As with the Czechoslovakia of 1968 and the Poland of 1981, the eyes of the world were on the Hungary of October-November 1956. The Hungarian Revolution was a turning-point, a lost opportunity for world change. Tragically, criminally perhaps, it showed the West prepared to respect the unprincipled provisions of the Yalta-Potsdam agreements. And three years after Stalin's physical death, it signalled the political death of the particular form of communism he had imposed on Eastern Europe in the late 1950s.

Hungary 1956 Revisited is not a descriptive chronicle of events; there are many of these. It is a radical reinterpretation of the Revolution in the context of world politics and Eastern Europe as a whole. It is radical in a double sense. It reveals totally new features and angles on an event which went beyond the simple question of a people having had enough of communism. Brand-new protagonists appear on the scene: General Serov, the first head of the KGB, Ambassador Andropov who started his career in beleaguered Budapest, Istvan Bibo, the great non-doctrinaire socialist and architect of a new consensus. Old acquaintances appear: the martyr of the Revolution Imre Nagy, the first Eurocommunist, who returned usurped power to his people – and the favourite of the Western Press, 'the liberal' Janos Kadar who betrayed and crushed the Revolution and gave at least his name to the reprisals.

At the same time, Fehér and Heller are radical in the other sense that they write from a resolutely Leftist position, relying on witnesses and participants for their rigorous documentary backing. Theirs is a passionate polemic, written with commitment to the greatest workers' uprising of post-war Europe. Theirs is a condemnation both of the West in 1956, and of Kadar's Hungary today – a regime which they insist has merely been consolidated, never legitimised.

Agnes Heller and Ferenc Fehér left Hungary in 1977, after a long record of dissidence. Agnes Heller is presently Reader in Sociology at La Trobe University, Melbourne, Australia. Both she and Ferenc Fehér are authors or joint authors of a number of books on socialism and socialist society.

Hungary 1956 Revisited

The Message of a Revolution – a Quarter of a Century After

Ferenc Fehér and Agnes Heller

London
GEORGE ALLEN & UNWIN
Boston   Sydney

© Ferenc Fehér and Agnes Heller, 1983.
This book is copyright under the Berne Convention. No reproduction without permission. All rights reserved.

**George Allen & Unwin (Publishers) Ltd,
40 Museum Street, London WC1A 1LU, UK**

George Allen & Unwin (Publishers) Ltd,
Park Lane, Hemel Hempstead, Herts HP2 4TE, UK

Allen & Unwin, Inc.,
9 Winchester Terrace, Winchester, Mass. 01890, USA

George Allen & Unwin Australia Pty Ltd,
8 Napier Street, North Sydney, NSW 2060, Australia

First published in 1983.

British Library Cataloguing in Publication Data

Fehér, Ferenc
 Hungary 1956 revisited.
1. Hungary—History—Revolution, 1956-
2. Hungary—Politics and government—1945-
I. Title   II. Heller, Agnes
943.9′052   DB957
ISBN 0-04-321031-7

Library of Congress Cataloging in Publication Data

Fehér, Ferenc, 1933-
 Hungary 1956 revisited.
Includes index.
1. Hungary—History—Revolution, 1956. 2. Hungary—History—Revolution, 1956—Influence. 3. Europe, Eastern—Politics and government—1945-. 5. World politics—1955-1965. I. Heller, Agnes.
II. Title.
DB957.F42 1983   943.9′052   83-10577
ISBN 0-04-321031-7

Set in 11 on 12 point Plantin by Bedford Typesetters Ltd,
and printed in Great Britain
by Billing and Sons Ltd, London and Worcester

Contents

Preface	*page*	vii
Acknowledgements		xviii

1 The Impact on the World — 1
   (i) The Hungarian Revolution and Superpower Politics — 1
   (ii) The Soviet Post-Stalin Internal Fight and the Hungarian Revolution — 24
   (iii) The Hungarian Revolution and the Western Left — 42
   (iv) The East European Context — 49
   Notes: Chapter 1 — 67

2 The Impact on Hungary — 75
   (i) The Hungarian Revolution: A 'Simple Matter'? — 75
   (ii) Was the Revolution Necessary? — 86
   (iii) The New Republic — 97
   (iv) Imre Nagy: A 'Kerensky in Reverse', an Inconsistent Bolshevik, or a New Type of Socialist Radical? — 115
   (v) Violence in the Revolution — 136
   (vi) Kádárist Hungary: The Product of a Crushed Revolution — 147
   Notes: Chapter 2 — 159

Index — 170

Dedicated to the memory of the victims

Preface

Generally speaking, adding any kind of preface to a book is a questionable practice – at least, any preface which contains more than technical information or acknowledgements. Anything else would seem to be a futile attempt to apologise for this or that feature of the text which, if it does not stand on its own, cannot in any case be protected by a preface. But in this particular case certain aspects of our presentation of the Hungarian revolution need some introduction.

First of all, we should like to dispel any appearance of Hungarian nationalism and a hypertrophy of Hungarian self-advertisement. True, we have stated repeatedly and from several viewpoints in this book that Hungary *in 1956* played a world-historical role. The Hungarian revolution was the first to assault the unjust and oppressive world-system created by the signatories to the Yalta and Potsdam agreements. It was the Hungarian revolution that taught the lesson, after too long a period of belief to the contrary, that a totalitarian regime can be toppled from within. Hungary in 1956 and her revolution put an end to the illusion of the Popular Front policy. The Hungarian revolution triggered the exodus of the communist intellectuals from their parties.

Is to say all this to say too much? Is this a fair description of the events within the limits of realistic assessment? There is an undeniable tendency in many (if not all) individuals to aggrandise the events of their own lives. Similarly, there is a tendency in the members of most (if not all) national communities to assign an exaggerated importance to everything that happens to them, while we have to admit that objectively there are in fact very few national communities in history whose 'life processes' exert continuous impact on humankind as a whole. Let us set the record straight at this crucial point: we have never entertained illusions regarding such a *continuous* world-historical role for Hungary; but we have two firmly held opinions on the matter.

The first is that there are national communities in the East European region under Soviet domination which have played –

once or several times – a world-historical role, and there are others which have not. This is said without the slightest sense of chauvinism or national superiority, but as a simple statement of fact. If there is one national community which has had a prime world-historical role in this region since the conclusion of the Second World War, it is certainly Poland. There was one moment – obviously between January and August 1968 – when Czechoslovakia occupied a similar position. In October–November 1956, Hungary had her finest hour. On the other hand – and this is said with full respect for the people living in these countries – there was *no* moment in which Bulgaria, Romania and Albania would have fulfilled such a function, and East Germany has her historical role elsewhere. But at least once the clock of world history ticked in Hungary, and it is about this moment that we have written our book.

Our second firm view pertains to Hungarian history in its strictest sense. For reasons which are partly clear and partly unclear to us, this history has always evolved in 'explosions', and it was between two such explosions that the clockwork of history seemed to have stopped. In contrast to geographically and numerically small, but politically continuously influential, countries (such as the Netherlands over nearly two centuries) Hungary made her appearance in modern history on only three occasions, in 1848, in 1919 and in 1956 – in all three instances in the form of spectacular political revolutions. Attitudes to these events can differ from one event to the next (ours is, for instance, a respectful distance from 1848, a most critical distance towards 1919, and a not uncritical but undeniably passionate identification with 1956), but the fact remains that Hungary appeared to an astonished world in the fury and fireworks of revolution, then disappeared again for a long time. If we were historical organicists, we should be inclined to say that such energies have been accumulating in the 'body' of this national community to explode with one powerful blast. In the period of accumulation not much is to be perceived; in the hour of explosion we are blinded by the released energies. But instead of such organicist rhetoric we simply state the fact of the 1956 climax of Hungarian national history: the interplay of inner and external factors was acted out on a level having universal importance.

A further problem dealt with here can be summed up as follows. We state – repeatedly but also separately in a concluding chapter –

that Kádár's regime, born out of a murdered revolution, is *not* a compromise but goal-rational oppression. It is, in our view, firmly consolidated but *not* legitimised. In contrast to this judgement, nearly the whole of the Western press hails János Kádár, undeniably the best statesman in Eastern Europe since the death of Tito, as the creator of the 'relatively freest regime in Eastern Europe'. Is, then, our verdict not a product of what the cynical German journalism calls *Dissidenteneifer*, the false zeal of the dissident? To begin with, let us state that we are not so much defending ourselves as we try to present our *case* convincingly in a book – written with affection and, undeniably, with hatred, too – but before we touch upon the crux of the matter let us make a *pragmatic* statement: if we had to choose a domicile, and if we had options only among East European nations, then we would also choose Hungary for our place of residence. But such a hypothetical–pragmatic decision cannot exhaust the matter entirely.

We believe that all people who insist on having *elected* governments at home and would not be satisfied with anything less, but who, nevertheless, suggest that we admit the legitimacy of a government which was endowed by foreign tanks and never went anywhere near the polls, make the mistake of confusing *pacification* with *legitimation through compromise*. Undeniably, Kádár's Hungary is solidly pacified (and that has been stated by us several times) in the deeper and very disconcerting sense that the majority of the population, quite obviously hostile to any variant of communism, is clearly convinced on simple observation that *within communist systems* this is the most tolerable that they can have. Therefore, a considerable part of the populace plays hand in glove with the government without accepting any fundamental principle of the regime. But this is *not* compromise, not even in the most problematical sense as was the nineteenth-century *Ausgleich* between Hungary and the rest of the Habsburg monarchy. In the text we have tried to point out certain features of a genuine compromise, such as the relative autonomy of the bargaining partners, social options guaranteed as rights, and the like. In this sense, and despite everything that should be criticised in it, Yugoslavia has, and Hungary does not have, a system based on the compromise between the ruling apparatus and the rest of the populace.

In addition, and more important, the Kádárist 'secret', or 'spell', does not, of course, lie simply in shrewd tricks, some of which have been mentioned in our essay. The main reason for the *pax Dei* reigning supreme in Hungary is the sociological constellation that *Kádár's Hungary is the only Khrushchevite country in a post-Khrushchevite environment*. This, in one word, is a summary of Kádár's statesmanship; and this 'Khrushchevite' feature is valid both in a personal and in a sociological sense. Kádár himself, even if with some reluctance, was 'hand-picked' by Khrushchev; and the two politicians, neither of them excessively sentimental, became so close that, after the *coup* against Khrushchev, Kádár committed what is a mortal sin for any politician in the Warsaw bloc: he spoke up *publicly* for the overthrown man. His 'anthropological contempt' for the troglodytes who came after Khrushchev can be seen in his remark to Dubcek at the last moment before the intervention, as reported in Z. Mlynář's *Night Frost in Prague* (London: Hurst, 1980): 'Do you *really* not know the kind of people you're dealing with?' he asked incredulously of his Czechoslovak colleague. In a broader sociological sense, in the darkness of Brezhnev's conservative social immobilism Kádár's Khrushchevism means the preservation of Khrushchev's experimentalist spirit, of at least the *claim* (not necessarily the practice) of some rationality, a limited but undeniable respect for the consumer in man, a cynical belief in the de-ideologised everyday life of the 'man in the street' (which, given the level of the officially obtainable ideology, certainly is a relief). All this, let us repeat, when measured against the background of Brezhnev's Eastern Europe, with its agricultural crises and famine mutinies arriving on schedule, certainly has a salutary air. But Khrushchev is a hero in our book, too, and *a fairly negative one* at that. It is one of the lessons of this book that the man who raised high hopes about the moral and political regeneration of socialism disappeared unlamented even by those who were originally ready to commit themselves to his policy objectives. Whatever Kádár's *relative* position as the only Khrushchevite may be (that is, relative to other, wholly insensible, regimes of oppression), he is not the proponent of, but a traitor to, any self-regeneration of socialism – through his role in 1956, his betrayal of the Prague spring, his regime of an enlightened police state which he himself describes as *essentially identical* with others in Eastern Europe. This is undeniably an argument of the socialist to other socialists. Those who are not susceptible to such arguments, but nevertheless praise Kádár's 'free Hungary', should ask themselves whether they would like to live in a police state, even if it is an enlightened one?

And here we come to our final point. Why do many non-communist Western observers lionise Kádár and his regime? In this respect we have to deal with several motives – and, frankly, few of them are particularly attractive. We once heard the strangest of all from an English gentleman: 'What is finally your problem with your government,' he exclaimed, 'a government which ensures order? The workers cannot make a damned Bedlam of the whole society as they can here in Britain.' In the given case the basis of elective affinities – namely, a reciprocal sympathy of the partisans of authoritarian governments – is very clear. But often we have to do with more refined motivations which are, however, not necessarily any better. 'Well, *down there*, this is the absolute maximum the poor chaps can have' – this is a typical version of Western attitudes which combines condescension, if not outright contempt, for this 'backward' area with a total indifference towards the fate of others. In addition, this condescension has an ominous history in Eastern Europe: a number of marshals, kings, regents and admirals were imposed on these countries following the First World War by similarly condescending Western gentlemen; by statesmen who believed that 'at home' everything must be liberal but 'down there' various forms of authoritarian rule are the absolute maximum the poor chaps can, and should, have.

A further, more complex, case is the Western feeling born out of the fiascos of anti-Stalinist revolutions and of the Western co-responsibility for such fiascos. The proponents of such views actually project their feeling of impotence into a positive channel – into the acknowledgement of the regime which, despite all, 'has produced something'. It is admittedly not yet freedom, they remark, but it may slowly develop into it. Thus they convince themselves. Poland, December 1981, will presumably not convince these partisans of 'gradual freedom for others'.

Finally, there are those who simply do not wish to put themselves in a Cold War position, and even if they are ready to condemn, say, Czechoslovakia or Honecker's 'workers' state' they are content to accept Kádár's *pax Dei*. They are not adopting a totally negative attitude towards Eastern Europe, *therefore* they are not adopting a Cold War position. The problem is too complex to be dealt with extensively here. Further, the assessment of the individual members of such a typology has, perforce, to be different.

In the last two cases, the motives are obviously respectable: people in such cases are led either by a feeling of guilt or by a desire to avoid placing themselves in a difficult position. None the less, we firmly believe that the cost of transcending the ideology and practice of the Cold War cannot be reimbursed, as it were, by finding a 'pet socialism' – a socialism which, if not actually humane, does at least have an acceptable face. To cut a long and very complex story short – perhaps too short – the critical, even hostile, attitude to 'real socialism' only becomes a Cold War attitude if it is coupled with, or channelled into, an attitude supporting inner repression in one's own country. Without this, a perfectly legitimate critical attitude need not purchase its clear conscience by adoring János Kádár's enlightened police state.

The Hungarian revolution is now a distant, nearly mythological event even for the people who followed its short and explosive course twenty-six years ago from newsreels and journals. In addition, this book is an interpretation, not a chronicle; so it would be only fair to give a brief summary of the main events and a short catalogue of the protagonists by way of introduction.

The story of the revolution started in March 1953 when Stalin died and his heirs, left alone without clear instructions for the first time, had to make decisions of their own. The first decision affected Hungary in June 1953. Three members of the so-called 'four-member leadership' of Hungary's arch-Stalinist dictatorship – Mátyás Rákosi, First Secretary of the Party and Prime Minister, Ernő Gerő and Mihály Farkas – were summoned to the Soviet Political Bureau in Moscow. The fourth member, József Révai, remained at home, but the other three were joined, on Soviet orders, by an unexpected companion, apart from István Dobi, the nominal head of state and Béla Szalai, Rákosi's secretary: Imre Nagy, then Minister of Natural Taxation. The result was a dramatic and quite unexpected leadership reshuffle. Rákosi remained First (or General) Secretary; but Nagy was now appointed as a partner in the leadership – namely, Prime Minister – by the June 1953 session of the Hungarian Central Committee. His 'new policy speech' in Parliament in July 1953 contained a wholesale condemnation of the Stalinist policy in Hungary, in particular the police terror and the forced collectivisation of the peasants' land.

The next two years were characterised by two events, one of them public, the other 'behind the scenes' (even if circulated by rumour to a very large extent). The public event was the famous 'revolt of conscience', the disobedience movement of Hungarian writers and journalists. The majority of them were communists in important positions in the ideological machine, some of them personally responsible for the Stalinist propaganda of the previous years. The participants in the movement felt that they were morally bound, both individually and as a group, to expose the official propaganda and its lies, including their own part in it. The struggle behind the scenes took place in party committees, primarily in the Central Committee and its apparatus. It was a fight between Nagy and his very small number of genuine supporters and the overwhelming majority of the apparatus, nearly all of them supporters of Rákosi, who had quickly recovered from the first shock of the decisions taken in Moscow and who embarked on a sabotage campaign against the new political course. For reasons which are to some extent analysed in our book, the latter were victorious and the March 1955 session of the Central Committee branded Nagy's policy as rightist deviation. Nagy was divested of all his official positions in April and expelled from the party in December.

The resolute measures of the Stalinists did not quell the mutiny, which took an organised form in December 1955. The public framework of revolt was provided by the so-called Petőfi Circle, a club for political debate which started its programme in March 1956 and went on attracting an ever wider audience until the day of the revolution. Leading Hungarian writers and journalists (Tibor Déry, Gyula Háy, Miklós Gimes, Tibor Méray, Tibor Tardos and others) and surviving victims of the Stalinist terror (Julia Rajk, widow of the executed party leader László Rajk, Ferenc Donáth, Géza Losonczy) made shattering speeches there to expose, in no uncertain terms, the crimes committed in the previous years as well as the personal responsibility of the Rákosi leadership for these crimes. The Writers' Association continued its revolt. The presidium of the Association condemned the institution of censorship in a memorandum demanding complete freedom of artistic activity addressed to the leading party organs in October 1955. In addition, the most prominent Hungarian writers took a public stand on behalf of the political comeback of Imre Nagy – beginning with Tibor Déry, who was expelled from the party for his 'anti-party activity' in the summer of 1956.

Unexpected and unintentional support was lent to the

Hungarian rebels by the Soviet leaders. Khrushchev's so-called 'secret speech' at the 20th Congress of the Soviet Communist Party, February 1956, condemning Stalin's 'violations of socialist legality' could only be interpreted in Hungary as a verdict in the case of Rákosi. The Poznan revolt of the Polish workers, in June 1956, and the promises of reform of the Polish leadership following closely on its heels – the first of their kind in a very long and far from concluded chapter of history – were regarded in many Hungarian circles as a forewarning of what course events would take if there were not a radical change of leadership. The Soviet–Yugoslav reconciliation was an added, accelerating factor. There could be no mistake about Tito demanding the heads of the organisers of the anti-Yugoslav campaign – in the first place, that of Rákosi, who with his show-trials proved indeed to be the best pupil of Stalin. All this resulted in a momentous but clumsy and unsatisfactory (because half-hearted) Soviet decision in July 1956. After too long a hesitation they dismissed Rákosi and appointed Ernő Gerő, the second man of the Rákosi leadership, as the First Secretary of the party. True, János Kádár, an imprisoned victim of Rákosi's terror and, in comparison with Rákosi, a moderate, joined the party leadership with some of his partisans, but that was not enough of a concession to a population whose spirit was nearing boiling-point. Events now proceeded irresistibly towards an explosion.

Once again the ultimate catalyst was Poland. When the news reached Budapest on 21 October that, even though the Central Committee of the Polish Communist Party had appointed Gomulka (as people then believed, the Polish Imre Nagy) as First Secretary of the Party, the Soviet army still surrounded Warsaw because the new leadership was no guarantee for them against 'counter-revolution' and was instead seen as an aggregate of doubtful, if not outright suspect, politicians, the Petőfi Circle and the university students decided to organise a demonstration in support of Poland. After a mass rally on 22 October 1956 the students of the Budapest University of Engineering issued a sixteen-point resolution demanding the democratisation of Hungary and the political return of Nagy. At this point an act of solidarity turned into the overture to Hungary's own revolution.

Next day, in the early hours of the afternoon, 300,000 demonstrators marched through the streets of Budapest. Initially, they demanded only the reinstatement of Nagy as Prime Minister, but the originally modest slogans were gradually expanded into a demand for political democracy in general and the independence of Hungary in particular. The official reaction to the demonstration was confused and hysterical. Party leaders and personal friends convinced an irresolute Imre Nagy, then still a private citizen with no official mandate, to calm the rebellious crowd with his personal authority – an action which nearly cost Nagy his political reputation. But a few hours later Gerő made an aggressive speech on the radio which the whole population took for what it was – an outright threat. In reply to this, a crowd which had gathered outside the State Radio building tried in vain to have their petitions broadcast. The rebuttal led to a clash between the by-standers, who had rapidly armed themselves, and the units of the secret police, the AVH, who protected the building. The siege ended with the occupation of the building. In the meantime the Central Committee of the Communist Party went into an all-night session during which Imre Nagy was reinstated as Prime Minister, with some of his supporters admitted to the Central Committee. None the less, the popular movement was branded counter-revolutionary in the communiqué issued after the session. More important, the Soviet army started – in all probability on orders from its own commanders and not following any appeal by any Hungarian authority – police action against the increasing number of armed insurgents in the early hours of the following day, 24 October. Between 23 and 24 October, Hungary trod the path to revolution.

The next day, 24 October, was spent under martial law, with street battles between Soviet army units and Hungarian insurgents, mostly in Budapest but also in the countryside and in the smaller towns. The turning-point came on 25 October when those taking part in a spontaneous demonstration in Budapest to protest their revolutionary spirit against the official slander about 'counter-revolution' were slaughtered by AVH machine-gun fire in front of the parliament building. When news of the massacre spread Hungary became ungovernable. The Hungarian communist leadership decided – obviously in a state of panic but in the presence and with the endorsement of Soviet 'advisers', Mikoyan and Suslov – to go further along the road of concessions. Gerő was dismissed, Kádár appointed First Secretary. The joint Nagy–Kádár leadership still spoke of counter-revolution but promised reforms. However, promises alone could no longer satisfy the crowds now permanently in the streets in open revolt. On 27 October, Nagy invited two non-communist politicians, Zoltán Tildy and Béla Kovács, but not yet non-communist political forces, into his cabinet. Next day he spoke on the radio of an agreement between the Hungarian and Soviet governments concerning the withdrawal of the Soviet army from Hungary. He also promised the disbandment of the AVH.

Parallel to the measures taken at cabinet level (which gained further momentum by establishing an inner cabinet with more non-communist members), three processes unfolded. The first involved the disintegration of the ruling Communist Party, the members of which either participated in armed resistance against the government which was led by the Communist Party, or were to be found in committees and general assemblies which condemned the policy of their own party, or simply evaporated. (Some of them, but only a tiny minority, fell victim to rightist atrocities. On 30 October the employees of the Budapest party committee were either killed in a siege of the party building or lynched after surrendering to an ultra-rightist mob.) The disintegration of the party became formal on 1 November when Kádár announced, in the name of an Organising Committee to which, in addition to Kádár and Nagy, György Lukács, Zoltán Szántó and Ferenc Donáth also belonged, that a new party, the Hungarian Socialist Workers' Party, had been founded to guide the Hungarian masses towards democratic socialism.

The second crucial process had already begun in the first days of the revolution, and it gathered momentum day by day. We refer to the self-organisation by the masses which took several forms, from establishing new political parties to publishing short-lived journals. Its most important manifestation was the creation of workers' councils. The councils were emphatically present in the last ten of the thirteen revolutionary days, but their decisive activity was felt in the crucial weeks following the second Soviet intervention when they stood in the forefront of popular resistance.

The third event was the gradual reintroduction of political pluralism. Nagy's partially reorganised cabinet already acted as the representative of a *national and revolutionary consensus* when on 1 November he declared that Hungary was leaving the Warsaw Pact to become a neutral country. The pluralistic character of his (second) government was formalised on 3 November when it was transformed into a temporary (and pre-election) coalition of the new Communist Party and the reorganised and newly legalised Social Democratic, Petőfi (Peasant) and Smallholder parties. Simultaneously with the revolutionary workers' councils the opposite extreme appeared with the arch-conservative forces whose spiritual leader was apparently Cardinal Mindszenty, freed on 30 October from his long-term and illegal imprisonment. Mindszenty gave his first, very aggressive and menacing, statement on the radio on 3 November.

In the early hours of 4 November, when the second and final Soviet attack was launched, the regime which had been installed by Stalin disappeared without trace; its institutions, emblems and insignia all completely gone. As we now know, the second Soviet intervention had been planned many days ahead. The Soviet Political Bureau conjured up a brand-new Quisling government, called the Revolutionary Workers' and Peasants' Government, headed by János Kádár, who only three days earlier had hailed the 'glorious Hungarian revolution'. Soviet army radio stations broadcast the manifesto and the first, very severe, decrees of the new 'Hungarian' authorities outside Budapest. Soviet army units enforced its first 'legal' decrees in the face of the resistance of nearly the whole Hungarian population. Soviet secret police, under General Serov, the first president of the KGB, arrested the Hungarian politicians and militants in the first days after 4 November.

With the exception of one event, neither a summary of these tragic days nor the epilogue to the revolution belongs to the subject-matter of our book. This event, the final act of this stormy chapter of Hungarian history, fell on 16 June 1958 when Imre Nagy, Pál Maléter and Miklós Gimes, following a sham trial condemning the *government* of revolution, were executed in Budapest. We suggest that all who are interested in the detailed history of Hungary 1956 turn to one or all of the following books, on which we have relied, and which are the best chronicles of this unique historical moment: Tibor Méray's *Thirteen Days That Shook the Kremlin* (1958), Miklós Molnár's *Budapest, 1956* (1971), and Bill Lomax's *Hungary, 1956* (1976).

Melbourne, FERENC FEHÉR
March 1982 AGNES HELLER

Acknowledgements

We should like to thank Brett Lockwood for his most dedicated editing of our text – a combination of conscientious revision and perceptive understanding. Without his help we could not have adequately expressed our intentions.

We should also like to express our gratitude to the office staff of the Department of Sociology, La Trobe University, and of the History of Ideas Unit, Australian National University, for typing our manuscript.

1 The Impact on the World

It would be a splendid opening to our essay to state that the Hungarian revolution of 1956 was a phoenix that rose from its ashes. Unfortunately, the statement would be inaccurate, for it did not. But this uprising is far from being the forgotten event that all its gravediggers, who now act out the roles of philanthropic and moderate statesmen, would like it to be. It is not a *historical symbol* guiding the decisions of social actors, but has become part of *popular historical mythology*. What this revolution meant and against what enemies it was fought (if not against the 'Russians', which is too vague a description) have become as much obscured for people all over the world – people whose memory has been indelibly engraved with scenes of jubilant crowds smashing Stalin's statue and Soviet tanks on the streets of Budapest – as has the exact meaning of every other important historical event. But at least all those who were sufficiently mature to comprehend these scenes in what was predominantly a pre-television era have not forgotten them, and the events of 1956 need surprisingly little explanation when mentioned in conversation, whether it be in Iceland or in New Zealand. It is our intention here to contribute to the transformation of the Hungarian revolution from a vague myth to a far more concrete symbol: a symbol that will promote the process of 'learning from history' for every interested reader, but for one in particular – the leftist socialist radical, who has an enormous historical debt in this respect.

(i) The Hungarian Revolution and Superpower Politics

The decade following the end of the Second World War – the era of the Cold War – was dominated by two apparently totally contradictory, but functionally almost equivalent, conceptions regarding the genesis, the character, and the prospects of longevity of the communist-ruled regimes of Eastern Europe. The first viewpoint stated with an air of doctrinaire superiority – and this was the dominant tone, particularly in the American press – that all East European and Asian communist systems were simply Soviet exports, and that if they did not enjoy Soviet military and secret police presence and support they would automatically collapse. Yet subsequent events of the most varied character and value-content in Yugoslavia, China, Albania and other countries testified to an infinitely more complex situation. In the first place, the proponents of this theory could not account for the truly astonishing fact that the Yugoslav communists, in a national war of independence which in itself would reduce rather than widen communist policy objectives, could attain the irrevocable communist course which the Spanish Republic, in a civil war the objectives of which were clearly social in character, could not. (And the Soviet presence in Eastern Europe is no explanation. It is well known that Stalin warned Yugoslav communists against 'rash' radicalism rather than encouraged it.) Nor, for that matter, could this theory provide any coherent interpretation of the Chinese communist victory – an event that was not a Bolshevik *coup d'état* like the Russian revolution, but a change preceded by a long history of communist administration of vast provinces, which meant a practical test for hundreds of millions of people, enabling them to choose between the communists and the Kuomintang. If we add to this that it was widely known then in the West, and has been amply documented since, that both changes of course, in the main, occurred *contrary to* Stalin's intentions, the poverty of this conception can only be accounted for by the fact that 'experts in politico-sociology', in their unassailable dogmatism, simply underestimated the real needs for socialism in Europe and for radical change of *any* kind in Asia which communist dictatorships thriving on these needs have used and abused. But Tito's post-1948 regime, stable and unchallenged, already undermined the self-confidence of this theory – a theory destined to be wholly refuted by the complete absence of any socially representative liberal–capitalist alternative in a China which had been gripped by a variety of powerful social convulsions mobilising and counter-mobilising tens of millions in a social dynamic unprecedented in communist regimes. And today Albania, repulsive and Orwellian as it is, still calls for an analytical and not a rhetorical explanation.

Taken all in all, the function of this conception was simple enough: it was the self-hypnotic technique of an intellectually sterile Cold War policy – a policy attempting to instil into its militants a confidence which was never really there.

Parallel to this theory, though diametrically opposite in content, there emerged an equally important, if less publicised, conception of the Cold War. This was the belief in the *indestructibility of communist systems from within*. The proponents of this view – generals, leaders of the Allied intelligence community, and ultra-conservative politicians – departed both from the idea that socialism was a 'perversion' and from the firm conviction that this creed, no matter under what name it appeared, would be unequivocally rejected by the masses if it were in their power to do so. Once a totalitarian system was established, zealots of the second position contended (and Churchill placed himself amongst them in accusing the British Labour Party of intending to introduce a 'Gestapo system' to facilitate its planning policy), such self-purging from within became impossible unless military aid was given to the enslaved nations. One particularly dangerous moment when this attitude gained control was during the Korean War, when MacArthur, who had been invested with enormous semi-independent military and political powers, and who had assumed the role of the arch-inquisitor of anti-communist crusades, allowed an unbridled zeal born of despair to provoke the Chinese intervention that brought the world to the brink of destruction. Such catastrophic scenarios would undoubtedly have been repeated had not the Hungarian revolution of 1956 eliminated for ever this idea of the indestructibility of the Soviet regimes from within. This was the first consequence of the Hungarian revolution which can truly and without exaggeration be called world-historical. It provided a number of important lessons that have not yet been digested by Western diplomats, East European statesmen, or Western leftists – lessons all the more important because *both* theories outlined above coincided as far as their practical function was concerned. Both of them catered, even if from opposite angles, for the ideological and practical demands of the Cold War.

Moreover, it has often been asked just what impact this uprising could possibly have had on the decisions of the policy-making bodies of a superpower that is impervious to the suggestions or warnings of the State Department. It is here that a few facts long forgotten by all but the experts should be borne strongly in mind.

To begin with, it was the Soviet government who, after being publicly accused by the Polish Government-in-Exile (in London) of perpetrating the Katyn massacres of 1940, after the Germans had uncovered the corpses of murdered Polish army officers, undertook in consequence of these developments to break off all relations with the representatives of a Poland fighting in a common cause. That government might not necessarily have been re-elected, but it undoubtedly stood in a relationship of some legitimacy with the Russians. No amount of pressure or supplication on the part of the Western Allies could bring Stalin to an apparent truce with – or, at least, a suspended hostility towards – the Polish leaders, and later he simply imposed the so-called Lublin Committee (a communist government with certain subsequent non-communist additions) upon the country, despite vigorous protests and without even holding formal negotiations with the émigré forces. Also, as we know from Churchill's vivid description, as well as from other sources, it was in an equally unceremonious way in 1944 that Vyshinsky, in the name of the Soviet government, 'dismissed' the government of their then ally, Romania, in order to install a more pro-Soviet one. In the following decade Soviet military power only increased. Nevertheless, for the thirteen days between 23 October and 4 November 1956, the Soviet leadership felt compelled to issue self-apologetic government communiqués. What is more, they entered into formal negotiations with – and made what proved to be false promises to – a social force and a government (Imre Nagy's *second* cabinet) which deep down they had always regarded as counter-revolutionary, and which they had outsmarted and deceived from the outset, and whose members they later executed or imprisoned. Nor did 4 November, the day of the second and final intervention, witness an end to such things. The Russians held numerous secret or semi-secret negotiations with various political forces. In Budapest these negotiations initially included the workers' councils, former 'rightist' and 'leftist' social democrats, writers and others, and former politicians of the post-war parliamentary system, the most representative of whom was the former secretary-general of the Hungarian Smallholders' Party, Béla Kovács, whom the Soviet military police simply abducted in 1947 *en pleine pluralisme et démocratie*, kept in the GULAG and released only shortly before the revolution. In Romania, where the sympathisers of Imre Nagy – mainly radical socialists no longer espousing specific doctrines –

were concentrated, equally endless negotiations were held with the aim of broadening the scandalously and dangerously narrow power-base of Kádár's new government. These negotiations were all conducted, either wholly or in part, by the Russians' Hungarian proxies, until such time as the Russian leaders judged some of them important enough to be removed from the hands of their emissaries. All of these things serve to illustrate that, in contrast to the opinions of several scholarly interpreters, the pragmatic Soviet leadership did not underestimate the crucial importance of tiny Hungary and her 'counter-revolution'.

Only when we have indicated – though we have not yet documented – the *global* importance of the Hungarian revolution can we establish its first element of significance: *the impact on the Western world*. Despite the 'false consciousness' of many Hungarians in revolt, their rebellion was directed against *all* signatories of the Yalta and Potsdam agreements, against the Western protagonists as well as the Eastern. In order to emphasise a point, sometimes it is best to turn to the primary sources – especially when the chronicler has the great capacity of laconically evoking the Shakespearian moments upon which history turns. Here is how Churchill describes the moment in which he made his fateful deal with Stalin concerning Eastern Europe, on 9 October 1944 in Moscow:

> The moment was apt for business, so I said, 'Let us settle about our affairs in the Balkans. Your armies are in Rumania and Bulgaria. We have *interests, missions, and agents* there. Don't let us get at cross-purposes in small ways. So far as Britain and Russia are concerned, how would it do for you to have ninety per cent dominance in Rumania, for us to have ninety per cent of the say in Greece, and go fifty-fifty about Yugoslavia?' While this was being translated I wrote out on a half-sheet of paper:
>
> Rumania
>   Russia   90%
>   The others   10%
>
> Greece
>   Great Britain
>   (in accord with U.S.A.)   90%
>   Russia   10%

Yugoslavia	50–50%
Hungary	50–50%
Bulgaria	
Russia	75%
The others	25%

I pushed this across to Stalin who had by then heard the translation. There was a slight pause. Then he took his blue pencil and made a large tick upon it, and passed it back to us. *It was all settled in no more time than it takes to set down.*

Of course we had long and anxiously considered our point and were only dealing with immediate war-time arrangements. All larger questions were reserved on both sides for what we then hoped would be a peace table when the war was won.

After this there was a long silence. The pencilled paper lay in the centre of the table. At length I said, 'Might it not be thought rather cynical if it seemed we had disposed of these issues, so fateful to millions of people, in such an offhand manner? Let us burn the paper.' 'No, you keep it,' said Stalin.[1]

In this memorable scene so brilliantly described by Churchill the most repulsive feature of the Yalta and Potsdam agreements comes immediately to the fore: the unassailable conviction shared equally by the 'Big Three' that they had the unquestionable right to decide the future of the world among themselves, without even going so far as to discuss the pertinent details with the parties (and sometimes the continents) involved.

Naturally, they produced several arguments in defence of this stance. The first was that only they, the superpowers, could serve as safeguards against the revival of fascism – an argument which of course neglected to take into account their original part in, and responsibility for, its emergence. The stories have been recounted many times of how Britain tried to use Hitler as an anti-Bolshevik weapon up to the very last, when the instrument turned against the apparent master; or how the Soviet leaders teleguided the German communist movement to do everything in its power to destroy the Weimar democracy and the Social Democratic Party, thereby becoming an accomplice, even if a suicidal one, in Hitler's victory, and how they shared the Polish loot with Hitler in 1939; or how the United States stayed away, as much in a selfish as in an aloof manner, and for as long as it was politically and militarily possible, from the European affairs in which an early intervention and an emphatic warning in the mid-1930s could have changed dramatically the state of affairs. Nor was there any indication during the Yalta–Potsdam period that any of them would behave in a wider or a more humane manner.

The second argument was moral in nature, strange as it may sound on the part of certain signatories of these agreements: since they had borne the brunt of the war, had suffered its greatest ravages, and had seen the greatest number of victims, they *therefore* had all prerogatives in the decisions of victory. Now, even if we disregard the questionable logic and the even more questionable justification of Stalin's crocodile tears over Soviet war victims – millions of whom were *his* victims, the waste products of *his* irresponsible and criminal unpreparedness for war emergency (as is sufficiently proved by Khrushchev's so-called 'secret speech' and A. M. Nekrich's famous book, *June 22, 1941* (Columbia, SC: University of South Carolina Press, 1968), on the first year of the Soviet–German war) – and even if we also disregard Churchill's not particularly refined racist propaganda directed against the 'Huns' – this alleged but mythical cause of all international ills for which a panacea was sought in the existence of thirty-five small German states instead of in a united one – then this statement about the 'greatest suffering' is true only in absolute and not in relative terms. For instance, there can be no doubt that in the war Poland suffered relatively just as much as the Soviet Union. Poland was, in addition, the focal point of the outbreak of the war, and one of the countries whose wishes, intentions or real desires were ignored in the most categorical and outrageous manner after it had ended. It is also worth saying that the particular group which in relative terms had not even a close rival in this nightmarish race of destruction, and whose victims in numerical terms were, to our knowledge, second only to the Soviet Union – namely, world Jewry – *was not even mentioned* by this 'wise and humanitarian' instrument of peace. Jews had to fight for another three years against the various powers of this 'wisely pacified' world to obtain a home for themselves, a safeguard of some sort against a new onslaught. (And if this procurement of a homeland did not happen in a manner free of contradictions, if it generated new tensions, the responsibility rests largely upon the shoulders of these 'moral' fabricators of peace.)

These considerations perhaps undermine to some extent the legitimacy and wisdom of the Yalta and Potsdam agreements – agreements to which, in a strange accord, all signatories stuck later on, even during their most bitter clashes. But two further elements should be added to the above. The first is related to the stubborn indifference to learning from history on the part of the great powers, the second to their somnambulist character with regard to the only instrument they already had in their power to preserve peace, miserable as both the means and the result are. As to the first, we need only point out that they simply copied the so-often-condemned Wilsonian technique of 'redeeming nations despite their own will'. They arbitrarily decreed new national borders, ordered – or, at least, promoted – forcible population-transfers, declared certain nations collectively criminal (even if not in so many words but by punishing them substantively), released others from the bonds of responsibility, created spheres of influence over nations that had sacrificed millions in order to make others independent, but in all of this had the immediate hindsight to change the agreed proportions to the detriment of others. As to the second, they simply failed to realise that it was the nuclear weapon alone (already in the hands of the Americans, well under way with the British, soon to come for the Russians) that would prevent them cutting each other's throat in a world cataclysm, and all their 'wise' decisions were just so many *obstacles* in the way of a miserable peace only guaranteed by the approaching nuclear stalemate.

It was against this general world constellation that the Hungary of 1956 revolted, though many or perhaps even most of its participants believed that they had the backing of the 'West' in their struggle against the 'East'. (But we shall see repeatedly in this study that at least one highly representative theorist *and* practical protagonist of the events, the great István Bibó, state minister without portfolio in Imre Nagy's last government, was perfectly aware of the *double anti-imperialist* character of the Hungarian revolution.) There was some vague knowledge of the Yalta and Potsdam decisions within the politically unskilled elements of the population, but their *full* impact was not immediately visible in the peace treaties concluded between 1945 and 1947 (for instance, in the Hungarian peace treaty of Paris, 1947). In addition, in the period *prior to* the communist takeover there existed in Eastern Europe a *popular myth* and a highly *questionable* and *ambiguous* attitude of the liberal parties of the region, and conjointly these two factors contributed to blurring the clear vision of large sections of the population. The popular myth consisted of the idea that the Western powers, now in an unassailable position of economic and military technological superiority, had only been 'temporarily outsmarted' by the Soviet leadership, and that very soon the balance of power would be restored to adequate and proper proportions. Yugoslavia in 1948 seemed to be verifying this interpretation. Without thorough strategic studies the 'man in the street' thought that it was mostly (if not solely) the American nuclear umbrella which sheltered Yugoslavia from Stalin's invasion. (We would add that the determination of the Titoist leadership and its popular support should be regarded as being of nearly equal weight.) The ambiguity, if not outright cowardice, of the liberal parties in Eastern Europe lay in the fact that their professional strata were fully aware of the hidden dimensions of the Yalta–Potsdam iceberg, but remained silent and behaved as if everything happened according to parliamentary rules. In spite of a growing desperation, the popular myth of this equilibrium soon to be restored by the Western powers persisted, and was projected into the period subsequent to the communist takeover. Let us repeat: it was Hungary 1956 *alone* that debunked and annihilated it. The North Korean military adventure had undoubtedly questioned the general lines of division drawn by the victorious superpowers, but it did not question – indeed, it rather confirmed on *both* sides – the *very rule* of the superpowers. The riots in East Berlin in 1953 were a famine-inspired revolt that failed to reach the necessary level of self-articulation that would call into question anything of the existing system of world domination. The same can be said for Poznan in 1956. The Polish October presented a far more complex case; but given what seemed *then* to be an exceptional piece of historical luck – namely, that a reform communist leadership could successfully channel these forces – the movement remained primarily concerned with the inner structural tensions of Poland, and showed an increasing, though hostile, indifference towards world events. But, on 23 October, Hungary exploded in the face of all those who in their boundless wisdom had created the collective Yalta–Potsdam system of superpower domination, and set a question mark next to it which has subsequently only increased in prominence and portent.

In a strange way, this explosion was achieved by the double character of the Hungarian revolution. It was a radical transformation eliminating overnight the seemingly immovable edifice of the Stalinist regime (an event characterised now by David Irving as a 'scatterbrained revolution') *and* a collective offer of *historical compromise* by almost a whole nation. While this first aspect is generally known, and forms part of the popular mythology, nearly everyone except certain experts is ignorant of the second. It is therefore time to shed some light on the *wisdom* of this revolution.

At its heretical and 'counter-revolutionary' height, when the 'traitorous Nagy government' decided to leave the Warsaw Pact, Hungary had *neutrality* as its topmost demand. There was no political force worthy of the name in the havoc of those days which would have suggested that Hungary join NATO. This may be called 'counter-revolutionary cunning' by the official chroniclers of the East – a cunning which shrewdly took into account the limits of Soviet patience – but, even if this were so, the same shrewd calculation has been working perfectly well for thirty-five years in Finland, to the utmost satisfaction of that same Soviet leadership. And it is not simply by chance that we mention Finland here, for the content of the Hungarian compromise, from the perspective of foreign policy, was precisely the 'Finlandisation' of Hungary.[2] The offer of compromise has to be understood literally. Nagy's second government repeatedly and officially assured the Soviet leaders of its intention to remain outside all military pacts and to sustain peaceful and preferably friendly relations with the Soviet Union. (It even refrained from stating publicly what had been stated privately to Andropov, the then Soviet ambassador in Budapest: that the *immediate* cause of the abrogation of the Warsaw Pact was the *return to Hungary* of the Soviet army from 1 November.)

But of more importance than this was the strange event that took place in the early hours of 4 November, the first day of the second (and final) Soviet invasion, in the Hungarian Parliament – a building occupied by the Soviet army and abandoned by the ministers of the Nagy government, who were mostly seeking refuge, in vain, in the embassy of Yugoslavia. It was at this moment that István Bibó, a man unknown to all except the élite, joining Nagy's government only a day earlier, and perhaps the greatest post-war leftist (non-doctrinaire socialist) political theorist of Eastern Europe, formulated, in his capacity as state minister of the last Nagy government, a final statement as 'the sole representative of the only legitimate Hungarian government left in the parliamentary building'.[3] This world, which produces and worships so many fashionable and empty idols, if it wishes to understand this part of its history fully, must become acquainted with this and other documents that testify just as much to the fearless inflexibility and revolutionary spirit of this truly great personality as to his political realism, his wide scope of vision, and his acumen. Bibó states:

> Hungary does not intend to follow an anti-Soviet policy. Moreover, it is her intention to co-exist in a community of free East European nations whose objective is to establish their lives on the basis of the principles of freedom, justice, and a society free of exploitation. In front of the world I reject the slanderous statement that the glorious Hungarian revolution was a hotbed of fascist or anti-Semitic escapades; in the struggle, the entire populace participated without class or religious discriminations.
> Moving and magnificent was the humane and wise attitude of a people in revolt – an attitude always capable of distinction, and which was turned alone against the oppressive foreign army and the squads of internal myrmidons . . . I appeal to the Hungarian people not to regard the occupying army or the puppet government eventually created by it as lawful authority, and to turn against it with all the means of a *passive* resistance . . . I am not in a position to order armed resistance. I joined the government only a day ago; I am not yet informed about the military situation. It would be utterly irresponsible on my part to dispose of the blood of the Hungarian youth. The people of Hungary have spilt enough blood to prove their dedication to the cause of justice and freedom for the world. *This time it is the turn of the world powers* to demonstrate the strength of the principles incorporated in the Declaration of the United Nations and the strength of the freedom-loving peoples of the world. I appeal to the great powers and to the United Nations for a courageous and wise decision on behalf of the freedom of my subjugated country . . . God save Hungary.[4]

This seemingly old-fashioned text, which must sound somewhat Risorgimento to the historically trained ear, was in fact a wise, circumspect, manifold and realistic document. It was by far one of the greatest constitutive acts of statesmanship in post-war Eastern

Europe, and already contained all the elements of Bibó's 'Draft of a compromise solution of the Hungarian question' – this most important document written by him during the following five days and later smuggled out of the country. The 'Draft' presented a compromise to the Soviet Union of a type that would have resulted in a course far freer from uprisings and revolutions than has been displayed in the last twenty-five years: a compromise which took into consideration the Soviet strategic interests in a quite circumspect way, and which at the same time, with its inflexibly democratic patriotism, did not yield one iota when it came to fundamental Hungarian interests. As such, and as a disgracefully forgotten document, it deserves a more detailed analysis. The more so since by virtue of its author, a politician totally uncompromised by the Rákosi regime (during which he had some subaltern clerical post), and a representative of a non-Marxist democratic party, the Petőfi (Peasant) Party, the 'Draft' was considerably more than the Don Quixotian daydream of a political fanatic. It expressed the views of most – perhaps even a vast majority of – sections of Hungarian society.[5]

The first three points of the 'Draft' provide a résumé of the immediate situation after 4 November: the *pretexts* (of restoring order) given by the Soviet army to legitimise its intervention, and the obviously false promises of the Kádár government to 'negotiate' the immediate withdrawal of the Soviet army with the Soviet government as soon as order was restored (as if they had a mandate at all to negotiate with their masters). The fourth point, however, must be quoted in full:

> It has become impossible to maintain socialism in Hungary *in the form of a one-party system* because the appeal to the Soviet army to intervene, in the first case made by the MDP [the pre-revolutionary name of the Communist Party] and in the second case by the Socialist Workers' Party [the name of the Kádárist organisation], annihilated the reputation of both parties and any governments eventually relying on them. Without a genuine multi-party system, having real authority, Hungary cannot be governed, the less so as the only communist who has preserved his reputation before the Hungarian people, Imre Nagy, has also accepted the multiparty system.[6]

The fifth point comprehensively covers the Soviet fears of a

Hungary that could become an obedient tool in the hands of Western power-centres, but it solidly rejects the view that the new coalition government could not have eliminated such threats to Soviet security. The morally and politically crucial sixth and seventh points, which amount to a sublime self-defence before 'History' of a butchered and slandered revolution, read as follows:

> A blocking of the road to an orthodox capitalist, anti-communist and arch-conservative restoration must not be a concern restricted to the Soviet Union and the communists, but it should also be a goal of the Hungarian youth, working class and army personnel who fought out the revolution, paid for it with their blood, and who in the main are not communist but overwhelmingly call themselves socialist. It would be morally inadmissible for the beneficiaries of a freedom won by the blood of revolutionaries to be forces of restoration placed in power by the votes of older generations. It ought to be considered as well that such a reactionary turn transforming Hungary – a nation located amongst communist countries – into a fifth column of the West would, on the one hand, become a constant stimulus to further aggressive plans and, on the other, a menacing sign for the freedom-loving communists of other people's democracies in planning the liberalisation of their own regimes. By contrast, *a solution which combined socialist achievement with the guarantees provided by free institutions* would set an example which would stimulate imitation.[7]

Before we begin a detailed analysis of these constitutional suggestions, a few additional remarks are necessary. First, what does Bibó mean, and what does he *not* mean, by 'compromise'? The text itself, with its moral pathos emphasising the primogeniture of the socialist (even if not communist) younger generations, of the creators for a short while of Hungarian freedom, leaves no doubt at all that the maintenance of what by habit we now call 'democratic socialism' was not part of a formula dictated by compromise but a sincere conviction of Bibó's. Secondly, his broadly based considerations both take account of and try to promote the whole process of de-Stalinisation sparked off by the 20th Congress of the Soviet Communist Party. It is precisely by virtue of such a broad political foundation that they could indeed become a draft for a *compromise* solution – something which the Soviet leadership could at least have considered (if it had wanted to) as a basis of negotiation. But, thirdly, speaking from the *Soviet* point of view, these considerations meant more than just 'Finlandisation': they went beyond what amounted to strict neutrality, and in effect meant governments whose existence would be endorsed by the Soviet Union, with certain mild restrictions on the press but an otherwise unlimited liberal market system and political pluralism. (That for the Soviet government this 'more' was rather 'less' is another matter: they dreaded, not needed, democratic socialism.) In this wide and internationally established capacity, Bibó's principles called for an (actual or virtual) referendum creating an *explicit national consensus* on which the compromise could be based.

Bibó's first point makes it very clear that the basis of the new legitimacy is *not* the 1949 sham constitution – a Soviet and Rákosi dictation – but the day of the revolution: 23 October 1956. *As a result*, the last legitimate Hungarian government is Nagy's second cabinet. The second point, the settling of the international status of a future Hungary, is one of the most interesting parts of the whole document, and absolute and irrefutable proof of its realism and willingness to compromise.

2 (Alternative A): A solution of foreign policy would be that Hungary leaves the Warsaw Pact but remains part of the consultative agreement dealing with European peace and security, provided that Yugoslavia joins it under the same conditions.
(Alternative B): A solution of foreign policy would be that Hungary leaves the Warsaw Pact and signs a bilateral agreement with the Soviet Union.[8]

Since we are chiefly concerned here with the impact of the Hungarian revolution on the general strategy of the West, and with the overall question of compromise, we shall only mention that points 3, 4 and 5 constitutionally guarantee the personal safety and career prospects of communists who would lose their power monopoly, and regulate the constitutional framework of a new Hungary, making it very explicit that the nationalisation of the main 'forces of production' and the agrarian revolution of 1945–6 must not be repudiated, while at the same time, and *for the first time in any country's history*, making the self-managed direction of factories a constitutional stipulation.

This somewhat lengthy digression was not introduced solely to throw light on the great personality of István Bibó, the potential architect of a democratic socialist Hungary – though this alone would be a worthy objective. We simply wanted to prove that the Hungarian revolution was not a 'scatterbrained undertaking', but a revolt against a world constellation created by the Yalta and Potsdam agreements – a revolt which, with its readiness to compromise, offered one single and never recurring opportunity for the West to redesign its whole post-war strategy and to establish with honour a situation equally beneficial both for itself and for the nations of Eastern Europe. We believe that this would certainly have meant better opportunities for a democratic socialist left as well.

Instead there obtained an ever widening and unbridgeable gap between the strident propaganda and the solemn promises made earlier to 'restore the freedom of Eastern Europe', and the absolute impotence – even reluctance – which followed the Hungarian revolution (apart from the later rhetorical exercises in the United Nations which did not even diminish the number of executions). The result was a major loss of face for the Western powers, a second moral Munich. Hammarskjöld performed endless manoeuvres to block discussion of the appeal by the Nagy government and, with regard to the United States, Miklós Molnár convincingly states that 'no diplomatic measures, no pressure, no offer of mediation revealed any desire on the part of the Americans to support Nagy's Government; there was even a slight decrease of interest from the moment when Hungary declared its neutrality!'[9] And Britain, the offended partner, spelled out this feeling. Sir Anthony Eden, himself responsible for the ill-timed Suez action, wrote concerning the procrastination over the Hungarian question in the United Nations:

> Five days passed without any further council meeting upon Hungary, despite repeated attempts by ourselves and others to bring one about. The United States representative was reluctant and voiced his suspicion that we were urging the *Hungarian Situation to direct attention from Suez*. The United States Government appeared in no hurry to move. Their attitude provided a damaging contrast to the alacrity they were showing in arranging the French and ourselves![10]

But as the Hungarian (and later other East European) masses very quickly got the message – or, rather, the lack of any response – this corroborates what we have said earlier: that the Hungarian revolution was a revolt against *all* signatories of the Yalta and Potsdam agreements. Let us quote Bibó again, this time from his essay 'The situation of Hungary and the international situation', written a few months later and only a few weeks before he was imprisoned for many years.

> The situation of Hungary became a scandal of the world. *The Hungarian situation is a scandal, first of all, of the Western world.* For ten years now the Western world has cried: 'The East European countries have not by themselves chosen a form of government based on a one-party system, but have had it introduced through the interference of the Soviet Union, and they are not satisfied with it.' The Western countries have been so informing the population in the hope that sooner or later they will have to create a new form of government. They have not promised the East European nations that they will launch a nuclear war on their behalf, nor have they appealed to them to initiate inconsiderate uprisings. But so much has indeed been included in these assurances that – provided it becomes possible through the international constellation and the resolute attitude of these very nations – the Western world will deploy its whole economic, political and moral weight in order to put the cause of these nations on the agenda and resolve it in a way satisfactory for them. *The Hungarian revolution has created both the preconditions and the legitimacy of such a global bargaining* . . . If this is not enough, what else would be needed to impose a conference on the world powers which would bargain, together with guarantees satisfactory for the Soviet Union, for the independence and freedom of Hungary? Instead, what is happening is a theatrical debate on the Hungarian situation in front of the plenary session of the UNO, with solemn and ineffectual resolutions . . . even though everyone has always known and knows now that the UNO as an instrument of peace is only as valuable as the power and the determination of the great powers participating in it . . . But what fails here is not the UNO but the political responsibility and the moral mission of the great powers.[11]

What are the actual political facts that validate Bibó's view (as well as our thesis) that the Hungarian revolution really did create the conditions (and the justification) for a global renegotiation of the Yalta–Potsdam situation? First, the Soviet Union was in a deep power crisis after Stalin's death, and at the time of the Hungarian revolution this crisis had not been even temporarily solved. Indeed, the revolution intensified this internecine strife. No Western Philbys were needed to know this. Secondly, at that time, when the rupture between the Soviet Union and China had not yet begun, an opening towards Asia was a possible option for Soviet policy – an option which, if taken, would have needed, and perhaps resulted in, a region of buffer states in Eastern Europe with an increased amount of inner freedom. Such consolidation was not an impossibility from a Soviet point of view, had the idea been presented to them by the Western powers. Thirdly, the United States was in an exceptionally good moral and political situation. America had not participated in that epilogue to French and British imperial escapades, the Suez campaign. Her prestige in Asia and Africa was therefore still very high, and she would have received, as a non-colonialist global power with a then unquestioned technological superiority, the support of a large number of non-aligned countries for her politics (a situation soon to change), had she tried to negotiate the proportions and, in particular, the methods of world government. Fourthly, and finally, whereas in the case of any intervention in German, Polish or other East European affairs, where the governments in question – governments still relying on raw power and with no real legitimacy at all – could have rejected a Western approach as 'interference with their internal affairs', this could not have been so with Hungary. Hungary, with a government as legitimate as any after the communist takeover, pleaded for an international collective negotiation. We do not wish to give the impression to the radical and socialist, to whom this essay is principally addressed, that such a change would have resulted *only* in a positive outcome. It could have channelled Soviet expansion towards Asia, creating new confrontations and new ('leftist' and 'rightist' or, more properly, anti-capitalist and capitalist) tyrannies, and that would have been disastrous for the nations of *that* region. It could also have introduced an early version of Kissinger's Holy Alliance, in which three white telephones would have decided amongst themselves all unsettled global matters, leaving no room for radicalism of any kind.

But all historical events imply negative options, and Hungary 1956 was not unique in this respect. It *was* unique in two ways: in the sense that it did create a new potential historical juncture, and that it also *exposed publicly* what had until then been a secret of the experts – the fact that from 1939 onwards there were two Western (predominantly British–American) strategies rather than one. The former involved a cynically clear level-headedness as far as objectives were concerned, and realism in the assessment of enemies' and the Allies' respective powers, but also, regretfully, a loss of the means to implement these objectives. The latter involved means in abundance but a cheap liberal sentimentalism mixed (in a dilettantish way) with the ruthlessness of the 'big stick policy', as well as only approximate ideas of the value and strength of both enemies and allies.

A description of a few features of these two unique aspects is in order, but since this is a study of Hungary 1956, and not of global strategy, these, too, will be selected according to their contiguity with the revolution. The British strategy can be summed up in the following manner. First, and despite Churchill's solemn statements to the contrary, the British leaders wanted to crush Germany via Italy and the Balkans, which would have resulted in the Western Allies arriving in central Europe *before* the Russians, thus containing Soviet communism within its already existing borders. Secondly, and very naturally, British Tory politics was aimed at keeping the British Empire intact, with possibly no concessions at all to the Asian independence movements. Thirdly, Churchill's intention of partitioning Germany into small states – the annulment of Bismarck's epochal deed – together with a weakened, because self-humiliated, France, would have restored in Europe, as far as foreign policy was concerned, the situation of the late *ancien régime*. This would have meant a continental equilibrium with a supreme British arbiter and a coalition of the Anglo-Saxon powers ruling the world. There can be hardly any question that this would be an illusory goal without active American aid (and Churchill must have known in the first year of American belligerence that he would never get that aid). It would also have been a totally negative attitude from an Asian point of view: the independence of the Asian countries was a joint result of the Japanese hurricane eroding the former colonial power-bases; the new, not directly colonial but 'protectionist', American way of governing the world; and the Chinese revolution, which demonstrated the irresistible power of popular movements in these countries. It would also have been a negative strategy for Germany.

Concerning the East European balance, the picture is less clear. On the one hand, the Greek lesson was instructive: that the British lent support to the worst sorts of tyrannical government (an old predilection of Tory politics, which has a long and ugly record in this respect), as against *liberals*, who could have found a middle-of-the-road solution. On the other hand, there can be hardly any doubt that under British tutelage the *majority* of the East European countries would have become liberal parliamentary systems with a wide range of more or less active elements of conservatism, and more or less active elements of radical social change – such as, for instance, a dramatic land reform. Czechoslovakia would, in all probability, have been transformed from the Masaryk system into something very like the Swedish regime of the welfare state; whereas Hungary, Romania and Bulgaria, in that order, would have had an increasingly conservative parliamentarianism, but not a police state with a parliamentary façade such as they experienced before the war. If such a situation had obtained in all the countries that were open to this second alternative, certain possibilities for democratic socialism would have come about as well. The fight against fascism not only radicalised huge masses, but also made all sorts of terroristic regime and police state hated by them, so that even the worst Stalinist communist parties had to pretend to begin with that they were the upholders of a 'more profound' principle of democracy. (And in certain cases – for instance, in Lukács' inconsistent but sincerely meant theory of a 'new democracy' – such a position had a hidden anti-Stalinist polemical edge.) The socialist and communist parties increased their electorate to an extent – and without necessarily using fraudulent methods and intimidation – where they felt themselves to be in relative safety, and nothing stirred the feeling in their ranks that they should have recourse to a dictatorship. This could (not necessarily *would*) have slowly transformed the Trojan-horse strategy into an early and candid version of Eurocommunism.

The American strategy has often been described as dilettantish. No repetition of the statement is needed. It will suffice to mention that in the late 1930s and early 1940s the United States had one ambassador in Moscow (Davies) who made reports to the President to the effect that Stalin's purges were fair trials of conspirators and possibly spies, and another in London (Kennedy) who in 1940 wrote off the British capacity for resistance and instead suggested direct talks with Hitler. It is more rewarding to scrutinise the aims and objectives of this policy.

To begin with, the American policy-makers regarded Britain as their main competitor in the post-Hitler period. This attitude was a strange compound of naïve but candid liberal feelings and anti-colonialist pride – the self-assurance that the United States, which had never had colonies, was destined for a worldwide mission. It also exhibited traditional anti-British resentment and an overwhelming amount of expansionist egoism. But, whatever the motivation, the selection of the main target was totally mistaken; and this misguided tack made the leading American policy-makers totally blind to the *real* power proportions. They systematically underestimated the strength of their real competition, Soviet and Chinese communism, and equally systematically overestimated the strength of their allies. The grossest example of their wishful thinking (about which Churchill expressly warned them) was their blind belief in Chiang Kai-shek's military and political reserves and future chances. Thirdly, they suffered from the typical American disease: the pragmatic overestimation of technological superiority, which they partly believed unchallengeable (and had a very bitter snub in 1949 when the existence of the Soviet nuclear weapon became known to them), and to some extent viewed as a universal remedy for complex social situations. In this respect, the British with their century-old colonial experience were far more realistic. Fourthly, even if they boasted about not being *ideologues* or fanatics, but down-to-earth pragmatists of a good traditional home-made style, the creators of the American strategy introduced a misplaced 'Hegelian dialectic' into their plans. They believed that un-freedom can serve the purposes of freedom; that liberal democracies can be effectively defended (without being irreparably compromised) by the most illiberal tyrannies. It was this complex in its entirety that was called the 'free world'. The road leading to the Vietnam defeat started at the moment they decided upon sponsoring several cliques of corrupt and cruel officers as allegedly effective safeguards against communism.

To give a brief account of the pros and cons of this policy, in all fairness it must be said that for all its crucial and inherent weaknesses it was still a better Western strategy than the British produced, if for no other reason than that it did involve the nuclear deterrent (an absolute prerogative for some time), which the

British strategy did not. As mentioned earlier, we have no doubt whatsoever that Stalin's surprising tolerance towards Yugoslav independence was mainly (even if not exclusively) due to the American nuclear umbrella. The American resistance saved Germany from being partitioned into a region of artificial and non-functioning small states, which we would have regarded as a definite historical regression. Still, though undoubtedly relying on powerful internal forces, it was American patronage that played a crucial role in the creation of the Japanese parliamentary–liberal system – a fundamental, new and positive development in Asia. If we add that this American competition thoroughly undermined the chances for survival of the British Empire, then the nations of Asia do not finish with a totally negative balance in their transactions with the United States. The chief fault of these ideas was, of course, the misconceived and arrogant idea of *pax americana* – a policy with the explicit purpose of American world domination. Motivated by the interests of American big business, this was both a reactionary strategy and one that, for a number of historical reasons, could not hope to produce the expected results anyway. The main loser in all this was Eastern Europe – a region where American propaganda daily promised 'freedom', in which it planted hopes, and for which it did not lift a finger.[12]

But the Hungarian revolution offered a real opportunity to eliminate certain structural weaknesses in the American strategy. Stalin, a man with whom fruitful negotiations were impossible after the war (whereas earlier – as his pact with Hitler demonstrates – he could be a flexible and even humble partner), was now dead. His heirs, deeply involved in in-fights, gave material proof of their limited readiness to talk. In 1955, after very long and loud propaganda to the contrary, they consented to the separate handling of Austrian neutrality, earlier bound up by them with the German peace treaty. As we have repeatedly mentioned, Hungary provided a legitimate excuse for the Americans to become negotiators of goodwill in this complex situation. This would have provided for them (and also for the world) the following benefits. First, at least one great power would have lived up to its word and its promises, and this by itself might have steadied an already very shaky United Nations. It would have presented the Americans as peacemakers, not as Cold Warriors, and would have undoubtedly eased the tension of the post-war decade. It might also have opened a new era in world government – an era that did not witness daily the threat of nuclear confrontation. Finally, there was the possibility which now seems to belong to the realm of fairy tales and childish utopias (or which is perhaps now the object of secret and sinister bargaining in complete bad faith on both sides – a bargaining evidently directed against both the West European alliance and East European efforts of emancipation): the reunification of Germany. This goal could at least have been attempted. No group was more acutely and anxiously aware of such a scenario than Ulbricht and his clique. Their relative restraint – no spectacular show-trials, forcing of a Popular Front cultural liberalism and the like – occurred *prior* to the beating they received at the hands of the people, and was mainly due to the nightmare of a united Germany, from which these super-Stalinists would have fled for good. Once the 'danger' had passed, these people became the model of conservative repression. Of course, in such a complex situation nothing is certain, but it seems to be at least a probability that a successful negotiation of the Hungarian issue along the guidelines worked out by Bibó could have opened the doors to negotiations regarding Germany.

But instead of this, according to all *available* and *public* evidence, the decision-making bodies of the United States considered during those tense days only two (and *not three*) options. One of them was undoubtedly a military intervention (symbolic or actual) planned for the days between 23 October and 4 November (but definitely not after). The result of such an intervention would certainly have been disastrous. A direct confrontation with the Soviet military would have been a strong possibility, if not an inevitable consequence, and the world would have been brought to the brink of destruction – to a far greater threat of nuclear confrontation than was posed by Korea. At the slightest sign of such preparations the Soviet leaders would have felt themselves directly threatened – the only psychological and social stimulus required for them to close their ranks and reintroduce Stalinism. (And that they *did* feel so, and that they *did* close their ranks, is proved by their secret talks with the Yugoslavs on 2 November, to which we shall return.) The system sponsored and endorsed by an American intervention would not have even resembled that described by Bibó. In all probability it would have been a replica of Greece after the civil war. At the same time, there is no evidence that the government of the United States had seriously considered the military option. There are two explanations of why armed intervention did not take place, though both are undocumented and even unreliable. The first is to be found in David Irving's book on the revolution, which has been quite aptly summed up by one of its critics as a 'bucketful of slime'. According to Irving, who claims that he had listened to secret CIA tapes, Dulles was most reluctant to side with the Hungarian 'mob'. Now, this explanation, apart from the fact that it stems from this man, is most unreliable for the following reasons. Not only the American press (which does not necessarily mirror the official position), but also the government agencies, after a hypocritical and tendentious delay, sided to a great degree and with much sympathy with this 'mob uprising' (as Irving calls it), both in their statements and in their United Nations declarations. Secondly, they have never been too fastidious with regard to genuine mob actions, as can be seen from the *official* American attitude after the Indonesian bloodbaths of 1964, which American diplomacy accepted as a 'natural' outburst of popular fury. The other explanation we have repeatedly heard in semi-official circles in Hungary, and obviously deliberately circulated, though not substantiated by documents, has both the authority of the (alas) too well-informed KGB and the general reasonableness of the story itself in its favour. According to this, the Pentagon, immediately alert to the opportunities offered by the situation, confronted Eisenhower with the option (or options) of a military action. Given, however, that American contingents could only have been deployed via Austria, this would have meant, even allowing for Austrian consent, the destruction of the first and only fruit of early *détente*: Austrian neutrality. Consequently, Eisenhower discarded all thought of military action and introduced the attitude which nearly twenty-five years later was sardonically applied to Carter: the 'no-win strategy'.

The second option, and the one that in fact the Americans – and with them all the Western powers, their allies and proxies – chose to follow, was just as treacherous and hypocritical as it was impotent. On the one hand, they increased the promises to and the militant spirit in the Hungarian population through non-binding propaganda channels and primarily through Radio Free Europe, which was under direct CIA control and administration and which was regarded as an *official* medium expressing government policies, though of course it was not official at all. This seemed to be a very ingenious scheme, but was in fact infantile and suicidal. The moment the Hungarian masses realised the deception (together with other nations of the area), they lost all belief in the credibility of Western promises and foreign policy. Moreover, the feeling of being deceived contributed to the collapse of resistance – a collapse just as swift and radical as it had seemed unbreakable a few weeks earlier. There was one particularly nasty aspect of American propaganda as relayed through Radio Free Europe: its spokesmen concentrated fire not so much on the actual Stalinists themselves as on the 'hidden Stalinists', and first of all on Imre Nagy – in other words, on all those who really broke with Stalinist traditions but tried to give a socialist-democratic turn to events, who tried to introduce a realistic and socially progressive course. By doing this, Radio Free Europe actively assisted Soviet propaganda in building up the image of a homogeneous counter-revolution, and fuelled the desperate bravado of small terrorist groups, sometimes even singling out targets for them. On the other hand, when the second Soviet intervention came, the Western powers (primarily the United States) did nothing – apart from helping the refugees – but stage theatrical performances in the United Nations sessions.

The third alternative of *real negotiation* and of initiating a period of global *détente* did not even enter their minds.

The American politicians obviously expected a twofold and glorifying result from this devious policy: a *mutual* humiliation of British–French and Soviet imperialisms without even having to employ the military, and the solidification of American supremacy. For a moment this indeed seemed to be the outcome of their strategy. The long-term results were, however, the total exposure of the 'roll-back' strategy as a purely verbal exercise and the missing of a historical bus – of the opportunity to end the Cold War. The only positive impact on Eastern Europe of this American perfidy can perhaps be seen a quarter of a century later: people can *now* grasp that freedom is only achieved through *their own* efforts.

(ii) The Soviet Post-Stalin Internal Fight and the Hungarian Revolution

The *impact* of the Hungarian revolution on the *Soviet Union* can only be understood if we consider, both logically and historically, the various strategies with which the Soviet leadership grappled between the time of Stalin's death and the actual outbreak of the Hungarian revolution. Yet, even after decades of 'scientific

Kremlinology', it is very difficult to tie up any particular option with any particular Soviet leader. All these men were deeply involved in the horrendous crimes of Stalinism (even if not to the same degree), and all of them tried to escape their past by alternately appearing as de-Stalinisers or as defenders of a continuity with the past, and sometimes as an incoherent mixture of both. Since an effective consensus operated between them on at least one important issue – that of not publishing any secret documents that might shed light on the actual state of events (Khrushchev provoked real hatred by repeatedly violating this sacred rule) – to some extent even the best experts are still groping in the dark. This state of affairs provides material for ingenious reconstructions, but little positive knowledge. Naturally, our reconstruction will not be exempt from such ills, either. It must also be remembered that, from early 1953 up until the revolution, Hungary played a *central* role *in every phase* of the Soviet internal power-struggles. While the first point is common knowledge, the second needs corroboration.

The turning of the tide in Hungary was signalled by a swift, unexpected and dramatic event: the people learned overnight in June 1953 that the Central Committee of the party (in a session not even the resolution of which was published) had appointed Imre Nagy, the scarcely known Minister of Natural Taxation and former Minister of Agriculture, as Prime Minister. Nagy's parliamentary speech on 'new governmental policy' (to which we shall return shortly) revealed him as a leader rather than a second man, and when the frightened party apparatus hysterically demanded guidelines Rákosi addressed them a week later at a Budapest party organisation meeting and gave an 'interpretation' of Nagy's speech that in plain Hungarian was equivalent to a counter-programme. This much is generally known, but the reasons for such a drastic leadership reshuffle are less clear, and an explanation is called for, given that Hungary was the *only* country where events led to such change. The Soviet trend was to the contrary, and was so marked that even Ulbricht, with his spectacular fiasco of the Berlin uprising only a week before Nagy was secretly appointed in Moscow, was able to save his head and his position.

In looking at the dramatic summoning to Moscow in June 1953 of Rákosi, Farkas, Gerő, and Dobi, who were all members of the Hungarian Political Bureau, and of Szalai (Rákosi's secretary) and Nagy (the unexpected companion who was *then not* part of this political body), the most plausible account of this event stems from

Nagy's Memoranda collected in *On Communism* (1957). The story amounts to the following. There seemed to be a far-reaching consensus (with the exception of perhaps Molotov and Kaganovich) between the otherwise warring factions of the Soviet Political Bureau regarding the necessity of implementing changes in Hungary, including a spectacular leadership reshuffle. The Soviet leadership was outraged by the Hungarian situation, and Khrushchev is quoted as saying that, without changes, Rákosi would be 'chased away with pitchforks from Hungary'.[13]

The same source mentions Beria's statement that Rákosi intended to be the first Jewish king in Hungary. Khrushchev seems also to have attacked the degree of power concentrated in Rákosi's hands (he was at that time both General Secretary and Prime Minister). If we finally add that Nagy's 'new policy speech' leaves no doubt about his (at least partially) 'Malenkovite' consumerist intentions, it is easy to imagine — an idea positively confirmed by Nagy in the *Memoranda* — that Malenkov was also instrumental in Nagy's promotion. The above remark by Khrushchev, which has a ring of plausibility, also gives some clue as to the reasons for the reshuffle. The 'pitchforks' indicate the danger of a peasant uprising, and Hungary was indeed on the brink of an agricultural collapse — a situation about which the Soviet leadership must have had some knowledge, considering that it was to the Soviet Union (and to the Soviet Union alone) that the Hungarian leaders must have turned for immediate aid. It is also widely accepted that Nagy himself had kept one unidentified member of the Soviet Presidium informed of the coming agrarian catastrophe. In the immediate aftermath of Berlin, and of the Pilzen riot, during which the portraits of Masaryk and Beneš had appeared in the ranks of the demonstrators, the last thing the Soviet leaders wanted was a further mutiny caused by famine. And so, reluctantly, they resolved upon the first fateful decision of their new collective rule.

However, the effects of this decision were beyond their immediate control, and raised totally unexpected problems for them. The 'new policy speech' was an event unprecedented in the history of communism since Lenin's inauguration of the New Economic Policy. First, here was a surprisingly sincere and outspoken statement condemning not single mistakes and occasional errors but the *overall political strategy of an entire period*. It was delivered by a man *not* responsible for the actions condemned therein (especially not for the crimes), and in effect became – without, of course, using Stalin's name – *the first de-Stalinising speech*. Secondly, it was not the usual Stalinist trick of making conciliatory gestures and false promises in order to defuse tension. It immediately opened up new social channels and provided opportunities for new lifestyles. Peasants could leave the kolkhozes they had been forced into (an unheard-of liberalisation), an accelerated industrial strategy of producing elementary consumer goods was set in motion, and the occupants of internment-camps were released. Thirdly, this final step evidenced an absolutely fundamental part of Nagy's policy: his determination to put an end to the rule of terror, the first show of which was the public admission of the existence of this very rule. Finally, certain 'nationalist' overtones indicated a receptiveness towards 'national communism'. In its entirety, the 'new policy speech' meant that the Hungarian genie was out of the bottle, and it had become a *Soviet* internal problem of the first order.

In February 1955, Malenkov was ousted from the post of Prime Minister, his politics of an accelerated growth of light industry (in order to produce certain essential consumer goods that were totally lacking) being branded as a rightist deviation; and somewhat more than a month later, during the March meeting of the Hungarian Central Committee, the same fate befell Imre Nagy. The connection between the two events was too obvious to escape anyone, but we have factual evidence from the same source – namely, from Imre Nagy, who had told the story to his closest friends – of the causes of the turn. 'Prior to the meeting of the Soviet Central Committee [which was to brand Malenkov's policy as Bukharinist] a Hungarian delegation had appeared before the Soviet Presidium in Moscow. The date of this confrontation is in doubt, but appears to have been in the first half of January 1955.' Once again, just as in June 1953, heavy accusations were made, but

> this time not against Rákosi, but against Imre Nagy. Nagy was reproached first of all for the economic failures of the New Course: the setback in industrial production, the collapse of most of the agricultural collectives, chaos in foreign trade, and hopeless indebtedness. All these were fields where the Prime Minister had very little control; the accusations were addressed to the wrong person. *There were also accusations of a different kind, more general in nature: unrest in the country, formation of factions and cliques in the Party, open*

activity of the 'enemy', too many liberties permitted to anti-Party and counter-revolutionary elements.[14]

In the main, the content of this dramatic encounter comes as no great surprise to either expert or layman. But one aspect of it sheds light on the fact that the 'Malenkovite' policy was not a one-way street. It not only came as a 'suggestion' from Moscow and found its adequate agent in Nagy, but things happened the other way round as well. The implementer of moderate changes turned out to be dangerously radical (this view is incorporated in the charges stressed by us), and his radicalism influenced negatively the position of his main supporter in Moscow. This is specifically stated by Váli:

> Malenkov's star was already in decline; for this reason he now showed much accommodation towards the views of his colleagues, and was willing to pose as spokesman, on behalf of the Presidium, in denouncing the Hungarian Prime Minister. *Malenkov had also been accused of endangering, by his economic and foreign policy, the orderly development of the People's Democracies.* In attacking Nagy, he had the opportunity to correct his mistakes.[15]

In our view, this is an irrefutable corroboration (via the witness, Nagy himself) of what we have assumed from the outset: that both the events leading to the Hungarian revolution and its actual outbreak had decisively influenced the Soviet internal power-struggle.

Nor were the Soviet leaders, slowly sizing up their chosen man, totally unfounded in their concerns. Unlike Malenkov, the Hungarian Premier combined four elements in his policy: an acceleration in the production of consumer goods; the transformation of several traditional Soviet institutions (especially in the field of agriculture); a demand for the rehabilitation of *all* Stalinist victims (years before Khrushchev's 'secret speech'); and another totally unprecedented gesture – an *open alliance* with representatives of the 'thaw' and, first of all, with certain dissenting intellectuals. All this could be a more than instructive parable, as well as providing Malenkov's enemies with a basis for accusations about where this policy would lead.

From the end of 1955 onwards, Hungary in general, and the

ever-strengthening Nagy group in particular, became direct challenges and an incessant problem for the whole system of Soviet societies.[16] During 1956 it seemed that the Soviet leaders were fighting a losing battle, constantly arriving with fatal delays at the battle scene. Moreover, for the first time since Trotsky, a near-blatant factional activity had appeared in a communist country – a constant and quasi-public pressure on the leading organs of the party in the form of an alternative programme. The Soviet leaders made consistently belated moves. They were resolved upon the 'secret speech' read by Khrushchev at the 20th Congress of the Soviet Communist Party (which in Hungary had lost all secrecy within two days), but immediately after it tried to save Rákosi, the one person who had been compromised up to his neck in the murders of the Stalinist era just condemned. When they finally sacrificed him, their choice of replacement fell on Gerő, a man hardly less responsible, and hardly more popular. To this, from Poznan onwards, not only the fact of the 'Polish thaw' had been added, but the interference of the Polish cause with the Hungarian – the increasing consciousness of *tua res agitur* on both sides. Considering all of this, it is hardly an exaggeration to say that this process – which was meant as a communist-led power reform but which concluded in a radical popular revolution – became an *internal factor within Soviet policies* that deeply influenced Soviet political strategies and the choices between them.

During this entire period the Soviet leadership was torn apart by these very real but unmanageable discrepancies between the Stalin and post-Stalin environments. On the one hand, the whole system of domination was in crisis. For a quarter of a century these leaders had been accustomed to *personal* rule, and even if they frantically strove to emancipate themselves from Stalin's personal tyranny, particularly since a new wave of purges was unmistakably approaching between 1951–3, they had no idea – and absolutely no experience – of how 'collective leadership' would work. They were all first-class executives of a despotic politics and, precisely because of this, were not *policy-makers*. All of a sudden, they were confronted with decisions of global consequence. In addition, Stalin's apparently unshakeable edifice showed dangerous signs of corrosion. A greater number of mutinies and open signs of deep dissatisfaction testified to this than reached even the experts at the time. On the other hand, the Soviet Union had experienced a long history the mould of which made certain options only *logically* possible – a history whose portent could only narrow the scope of the leaders' deliberations. Finally, this country, in what is only an apparent contradiction to what has been mentioned above, was externally very powerful, with a wide range of alternative openings for inroads into the power race for world domination. The Soviet leaders were just as eager not to miss this opportunity as they were desperate to get free of the grips of a dilemma created by Stalin. This mixture of despair and reckless global ambition characterised the years during which the Hungarian revolution had been fomenting.

It is more than a philosophical debate, and assumes an overwhelming importance for the understanding of the relentless growth and generation of the Hungarian revolution out of the inner power crisis of the Soviet system when we emphasise that Isaac Deutscher's analysis of the possible alternatives of Soviet development in his *Russia after Stalin*, made immediately after Stalin's death and apparently a spectacular example of successful political prediction, was, in our view, totally false. Deutscher trumped up three alternatives and tied them in with three names. The first was a return to Stalinism pure and simple, and the 'natural' candidate for this avenue was Beria; the second was military dictatorship or Bonapartism, perhaps with Marshal Zhukov at its head; and the third was reform, which at that time was naturally linked with the name of Malenkov, not Khrushchev. The very early *coup* in which the Political Bureau simply had its most dangerous colleague killed; later, Zhukov's somewhat increased, though very short-term, political role; and, finally, Khrushchev's reformism following Malenkov's elimination – a *volte-face* in which Khrushchev 'snatched', as it were, many elements of Malenkov's politics: all these seemed to support Deutscher totally. But this was only apparently so. Without becoming entangled in a general discussion of the social character of the Soviet Union, the following objections can be made to Deutscher's tripartite division of future alternatives. First, we shall argue that a return to Stalinism pure and simple was only a logical possibility. It was in every way a social impossibility except in the imminent danger of war. Secondly, in our view (and we can only state it here, not argue it in detail), Bonapartism or a military dictatorship was then, with a fairly underdeveloped armaments production, not even a logical possibility. With respect to a later stage of social affairs, and taking into consideration the important arguments by Cornelius Castoriadis in his *Devant la guerre* (Paris Fayard, 1981), the following can be stated in principle. In a society of a 'dictatorship over needs', in which all economic decisions are *directly political* in nature, economic leadership can not be implemented by the military for two, seemingly countervailing, reasons. On the one hand, a *formal* militarisation of the economy would rob the wage-earner, already over-dependent on the state, of even that small degree of relative autonomy that he indeed enjoys, and would transform labour into a state property. Such a change would immediately provoke mutinies, if not a revolution. On the other hand, such a move would deprive the regime both of its ideological legitimation invested in the party as a sovereign and, strange as it may sound, of its *only rationality* – namely, substantive rationality. The latter cannot be provided by the military, who can have only one substantively rational goal: war, with the ultimate goal of world domination. The well-known fact that it is only in the armaments industry that a relatively far-reaching instrumental–calculative rationality now prevails in the Soviet system does not really contradict the above thesis. This island of instrumental rationality can only exist within the ultimately irrational system of planning. Should it try to generalise and impose itself on society, it would become an even more dangerous form of dysfunctional irrationality. Of course, this is only true as long as the social structure is identical with a dictatorship over needs. But any social structure can be changed, for better or for worse, and with such a change the 'société militaire' predicted by Castoriadis with such verve could easily come about. Let us, however, repeat that military society was not even a logical possibility at this time. Thirdly, 'reform' is too vague a category to represent a concrete option. We have to specify what sorts of reforms (in the plural) are meant by it. The Hungarian revolution had to grapple with very different alternatives from those proposed by Deutscher.

In what follows we delineate *four options* between which Soviet policy vacillated for the three years between 1953 and 1956. It was obvious that something ought to be done, given the tensions of which the Soviet leaders were daily informed in confidential papers, but when it came to practical steps none of them wanted to admit the feasibility of the Hegelian dictum that, in order to *change* something, *something* must be changed. They frantically strove to defuse the tensions *and* keep everything as it had been, and it happened only in the confused in-fights between factions, the frequent *volte-faces* that introduced overnight brand-new political personalities to a surprised population, and particularly in the *dialogue* with a popular dissatisfaction imposed on them for the first time since the civil war that a politics of a *limited reform*, otherwise called Khrushchevism, was forged. It is not as a result of our national bias, but, we believe, an objective historical assessment, that this Hungarian rebellion, which could be neither halted nor retarded by any type of trick, played a constant and *crucial* role in the 'education' of the Soviet leaders, both in a positive and in a negative sense.

The first option of an early détente, in complete contrast to Deutscher's assumption, and according to mounting evidence, can be connected with Beria. It consisted of quick and spectacular gestures of *inner liberalisation and/or 'Finlandisation'*. It seems to be a fact that the exposure of the 'Jewish doctors' plot' – the first public humiliation of the MVD – was Beria's personal revenge on the functionaries of his former realm. During the last two years of Stalin's life, when Beria was already on the list of a new purge and virtually divorced from the organs of state security, these people had collected 'material' against him. We have seen him in his capacity as a supporter of Nagy against Rákosi, and the unsubstantiated rumour that he simply wished to 'sell out' the Soviet occupation zone of Germany to the Western powers had been persistently circulating in the well-informed areas of Eastern Europe.[17] But there were two problems with Beria, each of them sufficient to rule out his role as a 'redeemer'. He was, despite any temporary dissociation from the 'organs', the continuator of Yeshov's 'work', in both the popular and (what is more important) the official imagination. His roots in the secret police system were too deep to allow anyone to be convinced of his goodwill. But, secondly, and precisely for this reason, he 'overdid' what would have been immediately necessary for the apparatus. His sudden improvisations, lacking coherence and strategical conception, really did endanger the bases of domination of the Soviet apparatus. What he did perform during the short period of time that his other 'liberalising' colleagues allowed him in fact contributed to the destabilisation of a tyrannical system the stability of which he had worked at building up without the slightest hesitation at its human cost.

The second option was hallmarked by Malenkov's name (whose programme was partly snatched later, when he had already been overthrown, by Khrushchev), and consisted of *very limited* measures of an *exclusively* economic liberalisation, mostly along the lines of favouring light industry (producing consumer goods) to heavy industry (the more accelerated development of which was an alleged 'law' of the 'construction of socialism'). However, for two reasons, Malenkov fought a losing battle from the beginning. The first was in part conditioned by accidental factors. This man, who in the days subsequent to Stalin's death had both the position of a (first) secretary of the Central Committee and that of Prime Minister, for reasons which are not yet satisfactorily clear let himself be manoeuvred into the acceptance of the prime ministership alone, and from there tried to impose economic policy reforms on the party. An old-time *apparatchik*, he ought to have known better. In a Soviet society, where the party is indeed sovereign, this was no way to manage affairs. Malenkov's political fate was sealed.

Yet deeper still there was another factor, recognised by no one at the time. The social crisis pervading Stalin's system was so entrenched, and it had such severe effects on both the general social structure and international affairs, that it could in no way be solved with shallow consumerist measures. And to see what kind of a social reformer we have in Malenkov one fact will suffice, taken from the same source referred to previously. Marosán mentions in other unpublished parts of his *Memoirs*, in two *deliberately unconnected* phrases (the connection between which is fairly obvious), that, in early December 1956, Malenkov made a secret visit to Budapest, and the *next day* the Central Workers' Council, the brain and the headquarters of the workers' overwhelmingly socialist resistance to the Kádár government, was outlawed.

The third option was the policy of the hardliners, the option described by Deutscher as that of returning to – in fact, rather upholding the continuity with – Stalinism 'pure and simple'. Viewed formally, and taking into consideration what the Soviet Union has always been, and particularly what it was like under Stalin, these people *apparently* had the strongest chance of success. To begin with, they had the great historical names. While a surprised world was still learning how to pronounce the name of the Ukrainian first secretary, Molotov, for instance, had already been Communist number two for decades internationally. They believed they could rely on the sympathy or, rather, what is the substitute for this in Byzantine power games, the interest of the majority of the apparatus, and their proposal seemed to be the safe way, the path that history endorsed. We cannot here analyse in detail the social character of this immediate post-Stalin Soviet Union, though a short account can be given of the reasons as to why this hard option, this seemingly safe course, became a practical impossibility: a mode of action supported only by a few mass-murderers high up in the secret police, and accompanied by no positive programme at all.

Even as Stalin lived, and immediately after the victory which was even for many non-communist millions an overwhelmingly Soviet victory, the whole ideology of 'capitalist encirclement' – an ideology supplying an apparent legitimation and a psychological background to the terror – collapsed. Stalin's strategy of constant and self-repeating cycles of purges had outlived itself, and had lingered for some time because this type of regime can only be changed with the removal of its symbolic personal incarnation. And it is only the belief of increasingly paranoid dictators that a policy of terror can be implemented at any time, in any given medium, under all circumstances. If a terrorist élite cannot even themselves be convinced of the absolute necessity of total suppression, or if they lose the conviction for it (and there are many signs that this was the case with the Soviet apparatus after the war), a policy of terror becomes historically dysfunctional. On top of this, there was no longer any 'social space' for Stalinism in the Soviet Union. By this we mean that Stalinism was roughly equal to the 'original accumulation' of industrial relations (to use Preobrashensky's slipshod term, which simply means that costs, human or technical, did not count, only growth) *plus* a simple and forcible transfer of the necessary manpower from the villages, and for *internal economic reasons* there was no longer the rationale – and much less the opportunity – for these policies to be continued in the 1950s. Finally, it was obvious that the apparatus and, in a strange way, the Stalinist 'anti-party conspirators' – Molotov, Kaganovich *et al.* – too, were no longer prepared to live under a rule that meant constant self-decimation. In short, what appeared to be the strongest faction – a group whose views thus appeared to constitute the best option – was in fact the weakest: a group without any kind of policy recommendation and without any response to new historical exigencies other than triumphant jubilation when one of the other factions failed or suffered a fiasco. Thriving on their colleagues' numerous blunders, when they themselves initiated concerted action they were soundly defeated, even if not purged.

The fourth option was the *consolidation* of a structure in crisis, *conservative* or *liberal*, but in both cases *paternalistic*. Here, three initial remarks are necessary. First, given the Soviet leaders' abhorrence of any *actual* change, this faction advocating consolidation (which meant, by implication, that they admitted the *fact* of the crisis) must have had great difficulty in finding its identity. Even when it did, it concealed it behind ideological double-talk about 'continuity in discontinuity' and the like. Secondly, there is quite a controversy in Western Soviet historiography on the matter of whether Khrushchev was a willing and, as it were, a hidden agent of such a reform, donning the necessary protective guise for quite some time; or whether, on the contrary, he was an aspirant to the role of a new Stalin, and that it was only the interplay of historical circumstances that forced him to play, when he did, the role of benefactor and liberator. Of course, Khrushchev himself, in his *Memoirs*, claims the first role, while G. Pálóczi-Horváth, in an interesting but (unfavourably) partisan biography, tries to build up the opposite image. There is no need for us to take a stand in this debate: it suffices to state that the mask grew to Khrushchev's face, basically through his being credited by the world with the authorship of the de-Stalinising 'secret speech'. Thirdly, when we speak of consolidation, we do not endow the term with any messianic or even democratic connotations. The concept simply covers the following. The majority of Stalin's heirs understood that for several reasons things could not go on as they had before: that, owing to a burgeoning publicity both inside and outside the Soviet bloc, 'something had to be done'; that such a personal rule could not be continued without a new personal dictatorship, and this they dreaded; and that even their proxies were becoming most averse to being teleguided, as had become traditional and accepted under Stalin. Some of them were determined enough at least to grope in the dark for changes, and it is our firm belief that these people were (because they *had* to be) in constant dialogue with this Hungarian revolution-in-the-making, and drew many lessons from this process. A few changes which these proponents of consolidation introduced, with the constant intention of preserving the dictatorship system, can be mentioned. First of all, there was (after a short move to the contrary) a certain number of concessions made to the 'consumer' in the Soviet states.

Khrushchev's famous 'goulash communism' had been baptised after the consumerist leanings of this new leader. Secondly, the network of oppression has remained, both inside and outside (despite Khrushchev's boasting to the contrary, the system of concentration-camps had been reintroduced, even if not on a Stalinist scale and with a Stalinist cruelty). But for the first time in Soviet history there was a tendency to make repressions limited in number and to an increasing extent goal-rational.[18] This is the basic content of what was pompously called 'restoring the Leninist norms of socialist legality'. Furthermore, despite the reality of unresolvable inner tensions (one such tension being the structural impossibility of a normal regulation of succession in leading positions), the 'consolidators' had worked out a path of transition from personal rule to an oligarchy. Finally – and this will be analysed in detail later – they also introduced at least some methods of interstate communication; methods which, though they could never prevent these inner tensions from erupting in the most violent way, at least made the relations between the Soviet centre and its dependent countries functional, a situation that no longer held in Stalin's last years when these countries were increasingly run directly by the Bjelkin–Dekanozov apparatus of the MVD.

The four options now having been outlined, it may be added that there was a fifth, but this was only ever logically present; it never had any socially influential representative. This option would have been a 'revolution from above', either with an option of democracy which would have returned the country to the state prior to the Bolshevik takeover (which had not yet made *utterly* impossible a resurfacing of political pluralism), or in an egalitarian form – in the form of Mao's cultural revolution. For the latter possibility there was no 'social space' in an industrialised Soviet Union, and for the former there existed no resolute and influential social actor. There can be hardly any doubt that the radicalism of the Hungarian revolution, which promoted the possibility of the fourth option, but weakened that of the fifth option just mentioned, contributed to the latter being discarded for good. But there are no Hegelian necessities in history, and the limits of a system are more flexible than people are generally wont to think. The process can be viewed the other way round as well. Had the Soviet leadership been resolved at least to consider the various Hungarian proposals of compromise seriously, all of which were aimed at preserving some form of socialism together with political pluralism, such an attitude *could* have become a point of departure for similar experiments in the Soviet Union. Learning from history can be a two-way process. Yet, when the Khrushchevite Political Bureau had crushed all organs of the Hungarian resistance, instead of even trying to negotiate with them, and when, instead, it had unleashed a series of reprisals directed primarily against the representatives of political pluralism, it effectively sealed off an alternative for Soviet development as well. In the end, this is not merely a historical problem: it is a deep political and moral problem about which a lack of understanding can only lead to the slandering and distorting of the principles of the generation of reform communists; of *our* generation, who fought precisely for *this* option, though we did so obviously with many illusions, and obviously by 'misreading' certain actors, by projecting our wishes into their policy objectives. Reality, stripped of all appearances, verifies that there existed no 'world-historical necessity' that would have precluded social experiments in this direction *a limine*.

The impact of the Hungarian revolution on the warring factions and their slowly crystallising options, briefly summarised, is as follows. The option of 'Finlandisation' had been thoroughly rejected. As we mentioned in our discussion of Beria's recklessness, it did not seem to be a lucrative business: given the more theatrical, instead of down-to-earth and pragmatic bargaining, attitude of the West immediately subsequent to the Hungarian revolution, it simply proved to be a dead end anyway. This sadly lost and truly world-historical opportunity has been haunting realistic statesmen of the East and the West ever since. The option of consolidation, which was intended to be liberally applied for at least a while, subjected to itself the partial option of industrial consumerism. But in the form it eventually took, shaped by those who added the direct responsibility for crushing the Hungarian Revolution to their past Stalinist crimes, it succeeded in becoming an overwhelmingly conservative solution – one which promoted *paternalism* but did not tolerate any trend of self-articulation from below. In the relation between the communist states its most important result was the 'underground' victory of the principle of 'national communism'. This latter aspect needs further analysis.

A first and obvious point is that 'national communism' was *not* a Hungarian but a Yugoslav invention. Its first official – though only partial – acceptance was indicated at the historical meeting between Khrushchev and Tito in Belgrade in 1955 during the first stages of the Soviet–Yugoslav reconciliation. Yet it became very clear in 1955–6 that the 'Yugoslav bid', albeit inevitable for any de-Stalinising consolidating trend, was one of the least fruitful of Khrushchev's business ideas. Having undergone their rehabilitation as a socialist country and a communist party, the Yugoslavs became overnight not only an acceptable but also *the* natural model for all opposition elements who wished to remain within the framework of the Soviet system but who intended to change its structure and physiognomy. Since Khrushchev himself had admitted that the Yugoslavs had suffered much injustice, reparation had to be made, and up until the Hungarian revolution these people enjoyed an ever-increasing say in questions the decisions over which had previously been a jealously guarded Soviet privilege. For instance, all of politically minded Hungary knew that Rákosi's successor, Ernő Gerő, an exceptionally unlucky choice, had become accepted only when he 'accidentally' met Tito on a hunting party in the Soviet Union and had talks with him. The fact to which we shall return later – that the Yugoslavs themselves squandered their political capital – is another question. But, as matters stood in late 1955 to early 1956, the Belgrade deal sanctifying (or at least tolerating) 'national communism' seemed to be a bargain for the Yugoslavs alone, since they did not show the slightest inclination to join the Soviet sphere of influence (a step which in 1955 received official status with the agreement creating the Warsaw pact), yet still influenced – and in Moscow's view to a dangerous extent – the countries depending on the Soviet Union. So 'national communism' very much needed the joint Polish–Hungarian push during the historical autumn of 1956 in order to become a *practically accepted* policy, while *officially* it had increasingly become anathema.

This antinomy can be accounted for in a number of ways. 'National communism' means, first of all, the *relative* autonomy of the national communist apparatuses to develop their own short-term tactics, settle their personnel problems, and so on, though naturally within a framework set by the Soviet leadership and preferably without any kind of foreign-policy objective of their own. (From which it becomes immediately clear that the Yugoslav version was something above and beyond the Soviet-endorsed type.) This principle was so extensively disregarded in Stalin's last years that it became deeply dysfunctional for the 'mini-Stalins' as well. These countries were directly run by Stalin, Beria,

Abakumov, and later on the spot by other heads of the MVD and the Bjelkin–Dekanozov group of the MVD, who behaved as colonial governors. (Bjelkin called himself 'regent' in Hungary, which was Admiral Horthy's official title.) These people made the decisions on matters of life and death between factions (the clearest example is that of the Gottwald–Slansky dispute, with the defeat and execution of the latter), and opened up channels for other national mini-Stalins to interfere with each other's affairs, if these men were of good standing or showed themselves extremely vigorous in applying the policy of repression. (Rákosi, for instance, constantly sent messages and 'warnings' to his irritated colleagues in Poland and Czechoslovakia 'recommending them' to emulate his vigour in 'exposing espionage networks' in the party.)[19] All this created more and more dangerous confusion; it threatened and daily humiliated the national leaderships. After the death of Stalin, the only man whose authority the mini-Stalins begrudgingly accepted, this administration could not be continued. On the other hand, Poland and especially Hungary taught instructive lessons about what follows if the principle of national autonomy is taken too seriously. Accordingly, 'national communism' was publicly and ideologically outlawed, and yet clandestinely practised in the form of 'consultations' between the leaderships of Warsaw Pact countries and the Soviet Political Bureau. There can be hardly any doubt that Hungary became a turning-point in respect of accepting and implementing this new policy, and not only from a negative aspect. Despite the opinion that Andropov owed the real beginnings of his career as 'Mr KGB' to his astute reports about the gathering storm, the Soviet leaders had to realise that they got far too much misleading information from their omniscient secret police. For a long time, and practically up until choosing Kádár in Hungary, they made only incorrect personal decisions, always arriving late, their gestures turning out to be provoking rather than soothing or palliating. At long last, they decided to give their national leaderships a go at the therapy.

After a quarter of a century, it is about time to take an objective view of national communism, once the pet object of both reformist communists and anti-communist liberalism. But, because this creed helped to generate such a wide range of policies, these policies having varied goals and varied results, no overall appraisal can be given of it, though in our view it is beyond doubt that the most positive version, somewhat even *beyond* the original conception, is exhibited by Yugoslavia. Apart from acting to defend the country's national independence so dearly bought during the war (something of value in itself), the 'national way to socialism' led to a real compromise between the leading political group and the population – a compromise entailing not sham but genuine concessions. (This is why we decline to describe this deeply contradictory sociopolitical system as a mere ensemble of empty gestures.) Conversely, the most negative version is probably displayed by Albania, where the equally laudable aim of defending national independence has been perverted, and serves nearly exclusively the purpose of rationalising a system of terror – a system sustained in perfect isolation for so long only because it also preserved the politically vacuous rural backwardness of the country. China, on the other hand, is a most complex case – a large chapter of modern world history so full of puzzles that we are certainly pre-empted from evaluating it here or anywhere in a few lines. Yet two brief remarks should be made here about China's national communism. To begin with, whatever one's view on the proletarian cultural revolution may be (ours is a critical one but does not lie along the lines now so fashionable in the Western and Chinese press alike), this revolution became possible only via a nationalist form of communist dictatorship: it was only by deviating from the Soviet pattern of industrialisation that China could avoid the greatest famine and ecological catastrophe of world history. Secondly, China not only became independent, but also took on the shape of a *competition*, a juggernaut that has been struggling with its existence for twenty years, and one greatly dreaded by the Soviet leadership.

Apart from governments that remained proxies pure and simple of the Soviet Union, such as the German Democratic Republic (still a formally occupied country), Bulgaria, or Husakist Czechoslovakia (countries that occasionally blackmail the Soviet leadership for more material goods, but generally remain supplicants), or countries that became dependent allies in the pursuit of building their own empire, like Vietnam, there has emerged since 1956 a region comprising limited national communist countries. These nations – Romania, Hungary and Poland – seem to be constantly desynchronised with each other. Consequently, though up until now they have represented only variations of the same limited formula, they have either been critical of each other (as with Poland and Hungary) or openly at loggerheads (very much the case with Hungary and Romania). Now, compared to the countries discussed heretofore, the motivations for limited national communism of the countries in this compound are totally different. In Gomulka's first period in Poland, and with Kádár from the mid-1960s onwards in Hungary, it was a lukewarm anti-Stalinism of the Khrushchevite brand that prevailed. In understanding the Romanian case, though, we have come to accept the assessment of a dissident writing under the pseudonym 'Lázár', according to whom the motive for Gheorghiu-Dej and Ceasescu loosening the ties with Khrushchev's Soviet Union was the exact opposite of that operative in Poland and Hungary. These men were scared by the predictable gestures and rhythm of that form of de-Stalinisation exhibited by the First Secretary, and in order to keep their arch-Stalinist system intact they made slow movements towards separation that inflamed Romanian chauvinism.

History is underscored as a totally dialectical process when we see that the fruits of these different national communisms, whether they were powered with Stalinist or non-Stalinist ideas, turned out to be totally contrary to expectations. As is generally known, Poland experienced an unbroken series of crises and internal catastrophes, whilst the invariably repressive Romania was successful for quite a long period – at least, as far as its extensive (but very badly applied) industrialisation policy was concerned. But in what sense can these very different governments be equally labelled as *limited* national communisms? Well, all remain, though some only formally, some substantively, within the framework of the Warsaw Pact. Secondly, even if they have wholly different economic strategies (this is, first of all, why the claim for their *national* communist character needs no further corroboration), they have not left Comecon. Lastly, though they can be most disobedient on various foreign-policy matters (as Romania has repeatedly been with regard to the Middle East or world conferences of communist parties), they have never experimented with deep internal social reforms, not even of the Yugoslav type.

In the final analysis, one can say that the process which both led to and ended in the Hungarian revolution, and which in our opinion directly influenced the options chosen by Soviet policy-making bodies, had two main results: it promoted and favoured the option of *consolidation* in this gradual transition from a liberal to a conservative character, *plus*, subsequent to the Khrushchev period, that of a global expansionism. The reason for this path is clear when it is understood that those who implemented this policy were the same people who had crushed the most democratic result of all these social changes: Hungary 1956. Finally, and a point of great import, it resulted in the unofficial acceptance of national communism – a communism which sometimes could and at other times could not keep the nations concerned within the orbit of Soviet power.

(iii) The Hungarian Revolution and the Western Left

If we analyse first of all the impact of the Hungarian revolution on the *communist parties*, with a particular view to those who later became, for a shorter or longer period, either truly or only superficially 'Eurocommunist', at first sight the result is nearly totally negative. The communist parties seemed then (with such exceptions as the Larsen-led Danish Communist Party) to learn so little, if anything at all, from the Hungarian October; they were prepared to side so quickly with an occupying army forcibly suppressing the first post-war general strike of a working class in Europe that in retrospect the image of this 'automatic' solidarity is most depressing and humiliating for those who mean something radically different by the word 'socialism'. It is not our intention to lecture to political parties and movements, much less to remind them of their duty (which is at the same time their own interest) radically to revise their earlier position, but as radical socialists *and* Hungarians it is still painful for us to recall the contempt that communists the world over showed towards the practically full consensus of a fighting people whilst simultaneously admiring the military might which crushed the revolt. As far as communism was concerned, the cynical dictum of Frederick the Great seemed then to reign supreme: that God always sides with the stronger battalion. And if we compare this attitude with that obtaining after the intervention against the Prague spring, no doubt a cornerstone in socialist *annals* but an event which mainly occurred in party committee buildings rather than in the self-created organs of a people (with the latter destined supposedly to become the chief objective of socialism – or even its definition *in toto*), we can understand how profoundly successful the Stalinist bolshevisation of communist parties proved to be. Had they only accepted the Hungarian party demagogy, which at that time (in Kádár's speeches as well) often alluded to Kronstadt, the communists would have acted differently towards this country in 1956. But, of course, they had been taught for decades that socialism is identical with the rule of one party. We have read reports in the Italian press regarding Togliatti's efforts at accelerating the process that ousted Rákosi from power, rejecting any support for him before the revolution, and we have also read his (publicly known) *ex post facto* speech containing mild criticism of the collapsed leadership, though that was rather irrelevant in view of what had in fact happened in Hungary.

On the other hand, it would be unjust not to recognise a kind of bifurcation which partly took off and partly gathered momentum – in the process of preparation for and the actual events of the Hungarian revolution – between the communist parties wishing to remain loyal to the Leninist–Stalinist tradition as the only true source of inspiration and political strategy and those proposing to reconsider the whole problem of socialism. The most immediate touchstone was whether one supported the hardline policy of repression or, to the contrary, a policy that was not only more mild, but actually promoted de-Stalinising policies.[20] In this sense, the party leaders' different attitudes speak for themselves. Pálóczi-Horváth, in his book on Khrushchev mentioned above, quite coherently argued that Thorez fought actively for the re-Stalinising faction at the 20th Congress of the Communist Party of the Soviet Union (an action not at all surprising given his past and personality). Thorez became part of a movement aimed at halting the gathering momentum of de-Stalinisation. On the other hand, it is equally well known what hysteria Togliatti provoked when, in his interview in *Nuovi argomenti* in 1956, he raised the question of whether the system of the Soviet Union had become 'distorted'. Despite his predictably negative answer, he received an unprecedented public rebuke via a Soviet Central Committee declaration. The hysteria is totally understandable. People with even the slightest recollection of the history of working-class movements immediately viewed it as the ironical revenge of history that Togliatti, one of the most ardent opponents of Trotskyism, reformulated, in the form of a question, Trotsky's thesis about the 'perverted workers' state'.[21] Once again we cannot support our thesis with actual documents, but given the fact that the Italian Socialist Party broke its alliance with the Italian Communist Party precisely because of the Hungarian revolution (which proves that the Hungarian situation *was* on the minds of communists) it is highly unlikely that the Hungarian October did not subsequently play a considerable role in both the theoretical and political considerations of the Italian communists – a state of affairs which made them the only critics of Khrushchevism from the position of democratic socialism within communism.

But a connection does exist between a fundamental aspect of the Hungarian revolution and the best and most sincere elements of the trend nowadays called 'Eurocommunism'. This link is in the person of Imre Nagy, whom we once called the initiator and the first martyr of Eurocommunism. This view we retain. In the second part of this essay, we shall analyse his political personality in some detail. It will suffice here to mention in what sense he deserves this description. Even though ironically it was Kádár, on 1 November, who in the name of the 'new party' hailed this 'glorious uprising' in which the Hungarian people had shaken off the despotism of the Rákosi regime and had achieved 'freedom for the people', 'independence for the country', it was, in fact, Nagy's programme that was being voiced. And, more important, it was the symbolic gesture of a Bolshevism returning the power that it had usurped for nearly half a century to its only legitimate source: the masses so often alluded to by Bolshevik leaders; the people who were fighting for their free and unalienated self-organisation.[22] We know perfectly well into what a bloody and lamentable farce this majestic moment was degraded when a few days later this acclaimed uprising was suppressed and its leaders executed; but, should Eurocommunism have any future worthy of its original promise, it will, sooner or later, recognise the depth of Nagy's symbolic gesture, the pioneering role of his personality and his martyrdom.

The end of the alliance between the Italian socialists and communists *as a direct result of the Hungarian revolution* gives good reason to term the events of October 1956 the death-knell of the Popular Front policy. The break was given even more emphasis because one important element of the package deal that Khrushchev presented as part of his de-Stalinising programme at the 20th Congress was precisely the endorsement by Soviet communism of the 'parliamentary road to socialism' – a direct return to Popular Front phraseology. Of course, we cannot judge, but only distantly observe the *national* effects of this rupture: it is the task of Italian radical socialists (of all shades) to decide whether, in the form in which it occurred, it was a positive or a negative move, especially in view of the centre-left regime in which it resulted. To avoid all misunderstanding we emphasise that without unity in action the left has no chance in Europe or anywhere else. But, accepting all of this, on a global level we regard it as a positive and not as a negative development that the break between the Italian socialists and communists put an end to the Popular Front strategy, instead of revitalising it in a Khrushchevian spirit. If the Hungarian revolution triggered this development, it acted on behalf of long-term socialist interests. The Popular Front was a direct continuation of the *Trojan-horse strategy* formulated in the early 1920s (and spelled out as such by Dimitrov himself): a strategy based on perfidy, on promises never meant to be kept, on a blueprint for the silent encirclement and liquidation of a closest ally.

In this respect Hungary provided quite specific lessons. First of all, in Nagy's second 'counter-revolutionary' government, the social democrats, who had allegedly been discarded by the working class itself, resurfaced. They were represented by Anna Kéthly, a woman with the unusual record of not yielding to the physical and moral pressure of the Stalinist prison, of not betraying her own cause under inhumane duress. She was certainly no great theoretical proponent of socialism, her ideas about what socialism may mean being much too simple, many of them proving obsolete even when formulated; but these ideas did not entail a system of terror, and she added to them the force of an unbroken will and a moral determination. Equally important was the lesson ensuing from the fate of the so-called 'leftist' faction of Hungarian social democrats. These people, partly because of the belated fanaticism of their mythology of 'class unity', and partly – even mostly – because of weakness and ambition, helped Rákosi to eliminate their own party. (Marosán even boasts in the *published* parts of his *Memoirs – A tüzes kemence (The Heated Oven)* (Budapest: Magvető, 1967) and *Az uton vegig kell menni (A Journey Once Commenced Has to Be Completed)* (Budapest: Magvető, 1972) – that both at home and at international conferences he was Rákosi's spy against his own movement.) But they were paid in kind. A truly lunatic system of police terror imprisoned even these weaklings: men rejected by social democracy and never really accepted by communism. This event, which was not generally known but which became a public scandal in all its disgusting aspects before the revolution, taught a great lesson to those still needing it. This lesson did not simply amount to the conclusion that 'socialists must not give credit to communist promises'. Had it been so, things would never had ended in such new efforts at a socialist alliance between various forces and at this new communist self-criticism which *is* 'Eurocommunism'. What became ultimately questionable through this unmasking of coercive East European fusion between the two workers' parties was the very slogan of 'One class – one party'. And it is exactly this slogan that comprised the cornerstone of the Popular Front policy. Nowadays all communist parties who have at least some credibility in the eyes of their socialist allies have given up the option of homogeneous representation. Many considerations act against such a strategic alternative in general, and several of them extend far beyond what could be directly learned from the Hungarian revolution, but it *was* the Hungarian October which gave a final push in this direction.

One immediate consequence of the Hungarian revolution or, more precisely, of its suppression by the Soviet military was the *mass exodus of the intelligentsia* from practically all communist parties.[23] This, of course, had no impact on the electorate. It belongs to the unpolished view of the working class to know that wherever a considerable proportion of it voted communist (for instance, in France, where the Communist Party fulfilled to a great extent the role of an aggressive, nationalistic and, oddly enough, pro-Soviet Labour) they stuck to their party until the perfidy of a communist leadership, like the anti-Mitterand campaign in the late 1970s, affected them in their direct interests. But the effect of this gradual loss of intelligentsia – a process that up until now seems to be irreversible – cannot really be measured in quantitative terms, either. It had several by-products, one of which was that for the first time in thirty years (with the exception of the Trotskyite movement) there came about, in the form of the New Left intelligentsia, a leftist theoretical challenge to communism. Even if many defectors had abandoned Marxism, or whatever kind of leftist ideology for that matter, enough had remained to present a problem for the ossified communist ideological apparatuses. Actually, Hungary 1956 was also the final straw in this respect. For a long time a tacit revolt against the mummy of the once emancipatory theory of Soviet Marxism had been gestating – a revolt which now broke loose in several forms and which spread over many continents, primarily that of Europe. Also, as has been mentioned, the communist movement lost along with these defectors its bid for cultural hegemony. Of course, the concept in its deeper Gramscian meaning is more than a 'star list' which a certain party can present to a nationwide audience. Primarily, it means the capacity of a movement for generating the values and life-styles which became paradigmatic for the overwhelming majority. In this sense the theory of cultural hegemony is a radical–democratic theory of domination. But intellectuals, whether we like it or loathe it, are precisely the social agents who produce the blueprints (repeatedly revised and rewritten by practical movements) of such new values and life-styles, and when they leave a party they both testify to and partly create an incapacity of that party to produce new social solutions. Thirdly, the personage of the *fellow-traveller* practically disappeared. The fellow-traveller served Soviet communism in three ways: as the *unselfish propagandist* whose word sometimes carried a lot more weight than that of the committed–functionalised person (see the difference between Rolland's and Barbusse's impact and the weight of such a noble fellow-traveller as the Count Károlyi); as the secret 'fixer', the person who could contact people at important places who were otherwise inaccessible to official communists; and, lastly, as the *ideologically motivated* spy (Philby seems to be the greatest example of this type). In a world of 'either–or', when one either accepted and exalted the Soviet Union or was denounced as its enemy, the fellow-traveller influenced people exactly because of his or her flexibility. This person criticised many things in communism or in the actual state of Soviet affairs, but still – as Károlyi emphasised – regarded the Soviet Union as the 'nucleus'. After Hungary 1956 this attitude gradually lost its fascination in the West, and people rather viewed it as something dangerously inconsistent, particularly when leftist movements of the most different persuasions were prepared openly to criticise the Soviet Union. The Hungarian people's consensus against a regime which called itself socialist; the brutality and cynicism with which the revolt had been quelled; and a government simply forced on to a rebellious nation: these events also shook the fellow-traveller, many of whom had become corrupted, but who had all belonged originally to that passionate type of being – the person of conscience.

Finally, we must mention those representative intellectuals who in the radical left were practically alone in defending the cause of the Hungarian October. Foremost amongst these people was Sartre, and the Hungarian issue of *Les Temps modernes*. This journal, then at its height as far as its political influence and independent radicalism were concerned, made it very clear (something often now forgotten even in the liberal press) that October 1956 was not a mob uprising or a counter-revolutionary mutiny, but an event deeply rooted in the structure and the politics of the Stalinist years. Yet Sartre himself lived far too visibly under 'Stalin's shadow'. Even if he understood the reasons for this revolution he could not ultimately legitimate it via his philosophy of history, a philosophy for which the Soviet Union still remained the chief reference point, the moral datum line, the nucleus. Sartre, in effect, became the last towering example of the fellow-traveller. He was particularly unjust and condescending (an attitude unusual for him) towards the minuscule group of post-Trotskyites, the group of *Socialisme ou barbarie*. This band, whose most important members were Castoriadis and Lefort, is now at the centre of post-Marxist radical discourse, and its great achievement was then the unhesitating defence of the revolutionary masses in action and the latter's spontaneous genius in creating adequate organs of self-government. But a then equally lonely and hardly known representative of non-Marxist radicalism, Hannah Arendt, joined them, first in a booklet immediately following the events and subsequently a few years later in a brief but magnificent analysis of the Hungarian workers' council movement. In this essay, 'The revolutionary tradition and its lost treasure', she cites Odysse Barrot concerning the revolution of 1871:

> 'En tant que révolution sociale, 1871 procède directement de 1793, qu'il continue et qu'il doît achever . . . En tant que révolution politique, au contraire, 1871 est réaction contre 1793 et un retour à 1789. Il a éffacé du programme les mots "une et indivisible" et rejètte l'idée autoritaire qui est une idée toute monarchique . . . pour se rallier à l'idée fédérative, qui est par excellence l'idée libérale et républicaine . . .'

In order to prove what Odysse Barrot felt to be true, we must turn to the February Revolution of 1917 in Russia and to the Hungarian Revolution in 1956, both of which lasted just long enough to show in bare outlines what a government would look like and how a republic was likely to function if they were founded upon the principles of the council system. In both instances councils or *soviets* had sprung up everywhere, completely independent of one another; workers', soldiers', and peasants' councils in the case of Russia and the most disparate kinds of councils in the case of Hungary: neighbourhood councils that emerged in all residential districts, so-called revolutionary councils that grew out of fighting together in the streets, councils of writers and artists, born in the coffee-houses of Budapest, students' and youths' councils at the universities, workers' councils in the factories, councils in the army, among the civil servants, and so on. The formation of a council in each of these disparate groups turned a more or less accidental proximity into a political institution . . . The common object as the foundation of a new body politic, a new type of republican government which would rest on 'elementary republics' in such a way that its own central power did not deprive the constituent bodies of their original power to constitute. The councils, in other words, jealous of their capacity to act and to form opinion, were bound to discover the divisibility of power as well as its most important consequence, the necessary separation of powers in government.[24]

(iv) The East European Context

The summer and fall of 1956 were a unique phase in the history of Eastern Europe: a period unparalleled since the seventeenth century and Jan Sobieski, when the Catholic nobility of Poland and the Catholic and Protestant nobility of Hungary united to defend Christian Europe against the Muslim Turkish invasion. It was a brief but *synchronised* action in a generally desynchronised era. The traditional superpowers of the region – the Ottoman Empire, the Habsburg monarchy, and Russia, countries later joined by Bismarck's Germany – had experienced easy success with their politics of 'divide and rule'. The nations or national groups of the region had so divided themselves as to fall victim to any expansionism, and this was not otherwise after 1945: it *couldn't* be otherwise since in Eastern Europe the whole irrationality of the 1918–19 Paris–Versailles peace treaty system (a system condemned *then* by Soviet Russia and the Comintern) had been repeated once again, this time under the aegis of the Yalta–Potsdam 'superior wisdom'. It is very tempting to recount here the arguments of Bibó in another brilliant essay, 'The misery of the small nations in Eastern Europe', but it will suffice if we simply list the most detrimental factors influencing political life in this region to date. The first was the usual phony moralising of the victorious powers: the decisions as to which nations were 'guilty' and which deserved citations and rewards – a very questionable method in an international politics already laced with strong doses of Machiavellian cunning. Thus Romania, the only country not simply Hitler's ally, but under Marshal Antonescu having her own 'national way to the final solution', her own annihilation-camps, was declared not guilty. Indeed, for what were judged as her merits – amounting to nothing more than the shrewdness of her utterly corrupt and brutal ruling classes in deserting Hitler at the very last moment, a shrewdness and efficacy the equally brutal and corrupt Hungarian ruling classes did not display – Romania was given Northern Transylvania, a region overwhelmingly populated by Hungarians, and which since that time has been unceasingly a source of tension between the two countries. Though it has no bearing on the evaluation of this moralising injustice, it should be mentioned, for the sake of impartiality, that the democratic Hungarians must themselves bear a responsibility for not creating a resistance movement at least strong enough to tear *their* country away from Hitler's defeated cause (in a similar manner) at the very last moment. Even in the cases where it was debatable whether territorial changes were to the advantage or the disadvantage of a particular nation (as with Poland, where the argument is that the regions gained from Germany in exchange for those 'reunited' with the Ukraine were economically far more valuable), the changes themselves took place without a referendum, without even formally inviting the nation concerned to the polls. Poland, a valiant ally against Hitler and legally one of the victorious nations, was a chief victim of this process. Secondly, an inhumane policy of mutual and coercive population-transfer was encouraged – or, at least, certainly tolerated – by the victors (mostly by the Soviet Union). Public knowledge of this policy was suppressed. The Soviet press never wrote of it, and the East European press, working under Soviet military supervision, scarcely mentioned it, either, even during the brief quasi-democratic period of 1945–8. The expulsion of the German minorities from Poland, Czechoslovakia, and even from Hungary (Hitler's last ally) was an utterly hypocritical act exacting hundreds of thousands of victims from a national group literally driven out of their homes without the most elementary means of survival; and this act, together with the equally inhumane forced exodus of the Hungarians from Slovakia, was a policy of brutal and stupid injustice matched – rather surpassed – only by the Soviet post-war mass-deportation of parts of the population of the Baltic republics (or people such as the Crimean Tartars). Thirdly, Yugoslavia seems to be the only exception to the far-from-golden rule that it counted as 'pernicious nationalism' whenever minority national groups (Slovakians, Hungarians in Romania or in Czechoslovakia, and the vestiges of minority Germans in Poland and in Romania) tried to publicise either their sufferings or the discrimination directed against them, while it was 'progressive patriotism' when the leading nation, the 'nucleus', asserted its primogeniture and prerogatives over them. (This is said without the slightest intention of embellishing the Yugoslav situation, which deserves severe criticism in many respects.) Finally, this whole system of moralising injustice, of brutality on a massive scale, and of apparent irrationality had at least one instrumentally rational principle behind it, the only one that in the long run proved to be productive for the main victor, the Soviet Union: it divided these nations, in which new elements of disaffection have been added to traditional hatreds, and it divided them thoroughly.

A moment of accord was brought into this complex web of reciprocal mistrust, disaffection, and suppressed but unmistakable hostility by the unformalised but palpable alliance between Polish and Hungarian social forces in the autumn of 1956. This alliance demanded reforms that involved an independent and much more liberal Yugoslavia. As is always the case with movements under duress, it is hard to tell here, too, just how much of this alliance was due to cunning and tactical calculation, and how much to sincere sympathy. Undoubtedly the old hate against 'Serbs' was still lurking in the back of people's minds, and as a prominent Hungarian was said to have stated in those days: 'We have been a Russian colony long enough not to become now a Serbian colony!' On the other hand, we know from personal experience that, for all those who wanted a reformed *socialism* at the end of the road, Yugoslavia was *then* the model state, and for that objective our generation was ready to overlook obvious deficiencies in the Yugoslav political system, and we uncritically adored its resolute stance against Stalin; its (relative) internal rationality and liberality. The 'Yugoslav evening' of the Petőfi Circle was conceived of in this spirit. We simply have no knowledge of the hidden feelings of Poles about Yugoslavia, but on the visible political surface it was clear that, in the post-Poznan situation, all those who regarded Ochab as a Polish Gerő, that is to say, as a non-solution in the critical situation after the 20th Congress, held as a result of this attitude either looser or tighter contacts with the Yugoslavs.

Weighing up the impact of the Hungarian revolution on East European affairs, the immediate result could be said to be twofold and ambivalent. On the one hand, there can be no doubt that, having their hands full of Hungary, the Soviets decided to give Gomulka's team a go; and, whatever the lamentable outcome of this regime, it was still a better solution than a bloodbath. In this sense Hungary saved Poland. Bibó formulates this aspect of Hungary 1956 in the following way:

> It is now fashionable, both on the right and on the left, to regret the unreasonable momentum of the Hungarian revolution outrunning the self-imposed limits of the Polish action. Such a regretful reprimand does not make much sense, first of all for the reason that the Hungarian and the Polish movements were interdependent, and it was precisely this being nonplussed by the Hungarian events that made it possible for the Polish movement to stop where it did.[25]

A paradigmatic Polish radical democrat like Adam Michnik corroborates this statement word by word, a quarter of a century later:

> Of course, we have to keep in mind that at that time [October 1956] the burning Budapest testified that there is a very narrow range of possible changes, that the most important rules of the game are fixed by Soviet presence and they are not being vetoed even by the West. Imre Nagy's appeal for aid and the silence of the Western governments were much too clear a signal of *the substantial validity of the Yalta agreements* and of the fact that no one will help us if we do not help ourselves.[26]

On the other hand, the radicalism of the revolution, which to date has comprised a regulative idea but *not a blueprint to copy*, together with its equally radical defeat, disbarred from that point onwards all synchronised action and alliance in Eastern Europe. Never again (except perhaps for the historical interlude of condemning the invasion against Czechoslovakia on the part of the Yugoslav and Romanian governments, plus the protest actions of a few Polish, East German and Hungarian intellectuals) has this spirit of alliance, this happy moment, returned, and certainly not in the form of an influential political factor.

Turning to the issue of the varying impact of Hungary 1956 on different countries, it must be emphasised that the main loser (after Hungary, of course) was *Yugoslavia*, but also that the Yugoslav leaders were far from innocent in missing this historical moment for themselves and for other countries. Tito had such a unique opportunity in 1955-6. It is difficult to match the degree of self-humiliation to which the Soviet leaders exposed themselves when at Belgrade airport they publicly admitted that their policy was mistaken, though childishly blaming it on 'Beria and Abakumov'. Carried out by people accustomed to sending millions to the GULAG and to regularly purging their friends of yesterday, this was not an act powered by qualms of conscience. But if they wanted some sort of a change, a state of affairs which differed at least to some extent from that under Stalin – and they certainly did – then they had to settle the biggest public blunder of Stalin, the criminalisation of Yugoslavia by the Cominform. (They also realised that, as long as she remained penalised by her 'revisionism', Yugoslavia would remain a natural focal point of all elements of dissatisfaction.)

But this involved the immediate 'undoing' of the show-trials, where the chief and collective accusation against those charged was, nearly without exception, their criminal conspiracy with the Yugoslav Gestapo agent, Tito. In addition, it involved almost all first secretaries of the area, and first of all Rákosi, this busybody of the anti-Yugoslav witchhunt, and naturally Chesnokov, too, the Bulgarian Rákosi, whom Tito had received as a 'first gift' of the Soviet leadership. There were matters to settle in Poland and Czechoslovakia also, even though Bierut died (or committed suicide) right after the 20th Congress, and even if Gottwald was no longer alive, and the Czech show-trials had more than just anti-Yugoslav ideological foundations (for instance, anti-Semitic–anti-Zionist overtones). But the latter was still a file to be urgently opened. As to Gheorghiu-Dej, Stalin's main minion in Yugoslav affairs, he made the famous report in the name of the Cominform against Yugoslavia. Hoxha's murderous trials were equally directly aimed against Yugoslavia. Consequently, the Yugoslav leaders had totally legitimate reasons for setting as a condition of normalisation the exposure of all these Stalinist manipulations, the immediate dismissal of the main culprits, and the rehabilitation of the victims. Whether successful or not, such a resolute (and preferably public) demand would have made them the natural focal point of all the forces that were demanding changes in Eastern Europe and, without exploiting journalistic pathos, true champions of liberty in the region. There are many details we are unacquainted with, but there is no evidence, and not even any rumours, as to any resolute Yugoslav determination on this question, except perhaps for the cases of Rákosi and Chesnokov, regarding whom the Yugoslav leaders gradually gained ground with the Soviets, and Hoxha, in whose case they didn't because Hoxha was out of Soviet reach to the same extent that Yugoslavia itself was in 1948. Such lack of application on the part of an otherwise most energetic leadership is a mystery we cannot unfold, but this opportunity was missed, and it never returned. It is even possible that this apparent anomaly on the part of the Yugoslav leadership is connected with the fact that the Soviet Political Bureau was demanding too high a price for concessions, perhaps even the price of Yugoslavia's joining the Warsaw Pact, in exchange for the dismissal of all anti-Tito leaders and a partial liberalisation. If this was the price to pay, then the Yugoslavs had a strong case for declining to do business, and instead remaining distant observers of the events.[27]

But, if there were mitigating circumstances in the assessment of the political line taken by the Yugoslav leadership *prior* to the outbreak of the Hungarian revolution, nothing can defend its perfidy and narrow-mindedness *during* and *after* it: a deplorable approach of which then only the tip of the iceberg was visible to the layman, but about which more and more painful details have been revealed ever since. The two-edged character of the situation is best illustrated by Tito's famous speech in Pula, on 11 November, 1956, which was tantamount to the formal acceptance of the Soviet intervention and the Kádár government. This was the first official statement that left no doubts regarding just where the earlier 'radical' Yugoslav now stood. On the other hand, it was formulated in Tito's usual outspoken manner – something that did not detract at all from its most negative content, but which a Hungarian leadership hastily reverting to its original Muscovite style was most reluctant to publish. And when the *Népszabadság*, the rebaptised party-newspaper disseminating old-style lies embellished with a newly invented demagoguery, but having an editorial board which was then still sufficiently under the spell of the revolution to be, though Kádárite, rebellious enough to push the editor-in-chief, Lajos Fehér, into publishing the speech the official outrage at the top was so vehement that Fehér was immediately demoted. Even so, this report made publicly available the essential message – never forgotten – that one should not be deluded into relying on the political aid of Yugoslavia. Since then more important details have been printed, stemming from very different quarters but corroborating each other. From one angle Khrushchev, in his memoirs smuggled out to the West (containing, as expected, a pack of self-apologetic lies, but the ultimate reliability of which, to our knowledge, is not questioned by the experts), and from another angle Micunovic give a coherent story which we shall sum up with the words of Micunovic. The secret negotiations between the Yugoslav delegation (Tito, Rankovic, Kardelj and Micunovic) and the Soviet delegation (consisting of Khrushchev and Malenkov alone) took place from seven o'clock in the evening of 2 November to five o'clock the following morning. Khrushchev first informed the Yugoslavs that they were actually the last to be consulted regarding the Soviet plans for Hungary, to which all countries gave their consent, except for certain objections on the part of Gomulka. Then Khrushchev, who in later talks with the Yugoslavs in 1957 showed surprising and cold-blooded indifference about the fate of Yugoslav communists then recently murdered by Hoxha, obviously regarding such acts as a party prerogative, started off emotionally without giving any serious analysis of the course of events, saying that communists in Hungary were being murdered, butchered and hanged. He mentioned Imre Nagy's appeal to the United Nations and the four powers, and the withdrawal from the Warsaw Pact. It was a question of whether capitalism was restored in Hungary. Whether Nagy was just a tool or had himself long been an agent of imperialism was not clear at the moment.

'What is there left for us to do?' Khrushchev asked, meaning the Soviet Union. 'If we let things take their course, the West would say we are either stupid or weak, and that's one and the same thing. We cannot possibly permit it, either as Communists and internationalists or as the Soviet state.' He said they had assembled sufficient troops and that they had decided to put a stop to what was going on in Hungary. Khrushchev turned again to the question of intervention by the Soviet Army. He said that there were also internal reasons in the Soviet Union why they could not permit the restoration of capitalism in Hungary. There were people in the Soviet Union who would say that as long as Stalin was in command everybody obeyed and there were no big shocks, but that now, ever since *they* had come to power . . . Russia had suffered the defeat and loss of Hungary. And this was happening at a time when the present Soviet leaders were condemning Stalin . . . Malenkov let it be known that everything in the Soviet Union was ready for the second military intervention against the Nagy government to start right away. It is clear that the Russians are going to intervene frontally and with great force, because they are completely isolated from the Hungarian people . . . We explained that we were also concerned at the swing of events to the right, toward counter-revolution, when we saw the Nagy government allowing Communists to be murdered and hanged. There would have to be intervention if there was a counter-revolution in Hungary, but it should not be based exclusively on the weapons of the Soviet Army. There would be bloodshed, with the people of Hungary fighting against Soviet troops, because the Communist party of Hungary, as a result of what had happened in the past, had disintegrated, and no longer existed. We suggested that in the present situation there should be some political preparation, an effort to save what could be saved, and to set up something like a revolutionary government composed of Hungarians who could give the people some kind of political lead. A short discussion of the possible leaders followed, in which the Soviet delegates supported Münnich, the Yugoslav leaders Kádár. The Russians are obviously in favour of Münnich but are not against accepting our proposal. We pointed out that much depended on what the policy of the new government would be. Some of us suggested that the new government should condemn sharply and categorically the policy of Rákosi and Gerő as well as everything in the past which led to this situation: Khrushchev and Malenkov reluctantly agreed. Once again the debate about the First Man had been resumed, but when Micunovic pointed out to Khrushchev that Münnich had been somewhat compromised by being Rákosi's Moscow Ambassador in the anti-Tito times, Khrushchev gave his agreement to the Yugoslav request.[28]

With regard to the subsequent fate of Nagy, who was simply abducted together with his group, taken first to Romania and later executed, and the role of the Yugoslav leadership in it, Micunovic very valiantly (and more or less convincingly) defends his government's twofold aim: to protect the lives of his group whilst excluding them from political life for good. But on this issue it is very typical how Micunovic protests to Khrushchev on 19 June 1958:

> I raised the question of Nagy's execution. I told him that the whole world was shocked, and that an irreparable mistake had been made, and that it would be difficult for anyone to conceive anything worse for the Soviet Union and Hungary. *Nagy had meant less and less politically in Hungary, but they had now liquidated him physically but had resurrected him politically.* It was obviously a disagreeable subject for Khrushchev. He said it was Hungary's affair, and not the Soviet Union's [about which Micunovic, and rightly so, does not believe a word] but that he personally approved what the Hungarians had done and would have done the same himself. He reproached me as a Communist for referring to world public opinion, saying that Communists have other, class criteria in such matters.[29]

It is here most appropriate to quote the unfortunately evergreen Talleyrand: 'C'est plus qu'un crime, c'est une faute.' For, on the one hand, the Yugoslav perfidy did not pay them in terms of influence. In fact, just the opposite occurred. *The last moment* that top Soviet delegations discussed the political fate of Eastern Europe with Yugoslavia, or asked the Yugoslav leaders for any kind of advice, was precisely this fateful 2 November 1956. It would be a cavalier statement without foundation if we were to say that, had Tito and his colleagues vetoed the Soviet decision, a second intervention would not have taken place. We have seen that, in all probability, they never had that much influence over Soviet decisions. But a veto could have constituted a serious obstacle to the course of intervention. Not only would the Yugoslav attitude have then become unpredictable (Yugoslavia could even have served as a basis for protracted Hungarian resistance), but it could also have influenced the attitude of the West, whose ominous silence (except for propaganda exercises) not only did not escape Yugoslav attention but in all probability also had a crucial impact on the Yugoslav leaders. Yet the result, whatever the underlying strategic or tactical considerations, was that Yugoslavia remained anathema for all East European countries – practically just as suspect as in the good old Cominform days, though minus the unnecessary and compromising verbal acrobatics. In order to show what political capital Yugoslavia has nowadays in the Warsaw Pact countries, it is enough to quote a very short paragraph from *The History of the Hungarian Revolutionary Working-Class Movement*, published in 1979, which in its analysis of the 'crimes' of the Nagy faction says quite emphatically: 'It is a feature in common of the propaganda of the bourgeois reactionary groups and the revisionist faction to idealise the Western capitalist social relations, slandering the Soviet Union and other socialist countries . . . *They speak appreciatingly of Yugoslavia, first of all because it detaches itself from the Warsaw Pact.*'[30]

On the other hand, the motives behind the Yugoslav decision were most likely narrow-minded. First of all, it is obvious that for them leaving the Warsaw Pact could not qualify as a counter-revolutionary action. Secondly, in whatever light the character of the Hungarian events might have appeared to the Yugoslav leaders, and even if they regarded them as a genuine counter-revolution, nothing sanctified, in terms of *their own politics*, their offer of political support to the intervention in order to suppress the revolt. Ever since their break with the 'socialist camp' in 1948, the Yugoslav leaders had had to learn to co-exist with capitalist countries, and sometimes with those that were least liberal; and, if the worst came to the worst, Hungary would have been only one more on the list. At the same time, offering to help intervene in another nation's affairs on *ideological grounds* set up a very dangerous precedent regarding future prospects for Yugoslav independence. The only reasonable explanation is that the 'Djilas complex' of Tito and his associates had gained the upper hand. The moment Hungary returned to political pluralism, even if only for a few days, they felt the ghost of Djilas' programme knocking on their door. But as usual, and with this case being no exception, fear inspires bad solutions.

A far more clandestine but equally tortuous story is that of the

Romanian reaction to the Hungarian revolution. It is first of all remarkable that the Imre Nagy group had been deported to Romania, which was far from being the appropriate place. Why not the Soviet Union? Why not the reliably arch-Stalinist Czechoslovakia, which showed eagerness to support the invasion and Kádár's regime? The selection of Romania suggests that the Romanian leadership *volunteered* for this honour; that they were personally and directly involved in the speedy and obviously repressive solution to the Hungarian crisis. We know definitely from Lukács that, apart from Soviet and Hungarian emissaries, the Romanian 'supervisors' – the usual mixture of highly placed policemen and ideological inquisitors – played some role in the attempts at 'convincing' the Nagy group to give up its ideology, betray its promises and join the Kádár leadership. Gheorghiu-Dej and his Political Bureau very soon had reasons for having fears about Hungary 1956: for the first time since the war there were signs of pro-Hungarian political activity (at the universities of Cluj and Bucuresti), and this, even more ominously, could not simply be passed off as the predictable nationalist reaction of the Hungarian minority, for the swift wave of reprisals (arrests and rash sentences) hit young Romanian intellectuals, too. But the events of the Hungarian revolution instilled even deeper anxieties in the Romanian leaders. One Hungarian dissenter, now living in Romania and writing under the pseudonym 'György Lázár', in his study entitled 'Jelentés Erdélyből' ('A Report from Transylvania'), in *Irodalmi Ujság*, Vol. VII (London, 1977), states that the original concern over the 'rash' de-Stalinising gesture of Khrushchev's secret speech seems to have 'driven home the chickens to roost' in October 1956. He was of course speaking of the Stalinist Romanian leaders. Not wishing to risk their rule with Khrushchevite escapades, they pulled out of the Hungarian conflagration as swiftly as possible, afterwards going their own national (and rather chauvinistic) way of relentless internal repression.

Ulbricht remained true to his firm stance during the conversation with Marosán in the summer of 1956. He did not hesitate to regard the events as constituting a counter-revolution, and when, following the uprising (and probably even stimulated by it), Wolfgang Harich's ill-fated 'loyalist' opposition appealed against him to the Khrushchevite leadership he cracked down on the 'conspirators' without hesitation. In a way, Hungary 1956 was a final victory for Ulbricht. First, it confirmed his misgivings and warnings. He never had any doubts regarding the fact – corroborated by Manfred Hartwig, one of Harich's 'co-conspirators' – that Lukács was the intellectual foster-father of the heresy and, during their stormy encounter with Harich on 7 November 1956, three weeks before the arrest of the group, he made specific comparisons between them and the Petőfi Circle. Even though he had survived it, he had never really felt safe in his seat after the 1953 fiasco of provoking the first workers' revolt against the 'workers' state'. Shrewd politician that he was, he now understood that the Western impotence or unwillingness for the post-revolution talks that may well have resulted in the politics of *détente* (a politics the consequences of which might be very grave for him) would ensure the existence of his 'socialist East German nation'.

In Czechoslovakia, the only reaction was a secret resolution on the part of Novotny's leadership (and arrived at, of course, without any great moral qualms) *not* to launch an investigation into the show-trials, and not to instigate any kind of public rehabilitation (the memory of Rajk's funeral on 6 October 1956 in Budapest, the first mass-gathering that demonstrated the visible and increasing rage of even those who only desired the reform of the regime, was still very fresh in the minds of all observers). It was even decided to delay secret or unpublished acts of rehabilitation for as long as possible. In other countries, various courses of action were taken. Bulgaria, to our knowledge, played no part in this piece of history other than its usual automatic endorsement of Moscow's decision. Albania, on the other hand, was already in increasingly open revolt against the 'Khrushchevite treason' of the policy of the 20th Congress.

The Hungarian revolution very quickly became taboo in the Eastern bloc. It was never mentioned with any positive connotation, and was generally expunged from the records, pushed into total oblivion. To begin with, everyone had to pay tribute to the Soviet Union's intervention in the name of 'proletarian internationalism and solidarity'. Even Gomulka joined the chorus, and there is no reason to believe that he did so under duress. But after this an information blackout set in, and only so-called 'theoretical' documents analysed the 'lessons' to be drawn from Hungarian 'counter-revolution' – lessons that, of course, were never identical with those actually drawn by the leaderships involved. One important and real lesson was that of stepping up the 'divide and rule' policy. Moreover, the Hungarian revolution, an overwhelmingly *social* event, was translated by communist apparatuses into the language of anti-Hungarian chauvinism, mostly in Czechoslovakia and in Romania, but also in the Soviet Union (already Khrushchev had pointed out to Micunovic the bitter feeling of the Russian citizen towards the Hungarian who 'had fought against us' in two wars). In Romania, a decade of shameful cultural oppression of the Hungarian national minority was rationalised as 'justified suspicion' of these 'counter-revolutionary Hungarians'.

All of this, it should be understood, was only part of a wider setting, a setting to which Hungary herself, with her almost publicly pursued policy of anti-Romanian nationalism, was no exception – a policy which, for a change, is now used by the *Hungarian* government in Soviet service against the partially rebellious Romanians. But similar symptoms could also be observed in the Czech–Polish relations, which had never been all that warm. Equally, there had never been any effective obstacle to giving (not too public) vent to the expression of 'anti-Yugoslav' feelings, which were actually nothing more than revamped centennial hates and aversions. And one historical moment did arrive when the Soviet leadership could test the success of its desynchronising policy via inciting (or at least tolerating) mutual national hatreds: in August 1968. In 1956, they failed to mobilise the Warsaw Pact forces against a rebellious Hungary, and had to do the job alone. Obviously, this was not a military problem for the army that defeated Hitler's Wehrmacht, but a political matter of implicating others in the deed. We know from Pálóczi-Horváth's account that it was precisely Rokossowski's report to Khrushchev on the night of 19 October about the total unreliability of the Polish army which caused the First Secretary's abrupt *volte-face* the next day, a reversal that effectively endorsed the installation of the Gomulka group: so the Polish army could not be used. If anything, a Romanian presence (apart from the historical connotations: Hungary's Soviet Republic of 1919 was defeated by the white Romanian army) in the military action could have given rise to a peasant *guerilla* feeding on a deeply rooted nationalistic hatred. Similar considerations applied to the Czechoslovakian military presence. As far as the armed forces of the East German regime were concerned, even their symbolic presence (and Ulbricht's government could not, in all likelihood, provide anything more at the time) would have been a danger. A *German* occupying army, *anywhere* in the world, under *any* banner, little more than ten years after the war, might have raised grave considerations within the

Russian population as well. But owing to a carefully administered desynchronisation and division between the East European states these obstacles no longer required consideration by the Soviet leadership in 1968, and the privilege was granted to all the governments of Eastern Europe to soil their hands with the collective oppression of Czechoslovakian liberalisation.

It is against this background that we can formulate the *only norm* that Hungary 1956 provides for the *whole* of Eastern Europe. This is *not* the norm of a political revolution. It is perhaps too rigid a formulation when Michnik rules out any future relevance of the Hungarian experience: he does not seem to take into account the just as dangerously explosive elements inherent in the Polish *compromise* – elements that were, at least for a few days, eliminated from the Hungarian solution. But it will certainly be decided from nation to nation by the social actors themselves as to what form, if any, their emancipation will take. But, should Eastern Europe achieve any emancipation at all, it cannot afford again the total desynchronisation which it experienced for two decades. In short, the norm we speak of is the norm of *co-operation*. The need for collaboration in such emancipatory efforts had already been given expression by Imre Nagy in 1955, in a strange, but perhaps not accidental, stylistic and substantive resemblance to Bibó:

> Hungary has found herself for centuries to be the battleground of hostile forces, the target of adversaries, and she could not find her place among nations. The consequence of this was a series of national catastrophes. The great, but belated, historical conclusion had been formulated, after the defeat of our glorious war of independence [the revolution and war of independence of 1848–9], by Lajos Kossuth, by our national hero, and it was he who showed the way to follow. In order to ensure the independent, sovereign and free existence of the Hungarian people, Kossuth did not have in mind any kind of alliance with a great power or with a group of great powers, but a close co-operation between neighbour countries, in the framework of a federation of free nations enjoying equal rights. It is exactly these ideas that we have to return to.[31]

The idea of a confederation between the free nations of the region is, in our firm view, a very sound idea, and does not at all suffer from such a lack of realism as the Western reader would promptly believe. First of all, it has a *communist prehistory*. In 1947 the idea of a Balkan Confederation was discussed, and as a tentative suggestion, at least, publicised in negotiations between Tito and Dimitrov. True, this provoked the immediate rebuke of *Pravda*, then quite an unusual step in the case of such celebrities as the hero of the communist resistance, Tito, and the ex-Secretary-General of the Comintern. Nor should we necessarily believe that such ideas do not contain potentially oppressive elements: for example, under certain circumstances they could serve Soviet hegemonic interests in a better way than the existing system. But it is undeniable that ideas about a non-Soviet-led confederation have surfaced and resurfaced. F. A. Váli's generally very well-informed book states the following (without unfortunately giving the source of the information):

> Tito's ambitious projects [of playing the second role after Khrushchev in Soviet-led world communism – a conjecture by Váli] were not altogether favoured by more Western-minded members of his entourage. Kardelj and Bebler had never ceased to be suspicious of Soviet designs, and still hoped for *rapprochement* with a Hungary which had shaken off the shackles of monopolistic Soviet control, a relationship which they valued more highly than Tito's other leading project, the federation of Communist Balkan states.[32]

As becomes clear without a microscopic analysis of this passage, the idea of the Balkan Confederation had not only persisted among Tito's policy objectives, but could also have widened into one including Hungary, or could perhaps have been transformed into a dual – loosely confederative – pact with the former. The sympathy of Nagy and his group for Yugoslavia would certainly have promoted steps in this direction. Of course, we emphasise again that without perfect and radical inner democracy (a state of affairs which we identify with socialism) such a confederation would in no way be the *nec plus ultra* of political expectations. But since we regard superpower politics of *all* types as an acute threat to human survival it could have become a partial remedy, or a barrier to a military machine. Its historical neglect constitutes one of the great lost opportunities created by the Hungarian revolution.

This first part of our essay has dealt with the impact of the Hungarian revolution on the world at large, and to conclude it we should discuss its impact upon Asia. To a great many people the uproar in this tiny European country in 1956 has nowadays no influence at all on the political life of this gigantic strife-torn continent. Understandable as it is, this opinion is definitely mistaken. A point of first importance regarding Hungary 1956 and Asia is best illustrated by a long quotation from Miklós Molnár's book, *Budapest, 1956*, which, together with Bill Lomax's *Hungary 1956*, comprises our chief source of information as far as the reconstruction of events is concerned.

> China had shown a warm sympathy towards Gomulka throughout the Polish crisis, and preserved an equally favourable attitude towards the Hungarians. We do not know what the Chinese reactions were before the Soviet statement of October 30th, but the official Chinese government communiqué published on November 1st, apropos of the Soviet text, expressed a satisfaction which makes one feel that the Government of China had a say in this important statement. The Chinese Government declared that the five principles of Bandung should also be the basis of relations between socialist states, and that the claims made in the recent events in Poland and Hungary were 'perfectly justified'. In the last passages of the Chinese text there are even references without actually mentioning the USSR, to the 'bourgeois chauvinism' of certain great powers 'who neglected the principle of the equality of peoples', an accusation which, as we know, was to become one of the main grievances that Peking had against Moscow . . . In fact, Peking's sudden change of attitude towards Hungary took place on the very day when the first statement, which was still favourable to Imre Nagy, was broadcast . . . Jacques Levesque presents *two* versions of Peking's *communiqué* quoted above. In the first version which was broadcast by the New China Agency on November 1st at 15.06 hours GMT, there is a mention of Soviet errors committed in Yugoslavia, Poland and also in Hungary: 'The handling of the 1948–9 Yugoslav situation and the recent happenings in Poland and Hungary are enough to illustrate this.' In the second version which was published on the following day in *Jen Min Jibao*, Hungary had been left out.[33]

And, in fact, the Chinese leaders from then on fought in the forefront of international communist meetings and conferences in order to give a turn as negative and as repressive as possible to the Hungarian 'consolidation'. Without even offering an analysis, we may state that this is much more than an interesting item of documentation. Such a swift and dramatic change reflects upon all aspects of the inconsistency displayed henceforth in Chinese politics: on an anti-Soviet radicalisation which was not merely verbal, but which retained (and still retains) Stalin among its patron saints.

The second – and largely abortive – Asian reflex of the Hungarian events is recounted by Bill Lomax. He tells the story of Miklós Gimes, the former Stalinist journalist and later radical 'rightist' policy adviser of Nagy (executed together with the Prime Minister), who valiantly published, *after* the Soviet intervention, a journal symbolically entitled *October 23*.

> *October 23* now appeared as the official mouthpiece of the new movement, and in its earliest issues it carried the political platform drawn up by the Nagy group in the Yugoslav Embassy, giving uncompromising expression of the original demands of the revolution, and guidance on how to maintain the resistance struggle. . . . Gimes was also the main instigator in preparing a 'Draft Proposal' to be put to the Russians. This was drawn up jointly by the leaders of the Hungarian Democratic Independence Movement, in cooperation with the Revolutionary Council of Intellectuals, the Central Workers' Council, and the democratic political parties. The proposal embodied detailed suggestions for both a new Hungarian constitution and a pact with the Soviet Union which would guarantee the establishment of an independent and democratic Hungarian state that would be both *neutral and socialist*. In a most characteristic act of courage and bravado, Gimes presented himself at a press reception being held in the Grand Hotel by Mr Kumara P. S. Menon, who had been sent to Budapest as the personal representative of Prime Minister Nehru of India. Though Gimes was now a wanted man, the AVH did not dare to seize him in front of the Indian diplomats, and he was able to have a lengthy discussion with Mr Menon and to present him with a copy of the draft proposal. Needless to say, a few hours later Gimes

was arrested and imprisoned, but he had succeeded in his objective, and the draft proposal was subsequently put to the Soviet leader Bulganin by Prime Minister Nehru at a meeting in Moscow in early 1957.[34]

Naturally, Bulganin simply dismissed the whole idea of Indian mediation with a gesture of disdain (even though M. Molnár remarks with justification that the Americans were to the same extent uninterested in it). And with this action the entire Asian chapter of Hungary 1956 seemed to have been concluded. But, at the time and place that it was least expected, the phoenix did rise from its ashes. *Der Spiegel* reported that in the mass demonstration against the tyranny of the 'Gang of Four', the first mass demonstration in China demanding liberalisation and civic freedoms, the name and the photo of Imre Nagy suddenly reappeared.

Notes: Chapter 1

1. Winston S. Churchill, *The Second World War*, Vol. 6, *Triumph and Tragedy* (New York: Bantam Books, 1977), pp. 196–7 (our italics).
   There are certain literary advantages in the fact that the last great imperialist statesman was also a great writer with a Mandevilleian cynicism. There can be no doubt that Churchill deliberately used the language of a stockbroker here, just as there is no doubt that in recounting the story he still enjoyed the dark humour of his own hypocritical objections. This was old-fashioned Tory politics at its best. However, of most interest here are the developments and implications of this agreement. First, the political stockbrokers immediately went farther than was agreed upon in Churchill's proposal. After Romania, Bulgaria, Greece and Yugoslavia – a self-liberated country that still became a passive object of haggling and bartering in this trade-off – they drafted Hungary into the respective spheres of influence, and Stalin tacitly included Czechoslovakia, too. Secondly, it is remarkable that Churchill, being an expert on Leninist–Stalinist communism as well as the old fox he was, could believe for a moment that these proportions – regardless of whether they were conceived of in terms of government posts or parliamentary seats (a new concept in pre-fabricated liberal democracy conjured up by its champion) – could work effectively for any longer than a token period. Everyone now knows – and Churchill certainly did then – just what fate awaited their 10 per cent of agents, commissions and representatives under 90-per-cent Stalinist rule. That this was a cynical face-saving action on Churchill's part, rather than a serious attempt to safeguard the interests of the peoples of the Balkans, is a more probable explanation.
2. We shall return later in this study to the question of the content of the compromise offer, and particularly to the question of whether 'Kádárism' is an heir to, or a parody of, such attempts at a compromise.
3. In what follows we shall quote from this and other statements by Bibó from the Hungarian emigrant journal *Magyar Füzetek*, no. 4 (Paris, 1979).
4. I. Bibó, 'Statement of the Imre Nagy government', quoted in ibid., pp. 9–10. We shall later point to another equally representative draft of compromise stemming directly from the Nagy circle.
5. Of course, there is a point at which even courageous defenders of the Hungarian revolution – as, for instance, Castoriadis – would call such drafts figments of fantasy: that is, because of their appeal to the great powers. But, apart from determined resistance, a small nation can do two things: play *all* the cards, or commit collective suicide.
6. I. Bibó, 'Draft of a compromise solution of the Hungarian question' (1957), and further, in ibid., pp. 138. Many aspects of the problems raised here will re-emerge in our analysis, especially in the second part. Here it will suffice to state the following: (*a*) Bibó is, despite his Risorgimento mannerisms, a highly *realistic* and *sober* politician who does not depart from 'socio-ontological' considerations for or against the multi-party system, and who simply states (which remains a fact) that the communist organisations had completely lost their reputation before the Hungarian population. (Perhaps the only unrealistic element in him was that he overestimated the stamina and capacity for resistance of that population.) (*b*) The formulation leaves no doubt that Bibó wants to *maintain* socialism; he would even gain a black mark from certain present-day radical dissidents for admitting the socialist character of the communist dictatorships, though we would agree with them that he is incorrect in this. He only rejects the one-party system. These considerations, together with his possible important future role and electorate, should be very carefully noted by the Western leftists.
7. Bibó, in ibid., p. 139 (our italics).
8. ibid., p. 140.
9. M. Molnár, *Budapest, 1956* (London: Allen & Unwin, 1971), p. 220.

10 Quoted in F. A. Váli, *Rift and Revolt in Hungary* (Cambridge, Mass.: Harvard University Press, 1961), p. 355.
11 I. Bibó, 'The situation of Hungary and the international situation' (1957), in *Magyar Füzetek*, no. 4 (Paris, 1979), p. 144 (our italics). Once again, this disappointment can be called the just historical punishment of empty illusions. But we think that the Hungarian 'testing' of the trustworthiness of international institutions was a more democratic and more radical attitude than their sterile rejection *a limine*. Bibó's efforts to contact President Eisenhower directly in the early hours of 4 November when the second and final Soviet intervention had already been launched have to be added to these attempts at 'testing'. A few months ago Andor C. Clay (Sziklay Andor), American diplomat and intelligence adviser of Hungarian extraction, active between 1945 and 1972, published, as parts of an analytical essay, certain documents released by the 1966 Freedom of Information Act which included telex conversations between the American embassy in Budapest and the State Department in Washington, dated 25 October and 4 November. In the second text the representative of the American embassy reads the text of a statement handed over by Bibó personally during the telex conversation. The text had apparently been worded by Bibó and Zoltán Tildy (another non-Marxist, non-socialist minister of state without portfolio of the second Nagy government, ex-President of the Hungarian Republic). For substantive reasons which have been shown and which will become clear for the reader, we believe that the text was, in the main, the work of Bibó.

> In the present emergency situation Hungary turns with exceptional trust in the direction of the peace-loving policy, wisdom and courage which have been given voice by the President so often and so emphatically. Even if the Hungarian populace resists the attack with an ultimate resoluteness, there can hardly be any doubt that it will be defeated in this struggle against overwhelming odds, unless it gets support. At the moment, the most urgent support is political, not military, in nature. It is obvious that this new phase of Soviet plans stands in close relation to the British intervention in Egypt.
> The occupation of Hungary would not only mean a renewal of oppression in this area; it would also put an end to the trend of self-liberation that had been commenced in other East European countries in a way inspiring so much hope. It would undermine as well the American policy of liberation that has been practised with so much vigour and wisdom. It would also shatter the confidence in the United States of all East European nations; on the other hand, it would involve, under the adverse impact of the intervention in Egypt, a process of isolation of a kind that could only conclude in catastrophe. We are at the historical juncture that has often been alluded to by President Eisenhower and the Secretary of State, Dulles, when they have stated in their speeches that it is only through risking a world war that the road leading to a new world war can be blocked. Without the intention of advising the President, we have to call to his attention the possibility that, taking into consideration the mandatory necessity of avoiding the gravest consequences, he could, on the one hand, put an end to the intervention of Western powers in Egypt; on the other, he could appeal to the Soviet Union to withdraw its troops rapidly from Hungary. We are fully aware of the moral weight, as well as the practical difficulties, of such a double decision. (*Irodalmi Ujság* (*Literary Gazette*), no. XXXII (July–October 1981), Special Supplement, London, p. M10.)

12 As a general characterisation of the American policy-makers we can safely accept as objective the words of Tibor Méray, author of *Thirteen Days That Shook the Kremlin* (New York: Praeger, 1959), the first significant chronicle of the revolution, a convinced liberal conservative who cannot be accused of leftist antipathy to America: 'it has never occurred, not for a single moment, to the leaders of the United States to do

anything tangible in support of or to rescue the Hungarian revolution. They have undeniably felt sympathy to it, but this sympathy never went beyond a few humanitarian gestures or statements. They had neither plans nor intentions to lend effective aid or to bind the hands of the Soviet Union' (*Irodalmi Ujság*, no. XXXII, p. M2). More particularly, the analytical article by A. C. Clay, and the documents collected and first published in it, allow for the following conclusions. First, both in their exoteric and semi-exoteric considerations, the chief American policy-makers – President Eisenhower; Secretary of State J. F. Dulles; R. D. Murphy, Political Secretary of the State Department; Bohlen, the American ambassador in Moscow; Henry Cabot Lodge, United Nations chief delegate of the United States – considered, if anything beyond general and non-binding statements, only the military action and immediately came to the same conclusions to which Joe Citizen would have instinctively come: namely, that (*a*) it was too dangerous and (*b*) they would have to contact the Hungarian insurgents through impenetrable channels, countries which were either Warsaw Pact members or communist or non-communist neutral states (Yugoslavia and Austria). In other words, they realised that access was, in a simple geographical sense, denied to the American armed forces. Unfortunately, and taking into consideration both Eisenhower's main consideration of his re-election on 4 November 1956, and the departmental and personal in-fights so amply documented even in these days, the satirical tone of the above sentence is not a piece of cheap and frivolous anti-American propaganda but a relatively restrained description of a very sad state of affairs. The only option beyond the military, which, however, hardly deserves the denomination 'political', has been reported by Bohlen (in the same article by Clay, ibid., p. M13): '[On 29 October] I received a cable from Dulles instructing me to forward an urgent message to the Soviet leadership to the effect that the United States do not regard Hungary, or for that matter, any member of the Soviet bloc, as their potential military ally . . . The same afternoon I had an opportunity to forward the message to Khrushchev, Bulganin and Zhukov; but the American guarantee had no impact on the Soviet leaders; they had already made their decision: the revolution had to be crushed.' Now, this is a serious moment worthy of analysis in some detail. We know almost certainly – and we shall come back to this at a later stage of the analysis – that 29 October was *not yet* the moment when the final decision was taken. As a result, American foreign policy still had a chance. In addition, we need not have a pro-Soviet bias to see why Dulles' suggestion was unacceptable, even unfit for serious consideration on behalf of the Soviet leaders. For Stalin's heirs it was small consolation indeed if the American Secretary of State assured them that he did not intend to include *their* East European vassals in the Western military alliance. If the Soviet Political Bureau was ready to negotiate at all (which is questionable), its members wanted something incomparably more substantial as a first step. No single suggestion, only a *package deal*, could have helped (this was the time when the Soviet leaders wanted 'linkage'), and it will become immediately clear to the reader that Dulles did not even mention Egypt; in other words, he did not even suggest a share in world government for the Soviet leadership, and *less* was simply not satisfactory for them. It is very difficult, however, to believe that this idea simply had not occurred to Dulles. It is incomparably more likely that the whole Bohlen message was an empty gesture for posterity.

But, secondly, a dominant weakness of American diplomacy comes to the fore in these documents, a weakness for which the political élite of the United States has repeatedly (most recently in Iran) paid such a heavy price: American experts simply cannot read the accelerated events of a revolution. Obviously there is a historical reason for this: the total absence of a tradition of political revolutions from the American scene, together with a lack of appropriate experience. But the result is that a habitual attitude of 'take your time' prevails in a situation where usually there is no time at all, except for a few minutes the potential of which never returns. Let us quote an interesting passage from the telex conversation between the American embassy in

Budapest and the State Department on 25 October. The actual impact of the hesitation so characteristic was nil, precisely because of the predetermination, analysed above, not to take any step at all, except gestures of a mere propaganda value. But had the proper authorities of the United States intended to act they could not have relied on their main source of local information, their political assessors in the embassy. Here is how they sized up the situation in a crucial hour: 'It is impossible to predict developments. Yesterday we had the impression that he [Imre Nagy] would be blamed for the appeal to the Soviet Army and he would lose his popularity enormously. Today we don't know where he stands and how the population will judge upon the line of demarcation between Nagy and Kádár . . . I repeat, we do not know but we assume that Nagy is in fact Prime Minister. Should the blame for the appeal to the Soviet Army be put on Gerö, and should he become the scapegoat for all what happens now, and should Nagy make further concessions, he could yet have a chance. But we don't have enough knowledge for stating anything with an air of certainty' (*Irodalmi Ujság*, no. XXXII, Special Supplement, p. M10). Now, this is a conscientious dissertation cataloguing all logical alternatives but definitely not a political document which simply *must* run the risk of making policy recommendations then and there. We have already seen, and will see later, that the situation was, in fact, difficult and hardly scrutable; equally, that the American leadership did not intend to act. But, with all this, 'no recommendation' suits only the purposes of a 'no-win policy'.

13   The source of all accounts – those of Méray, *Thirteen Days That Shook the Kremlin*; Miklós Molnár and László Nagy, *Imre Nagy: réformateur ou révolutionnaire?* (Geneva Paris: Librairie E. Droz/Librairie Minard, 1959), G. Pálóczi-Horváth, *Krushchev: The Road to Power* (London: Secker & Warburg, 1960), and the book by Váli mentioned above on which we here rely – take their information from Imre Nagy, *On Communism: In Defense of the New Course* (New York: London: Thames & Hudson, 1957), which contains various memoranda that Nagy had circulated in Hungary during 1955 and 1956. The most laconic summary of the general atmosphere of the meeting is given in the following words: 'The shocking situation was described by the key members of the Soviet Communist Party, who declared that the mistakes and crimes of the four-member Party leadership in Hungary, headed by Rákosi, had driven the country to the verge of a catastrophe, shaking the People's Democratic system to its foundations, and that, unless prompt and effective measures were taken to bring about a change, the people would turn against them and, to quote Khrushchev, "we would have been booted out summarily" ' (Váli, *Rift and Revolt in Hungary*, p. 4).
14   ibid., pp. 156–7 (our italics).
15   ibid. (our italics).
16   Not only for the Soviet leadership *sensu stricto*. In an unpublished part of Volume 2 of his *Memoirs*, which we had the opportunity to read, G. Marosán, later number three in Kádár's first leadership, describes a conversation between himself and Ulbricht during the summer of 1956. Ulbricht, an arch-Stalinist with both great experience and also an over-refined sense of the interests of the regime, deemed it narrow-minded that the Hungarian leadership did not arrest Nagy, the leading members of his faction and possibly Lukács as well.
17   Selling out Germany was, perhaps, too far-fetched an idea even on the part of such an uninhibited adventurer as Beria. But it was at least partly corroborated by the fact that Zaisser, the Minister of State Security in East Germany, who was 'apparently backed by Malenkov and Beria in Moscow', who 'was an unlikely security chief, a secret policeman with mild manners who believed in a *united and neutral Germany*' (as J. Steele characterises him in his *Socialism with a German Face: The State That Came in from the Cold* (London: Cape, 1977), pp. 86, 97), belonged to the forefront of the anti-Ulbricht opposition in the Political Bureau. Both before and immediately after the Berlin uprising he blamed all ills on Ulbricht's policy. Vague as this reference is about his being backed by Beria, and despite the fact that the latter in the last years of Stalin had only formal contact with the security organs, if we consider that his lines of

personal connections had been kept constantly alive, then Zaisser, a Minister of State Security, with views of German unity and neutrality, *could* have been the spokesman of Beria's short-lived policy.

Yet there is still further documentation of a possible deal with the *Western Powers* aimed at the exchange of *Ulbricht's East German state*, perhaps for an early version of *détente*, and allegedly initiated by *Beria*. In his excellent *Histoire de la guerre froide* (Paris: Fayard, 1965), pp. 83–4, *André Fontaine* mentions the following crucial and, if not entirely conclusive, none the less very likely piece of evidence:

> If one can believe the old-time Italian communist, *Giulio Seniga*, a secret meeting of the *Cominform* took place in the Kremlin between 12 and 14 July 1953. Italy was represented by *Pietro Secchia*, whose notes have been reproduced by the author. At the meeting, *Malenkov, Molotov* and *Khrushchev* presented a report on the crimes of *Stalin*, which anticipated that of Mr Khrushchev submitted in 1956 to the 20th Congress of the Communist Party of the Soviet Union. From this, they proceeded to the case of Beria, who allegedly 'had attempted to dissolve with his perfidious acts of intrigue the leading *Leninist* nucleus of the party in order to augment his personal prestige and to realise his criminal anti-socialist projects'. His proposals regarding the German question '*could allegedly be summarised as the toleration of the transformation of the German Democratic Republic into a bourgeois state*'. They confirmed the exposure 'during the last days' of the criminal projects of the Minister of the Interior [an incorrect description of the official function of Beria], 'who had wanted to establish, with the mediation of his agents, a personal contact with *Tito* and *Rankovich* in *Yugoslavia*'. (Our italics; quoted from Giulio Seniga, *Togliatti e Stalin* (Milan: Sugar, 1961), pp. 39–43).

While not absolutely irrefutable proof, the passage quoted above is a very strong indication of Beria's *fuite en avant*. The apparent incoherence of the accusations (first of Stalin's 'crimes', then of Beria's equally criminal intention to establish contact with Tito) confirms rather than invalidates the authenticity of the account. In terms of Soviet logic, as long as the *Political Bureau* had not decided that Tito was a comrade and Yugoslavia socialist, the former remained an enemy, no matter what crimes of Stalin had been admitted by the Soviet leaders. On the other hand, the combination of the sell-out of the German Democratic Republic with a rash reconciliation with Yugoslavia, and the swift and ruthless extermination of what the speakers at this meeting called the Leninist nucleus of the party were acts that would be thoroughly consistent on the part of Beria, just as consistent as was *his* extermination and the instigation of a policy of moderate consumerist reforms by this 'Leninist nucleus'.

18 A blatant example of goal-rational oppression is the following. For many years after the revolution, rumours about people captured by the Soviets after the barricade fights in Budapest put in closed wagons and deported to (but later returned from) the Ukraine were stubbornly circulating in Hungary. We cannot either substantiate or invalidate them. But the very fact that a coercive and *massive* population-transfer – a logical step in earlier Soviet politics, and a practice affecting millions in the Baltic republic and in the occupied territories in Poland in 1939 under the leadership of Khrushchev – did not occur demonstrates the increasingly goal-rational character of Soviet oppression.

19 A classic example of Rákosi's arrogant interferences is the following: 'He disapproved of Polish methods of relative tolerance. "I told Bierut that they [the Poles] were rightist deviationists. I told them the way they were doing it was wrong, and that they must do it my way: arrest one Church dignitary, and bribe the rest. And that's all there is to it"' (Váli, *Rift and Revolt in Hungary*, p. 65). Rákosi similarly tried to interfere with the 'final shaping' of the Slansky trial to obtain further corroboration *a posteriori* to the Rajk trial.

20 As to the former aspect, one episode (which also has some general relevance) should be

mentioned here. Many years after it happened Kádár mentioned at a session of the Hungarian Central Committee that he and the party had been fully aware that it was Lukács who turned clandestinely to Togliatti for aid on behalf of the imprisoned Hungarian writers. In the latter's long-lasting detention there was a particularly dangerous period in which not even the death sentence (and its actual execution) seemed to be out of the question. We can confirm that Lukács did write a letter to Togliatti and successfully smuggled it out of the country, and Kádár's unfriendly remark at least suggests – and this perhaps can be corroborated by documents – that Togliatti found some means of making the Italian communists' disagreement audible with such a turn in advance. On the other hand, there was not even in the popular accounts circulating in Budapest any mention of such or similar acts on the part of the French communist leadership, except for one individual action: Aragon's personal intervention to Kádár when two Hungarian writers did get the death sentence. *L'Humanité* gave continuous and unqualified support to what is euphemistically called the 'politics of administrative measures' in post-revolutionary Hungary.

21 A word about the attitude of 'genuine' Trotskyism to the Hungarian revolution is appropriate here. One need not accept Castoriadis' characterisation of Trotskyism as a faction of the Stalinist bureaucracy in exile – at least, not as an all-embracing description of all shades of Trotskyism – in order to admire the quotation by Mandel (in *Quatrième Internationale*, December 1956):

> Socialist democracy will still have to engage in more battles in Poland. But the main battle which allowed millions of proletarians to once again identify with the Worker's State, is already won . . . The political revolution which, for a month now, shakes up Hungary, has shown a more spasmodic and unequal development than the political revolution in Poland. It did not, like the latter, fly from victory to victory . . . This is because, contrary to the situation in Poland, the Hungarian Revolution was an elementary and spontaneous explosion. The subtle interaction between objective and subjective factors, between the initiative of the masses and the building of a new leadership, between pressure from below and the crystallisation of an opposition faction above, at the summit of the Communist Party, an interaction which made possible the Polish victory, has been missing in Hungary. (Quoted in Castoriadis, 'The Hungarian source', *Telos*, no. 29 (St Louis, Miss., 1979), p. 6

What is really depressing here, and what foreshadows the totally negative role played, for instance, by the neo-Trotskyism of the *New Left Review*, which pays some lip service to anti-persecutionist ideas but consistently defends the system of oppression in Eastern Europe, is not the caricature of prediction. Everyone can make false predictions. It is the value choice that counts. For Mandel, a compromise that is solidly supported by Soviet armour is automatically more valuable than the self-organisation of a people, which shows the apologetic function of the theory of the 'perverted workers' state'. It is also very strange that Mandel's memory so characteristically fails: the interaction between an opposition faction and 'the initiative of the masses' was *not* missing from the Hungarian revolution; with many difficulties, it finally came about. But the opposition was abducted, and the mass initiative crushed by a more powerful 'perverted workers' state'. In order to document further the total failure of Trotskyism in the face of the radical action of the masses we will briefly return later to Isaac Deutscher's analysis of Hungary in 1956 – this major disgrace of such a great historian.

22 It is precisely *this* gesture that provokes Deutscher's aversion for Nagy (Deutscher calls him a 'Kerensky in reverse').

23 We do not have any statistical survey tabling the proportions of these 'defectors': it is therefore our *impression* that the largest outflow took place in the French Communist Party, in the party *sui generis* of representative intellectuals, and that the smallest

exodus hit the Italian communists, now the only party that can claim cultural hegemony in its nation. But, even if our assessment is not correct, the fact of the intellectual mass exodus is.
24 Hannah Arendt, *On revolution* (New York: Viking, 1963), pp. 270–1.
25 Bibó, 'Situation of Hungary', p. 183.
26 Adam Michnik, 'What we will and what we can', address to the oppositional Free University in Warsaw, 14 November 1980, in *Magyar Füzetek*, no. 8 (Paris, 1981), p. 16 (our italics).
27 This assumption has not been proved but it is strongly supported by the *Moscow Diary* of Veljko Micunovic, Yugoslavia's ambassador in Moscow from 1956 onwards, a party to Tito's most secret decisions, and from whom, as a reliable authority, we shall quote extensively in what follows. As to the actual position of the Yugoslavs and the demands set against them by the Soviet leadership during the crucial summer of 1956, Micunovic informs us that in September 1956 a top secret letter by the Soviet Presidium on the attitude to Yugoslavia was circulated. The letter reformulates the interstate relations in a fairly objective manner, but it describes the Yugoslavs in ideological terms and, further, as opportunists who demand relations between the communist parties that are 'acceptable to Social Democrats but not to Communists' (Veljko/Micunovic, *Moscow Diary* (Garden City, NY: Doubleday, 1980), pp. 107–9). Now, this qualification tells a very long story. Obviously, the Yugoslavs would have ceased to be opportunists only if they had joined, in exchange for some minor and insignificant concessions, the 'socialist community'.
28 ibid., pp. 133–44. This is such a straightforward story that it requires no comment, at least as far as Yugoslav claims to democratic socialism and a policy of non-interference are concerned. (Whereby we do not deny the East European relevance of their system based on genuine compromises between the leading élite and the population.) But a couple of additional commentaries are needed here. First of all, from the whole course of negotiations it became clear that the Soviet leadership was genuinely scared of a possible Western intervention, which shows that they were not contacted by the United States for serious negotiations and which corroborates our earlier point about the fatal mistakes of the West. Secondly, and if we disregard the phony commiseration of people for their 'comrades' who had had a thousand times as many communists murdered in their own time as were lynched by Hungarian insurgents, at least some of the real reasons become visible. There were, in the main, two considerations inducing the post-Stalin Soviet leaders to the final decision – neither of them, of course, involving ideological double-talk about the restoration of capitalism. The first was the fear of their own apparatus, which anyway was scrutinising the de-Stalinisers suspiciously; the second was the fear of the crippled reputation of the Soviet State. Finally, it becomes clear from the chronicle that even the initial formula of Kádárism, that is to say, distancing the leadership equally from the 'mistakes of the past' and the 'treason of those supporting the counter-revolution', was in the main a Yugoslav invention. The Russians simply wanted to 'restore order' and reprisals.
29 ibid., p. 396 (our italics). There are two important features of the Yugoslav attitude worth mentioning. The first is that only then had it started to dawn upon them that their attitude in the Hungarian question just did not pay in terms of pragmatic policy, either. On p. 395, Micunovic remarks: 'Some of the charges which are laid against Nagy can apply to us: his appeal for the "liquidation of military blocs" and his support for "national communism", as the West used to describe the internal system of Yugoslavia. Many Hungarians could have suggested to the Yugoslav leaders in time that, should they yield and deviate from their self-professed principles in the Hungarian question, they would find themselves on the same bank of accused as the victims of the Hungarian revolution. The second remarkable feature of this most remarkable conversation is that Micunovic uses Khrushchev's cynical argument against Stalin, this time against Khrushchev. As Khrushchev stated in the 'secret speech' that, for instance, Bukharin's execution was 'superfluous' since he no longer

represented political power, Micunovic now stated that Nagy's execution was superfluous for the same reason. This means by implication that the Yugoslav still felt it legitimate to murder one's political enemies in a 'legal' way if this was deemed necessary by a certain authority possessing superior wisdom; and also, by implication, that the principle of dictatorship and goal-rationalist–Leninist (instead of increasingly irrational Stalinist) terror had remained valid for the Yugoslav leadership.

30 *A Magyar Forradalmi Munkásmozgalom Története (The History of the Hungarian Revolutionary Working-Class Movement)*, ed. the Institute of the Party History of the Hungarian Socialist Workers' Party (Budapest: Kossuth, 1979), p. 561 (our italics).
31 Quoted in Molnár and Nagy, *Imre Nagy*, pp. 51–2.
32 Váli, *Rift and Revolt in Hungary*, p. 257.
33 Miklós Molnár, *Budapest, 1956: A History of the Hungarian Revolution* (London: Allen & Unwin, 1971), p. 230.
34 Bill Lomax, *Hungary, 1956* (London: Allison & Busby, 1976), pp. 180–1. This quote serves to emphasise that not only Bibó, but also circles closely associated with Nagy, had worked out reasonable drafts of a compromise – a compromise that equally took into account Soviet interests and those of a Hungarian socialist system.

2 The Impact on Hungary

(i) The Hungarian Revolution: A 'Simple Matter'?

There is a tendency among professional and non-professional interpreters of the Hungarian revolution to simplify matters with regard to its meaning. Some call it a 'simple matter' of restoring national freedom, a 'national revolution'; others an equally 'simple matter' of restoring political liberties, a 'liberal revolution'. But the two concepts are not, and never have been, co-extensive, and this 'simple matter' is somewhat more involved. There is a third interpretation, the simplest of all. Cardinal Mindszenty, in a speech broadcast on the evening of 3 November, radically denied the revolutionary character of the events. (Apart from its arch-conservatism, the speech was notable for its being perhaps the most monumental blunder in the histories of modern revolutions in that it provided inexhaustible material for the enemy – in this case, for the Soviet and pro-Soviet propaganda.) For Mindszenty, it was a 'fight for freedom'. Though it is of course true, and understandably so, that for the genuinely restorative and conservative forces the term 'revolution' was unacceptable in *any* sense, given that the overwhelming majority of the population unhesitatingly termed the events 'revolutionary' we are still left with a problem, and one that is far from being of a purely semantic nature.

In judging the arguments for and against the thesis that characterises October 1956 as a 'national revolution', we must set aside any formal definition of the term 'revolution' (as against 'rebellion', 'revolt', 'uprising'), as well as the verbal pyrotechnics distinguishing wars of national independence and social revolutions: these are grossly sterile enterprises. It is beyond all doubt that the *fight for national independence* stood at the pinnacle of those celebrated thirteen days for the very simple reason that every change had to be fought for against the military presence and oppressive role of the Soviet army. At this point it must be understood as absolute fact (this issue was much debated in the assessment of Imre Nagy's political character) that the Soviet army intervened *prior* to any Hungarian appeal that it received, and particularly *prior* to any consent to intervention given by Nagy (to put his name to the appeal), and that the Soviet Presidium and their Hungarian emissary, Andropov, were already the real repositories of power on the night of 23 October.[1] Apart from a few murderous attacks of the hated 'Blues' (the AVH commandos) upon peaceful demonstrators, which left far more victims than the number of 'Blues' later lynched by infuriated crowds, the Hungarian armed insurgents nearly always fought against Soviet armed forces, and hardly ever against Hungarian units. (Miklós Molnár, in his *Budapest, 1956*, amply verifies that the attitude of the Hungarian army covered the whole range from passive non-interference to active support – the latter less frequently – with sporadic instances of hostility against the masses.) Apart from the wider socio-political setting, this fact naturally made the revolt *prima facie a national issue*.

But the 'wider socio-political setting' was very much present, and not only objectively, but also subjectively – in the consciousness of an insurgent people. The fact so often mentioned in this study, that Hungary 1956 was a revolt against the whole system of the Yalta and Potsdam agreements, was a fact reified in a manifest national opinion – in the belated conclusion of the defeated revolution and its miserable theatrical aftermath.[2] Unaware as the (mostly young) insurgents had actually been of the unassailable strength of the pact agreed upon between the great powers, they were to some extent even propelled onwards by their naïveté. Millions of Hungarians daily generating revolution still had good reason to believe that their national separation from the Soviet bloc, provided it was successful, would be most welcome to the West. After an eventual victory, Hungary, as a nation, would receive the consideration and understanding from the West that it so painfully missed in the peace treaties of 1918–19 and 1947; the first treating Austria, the kernel of the Habsburg Empire, much more kindly than the mutilated Hungary; the second giving considerable territorial priority (after the real victims of Nazism such as Yugoslavia and Czechoslovakia) to Nazi allies such as Romania, and even to Austria over Hungary. Indeed, this was not an exaggerated optimism, if the Hungarians believed that a victorious anti-Soviet revolution would incline the West favourably towards them for the first time in a century. And it is this unvoiced expectation alone in regard to which the 'conspiracy theory' applied to the Hungarian revolution holds water – a theory applied in such an abundance of either sociological simple-mindedness or premeditated political malevolence. This insurgent nation in its entirety – or, at least, nearly all its adult citizens – understood perfectly well (and this is widely corroborated by our personal and casual conversations on the streets of revolutionary Budapest) that even the slightest public mention of a revision of the peace treaties would be fatally counter-productive to the Hungarian case. But the same people expected, in an often undefined and generally unarticulated manner, that after victory the 'era of injustice' would be abolished. In our estimation, it must have been a very insignificant and foolish minority that seriously considered borderline revisions; and it very rarely happens that nations are *that* ignorant of general trends. The majority of Hungarians thought in terms of material–financial compensation for the injustices suffered at the hands of a biased world; they thought in terms of concrete rewards for the valiant deeds of national revolution.

Here we come to the third major point of this part of our essay, to a characteristic feature of the events which will repeatedly resurface in our further analysis: that is, to the language, the symbols and the atmosphere of an *almost compelling but certainly very imposing national consensus* which predominated as the most immediately visible symptom of those thirteen days, and which was practically the most repressive feature of a tremendously emancipatory historical juncture. The unceasing singing of the national anthem; the continuous emphasis on the presence of the national tricolour and the traditional Kossuth blazon on all public buildings, in lieu of the symbols created by the communist regime (which represented for the population Soviet occupation *tout court*); and the endless repetition and recital by the masses that 'we all are Hungarian': all this was a display of gestures which often seemed either quite infantile or plainly obsolete to Western visitors, for whom the question of a people's national existence, despite the Nazi intermezzo, seemed to be a matter settled a very long time ago. For our generation, for reformist socialists who had been brought up with a traditional – and far from unfounded – suspicion of Hungarian nationalism, this was an irritating symptom, and even a dangerous signal. Of course, in the moments of a nationwide crisis of the type where both those at the top and those at the bottom try to bridge a most dangerous gap and avoid a civil war, the national community seems to be the most expedient common denominator for unifying the warring social forces. Jagielski, the Polish Deputy Prime Minister, in the historical days of August in Gdansk when he signed the agreement between the workers and a communist government concerning free trade unions, left the scene with the statement that 'We all behaved in a manner worthy of Poles'. Yet, although all these actions had a *directly political* function, where national consensus did emerge in the Hungarian revolution (primarily on the part of certain followers of Imre Nagy) this was not its prime feature. Rather, this national consensus served as a *defensive shield* for a nation that – apparently pathologically, but in actual fact with very good reason – distrusted everyone who had the slightest connection with a dictatorship being toppled by a process of stubborn demonstrations and street fights, whatever the newly acquired political physiognomy of the latter may have been. Even Imre Nagy, as a result of his signing the appeal to the Soviet army (a gesture we shall discuss later), seemed to have lost popular sympathy for a short time. And if one considers the strange course of events during which Kádár gave his radical speech (analysed earlier) on 1 November, and was then mentioned little more than a day later by Khrushchev and Malenkov as the possible chief representative of an authority overseeing Soviet military administration, one perhaps will not regard this general mistrust as all that paranoid. A nation constantly misused and betrayed, a nation accustomed to the fact that the more radical its left, the less sympathy it feels for its *grievances as a nation* (a story which started on 1 August 1919, when a communist government, instead of perishing on the barricades like the *communards* of Paris in 1871, fled from a *Romanian* army, thus losing both its national and revolutionary respectability) – this nation wanted to *implicate* everyone in the common cause by employing the forceful gestures of a national consensus. Though this is a very questionable method of creating freedom, the problem with its general communist condemnation is that radical revolutionaries should be the last people to criticise such an ideological practice of forced collective implicating. It is precisely this that happens in all revolutions. Loyalty to the *nation* and collective implication in regicide were similar devices serving the same purposes for the French revolution.

All of the foregoing seems clearly to support one 'simple' solution: that the Hungarian revolution was 'simply' national. But such a statement, especially considering the very marked presence of an aggressive impetus for national consensus, raises immediate explanatory problems with regard to the other, equally 'simple', principle of explanation: the liberal one. Eastern Europe hardly ever witnessed the generally happy marriage of early-nineteenth-century liberalism and nationalism. The Czech example, where an overwhelmingly tolerant liberalism led the nationalist struggle, was the exception rather than the rule. In early-twentieth-century Hungary, nationalism, as far as the majority of its representative types was concerned, was illiberal and parochial, with strong authoritarian leanings. Later, a more plebeian version of nationalism appeared (in the movement of the populists in the late 1920s and early 1930s) which, although it displayed enduring merit in shaping a radical collective consciousness, especially regarding the peasants' lot in a 'country of three million beggars', was from the start outrightly sceptical towards – if not a total rejection of – liberalism. Liberalism, on the other hand, was leaning towards the compromise, the famous *Ausgleich*, in the nineteenth century, and not as to the 'lesser evil', but as to the proper order of things. In other words, it was Jewish–cynical–cosmopolitan, or it was confederalist, and time and time again it undertook intellectual experiments with the dream of Kossuth's old days, the Danubian Confederation. Even if remarkable mediators between the two poles can be discerned (the most representative of whom was László Németh, by far the best intellect of the populist movement), the opposing extremes were *not* limited to the intellectual life and the intelligentsia. Consequently these two apparently 'simple' solutions are both relevant to an extent, since elements of both were present in the events, but they are mutually incompatible if either of them is used as an *exclusive* explanatory model. And there is a particular reason for their mutual incompatibility. Liberalism is by definition a *contractual* arrangement of the state of social affairs, whereas nationalism (mostly) in the case of nations experiencing a dangerously and coercively delayed national existence is, for historical reasons, an *organic* arrangement of the state of social affairs.

There is no need to raise the centennial debate about the character of social contract to understand this basic difference between these two conceptions. Whatever form the contract should assume (it may be, in exceptional cases, a preceding one creating a total national *tabula rasa*, as with the United States of America; it may also be, and mostly is, partial and tacit consensus by the act of not questioning the rules of the game, and the like), in all cases it *ideally* turns to the individual to gain his or her consent to the politics pursued by the government – a government whose (equally ideal) objective is the common weal. This structure assumes the right of – even if it does not necessarily produce the preconditions and the guarantees of – changing policy objectives on the part of the citizenry, and also of leaving the framework of the contract, of substituting one nation state for another one. Organic nationalism is by its very nature intolerant towards the idea of choice, elective affinities, contract, and especially towards the cancelling of contracts. It considers the fact that one is *born into* a nation, which is viewed, to use Tönnies' categories, as a *Gemeinschaft*, and not as a *Gesellschaft*; as *destiny* and *moral duty*, a *Gemeinschaft* in which all rights are invested with the impersonal entity called 'nation', to which the individual really is only morally bound *accidentia*. A line of a famous Hungarian national poem, 'You must live and die here', expresses unequivocally this organic–irrational intolerance which can lend cohesive force to a group of otherwise egoistic individuals in emergency situations but which necessarily generates the intolerance of the general against the particular. Now, the drive to national consensus that surfaced in the Hungarian revolution was unambiguously organic in nature, which very strongly contradicts its interpretations as a 'liberal revolution'. But it has to be mentioned for the sake of impartiality that one of the main protagonists of the revolution who has repeatedly appeared in our analysis, Bibó, was at the same time the principal theorist of transforming intolerant–irrational organic nationalism into a kind of contractual patriotism. He certainly was not a cosmopolitan, and he bore a special responsibility for, and displayed an unusually strong emotional attachment to, his much suffered little nation, but it was one of the prime objectives of his theoretical efforts to eliminate all elements of (national or racialist) discrimination and irrational–coercive obligation.

This tension between the two tendencies holds true in spite of the fact that the trend which we called the 'aggressive drive to national consensus' had never reached the truly tyrannical level of fundamentalism. Of course, all considerations regarding a revolution and a social upheaval which lasted for thirteen days have to be very cautious with their (obviously far-reaching) generalisations. Nevertheless, we think that there is a straightforward explanation of the non-fundamentalist character of this constellation: in contrast to Irish and Polish nationalist movements, the Hungarian movement *was not religious*. Of course, we do not mean to say that there are no religious people in Hungary, and not even that a majority of the population were not religious. In all probability the majority were, and still are; and if there obtained a full, and not a restricted, religious freedom in Hungary (though, of course, the latter is far more preferable than the overt persecution of religion in the Soviet Union) people would profess their religious creeds publicly and in great numbers. But the idea of a non-religious–democratic Polish opposition, regardless of whether it conforms to the facts – a thesis according to which the church has a far greater cohesive force and *therefore progressive role* in Poland than elsewhere because it had been for centuries the only substitute for a national independence and a separate cultural existence (and there are similar explanations of the Irish historical development) – such a thesis was *never* characteristic of Hungarian historical development. True, Transylvanian Protestantism caught between two world powers, the Ottoman and the Habsburg, became a bastion of what we call now, with a considerable amount of arbitrary modernisation, 'genuine Hungarian substance'; and, equally true, Hungarian Protestantism, under constant duress, developed an ethic of bearing vicissitudes with manly dignity. It helps to explain matters when we see that both Bibó and Nagy came from families with such a Protestant background. But this 'genuine substance' and this ethic of 'dignified endurance' became a *national pattern* with an ever-declining (or perhaps totally lost) religious colouring. As an example, the life and especially the death of Imre Nagy (and of other communist martyrs) verify that such a process became widespread even on the left. Further, and more important, in the storms of Hungarian history there had occurred a dramatic break between ethics of a religious origin and the actual religious institutions. Whereas in the seventeenth century it was relatively easy to locate where the Hungarian Catholic Church stood (it sided unhesitatingly with the Habsburgs), just as it was with the various Protestant churches, which were so many hotbeds of constantly fomenting Hungarian rebellions, one of the great deeds of the Hungarian war of national independence of 1848 (which, to the utmost grief of Cardinal Mindszenty, was a social revolution as well) consisted of an amalgamation of Hungarians of all religious persuasions (including the Jews emancipated by the revolution, who in great disproportion participated in the Hungarian insurgent army) in one nationalist enthusiasm. From this time onwards it became very difficult – if not impossible – to identify one or the other church fully with the cause of Hungarian nationalism, or, conversely, to separate fully any church from this cause. The positive result of this situation, detrimental to the church's intellectual and emotional dominance of souls but most encouraging as regards the prospects of a radical enlightenment, was the fairly widespread separation of nationalism and religiosity. Individual nationalists could be, and eventually in their majority perhaps were, religiously inclined, but their actions were not motivated by religious considerations and they were certainly not guided by religious institutions. In modern Hungarian history it happened rather the other way round. And to show just how many people are blatantly ignorant of this Hungarian past and present who should not be so ignorant we need only quote the following paragraph of Isaac Deutscher's personal version of the Hungarian revolution (from *L'Espresso*, 25 November 1956):

> ... a religious peasantry had risen and thrown its weight behind the anticommunists ... The ascendancy of anticommunism found its spectacular climax with Cardinal Mindszenty's triumphal entry into Budapest to the accompaniment of the bells of all the churches of the city broadcast for the whole world to hear. The Cardinal became the spiritual head of the insurrection.[3]

This historical picture of the 'white' Cardinal entering the capital to the accompaniment of bells is not only a painful reminder of the bad taste of nineteenth-century chauvinist Hungarian frescopainting (which Deutscher did not have the luck to see but somehow expresses the capacity of imitating), and is not only, to be more serious, part of an unacceptable analysis of the Hungarian revolution (we regret having to state this of a historian whose work, despite this and other faults, we highly appreciate), but is moreover, and without any doubt at all, *fatally ignorant of Hungarian realities*. Since Pázmány in the seventeenth century, no Hungarian cardinal has played a central – or even important – role in Hungarian politicis. For, since that time, there has not existed the foundations for (any) Hungarian fundamentalism that would enable him to do so.[4]

Of course, the idea of a *nationalist* and at the same time *liberal* revolution, the combination of both 'simple' explanations, is not as absurd in the twentieth century as it was, for instance, in earlier periods of Hungarian history, when a weak Hungarian liberalism sought at one time the shelter of the Habsburgs against the brutal anti-enlightenment attitude of the nationalist gentry, at another the protecting influence of the Western democracies against the pre-fascist inclinations of chauvinistic urban lower-middle classes. The Stalinist regime in Hungary, just as elsewhere, succeeded in violating the human integrity of the individual in both capacities: as a member of a national community and as the repository of individual freedoms. A *joint* revolt in *both* areas was thus on the cards. But there are a number of symptoms, a series of social problems, which in fact constituted the main concern of the short-lived Hungarian revolution, and which cannot be accounted for either by nationalism or by liberalism, and not even by their simple combination. It is this complexity that makes such an apparently simple revolution one of the truly radical and most complex social occurrences of this century. And there are many lessons still to be drawn from it. In what follows, we shall point out the phenomena that cannot be explained by a purely liberalistic account. But all of what we say is concerned with the complexity of Hungary 1956.

The primary obstacle to a full-blooded and orthodox liberal transformation of Hungarian society consisted in the circumstance that, in arranging the complex affairs of the Hungarian agenda, the *formal* and *substantive* aspects of freedom simply could not be separated. Liberalism, traditionally and formally, is concerned about, on the one hand, the constitutional guarantees of individual freedom and, on the other, the duties which follow from and are collateral to such civic liberties. The primary concerns of any consistent liberalism are the freedom of property (in a preferably unspecified way) and the form of government that has the duty to implement and safeguard civic liberties. It is precisely this which comprises the *formal* system of liberties: formal in the sense that the more sound a liberal constitution is, the less explicit it remains regarding any particular substantive organisation of the socio-economic order of the given society, as long as any such order guarantees constitutional freedoms, including that of pluralism. Now, in the post-revolutionary and, as it seemed at the time, post-communist Hungary, no liberal arrangement of social affairs was possible, because the fundamental document, the Constitution, or any draft of a constitution, had to be explicit and unambiguous regarding the crucial point – namely, *how it interpreted the freedom of property*. And we saw earlier when briefly analysing Bibó's 'Draft' that his solution was specifically and explicitly *democratic socialist* in this respect, while there is good reason for interpreting Cardinal Mindszenty's speech as an appeal to an offensive against all expropriated forms of property. We shall come back to the fundamental problem of property later, but it should be remarked here that, whilst there was a general discontent with the form of property that the communist regime introduced, no objective observer of the events can state that the popular majority wished to return to the pre-1945 situation. This certainly was true concerning the outcome of the agrarian revolution (the main loser of which, together with the aristocracy, was Cardinal Mindszenty's Catholic Church). Ferenc Donáth, the leading Hungarian communist expert on agrarian problems, who was the victim of a show-trial during Rákosi's period, and a later victim of a not more 'legal' trial of the leading members of the Nagy group (he received twelve years' imprisonment for his role as a state minister without portfolio of the second Nagy government), proves beyond any doubt, in his brilliant book on the 1945 landpartitioning process, *Reformés forradalom: a magyar mezőgazdaság strukturális átalakulása, 1945–1975 (Reform and Revolution: The Structural Transformation of Hungarian Agriculture, 1945–1975)* (Budapest: Akadémiai Kiadó, 1977), that this had been a genuine revolution. This partitioning had been implemented by spontaneously created peasant committees (who professed several different political creeds but whose members were equally revolutionary-minded), and mostly happened not with the help of but *in spite of* the coalition parties, all of whom of course had different attitudes to it (the communists were ardent zealots; influential factions of the Smallholders' Party were sceptical and even hostile), but who all agreed that it was a matter for 'experts' and had to be taken out of the hands of 'ignorant laymen'. In industry, the dissatisfaction of the workers with the actual state of affairs and the existing forms of expropriation in 1956 was aggressively overt and explicit. Nevertheless, the goal of new forms of *socialisation* remained a postulate, as did important parts of the goal of *workers' control*. Early forms of the latter, in the triad of owner, trade union and factory committee (more or less freely elected), were achievements of the 1945–8 period which the majority of the working class were not at all ready to relinquish. These were all matters *far beyond* the conceptual framework and the solutions characteristic of any orthodox liberalism, but were precisely the matters which had to be deliberated upon and resolved before a new Hungarian constitution could be drafted.

In addition to the formal–substantive issue, all liberal arrangements of future social affairs raised a question which no honest liberalism can avoid: what will be the *basis of legitimation* for the new, allegedly liberal, social order? Viewed from this aspect, there were only two straightforward answers to the question during the revolution, *neither of them liberal*. The first had been provided by Cardinal Mindszenty. His insistence on calling the events a war of independence, instead of a revolution, was more than just terminological hairsplitting. The implication was that the independent (i.e. pre-1945) Hungary had its accepted traditions, values, historically legitimised social order, and that all revolutions are necessarily directed against this order. Indeed, Mindszenty tacitly returned to Admiral Horthy's consistent use of the word 'counter-revolution' (the *tacit* reference to which was the only tactful feature of his memorable speech). For the Cardinal, Hungary had her unbroken tradition, and the catastrophe had quite obviously only been caused by her losing her independence. Once this was restored, no new social considerations or reforms would be necessary. Despite certain references to rights and liberties, this was the undiluted lingo of a counter-revolutionary *conservatism*, and one accompanied by very little liberalism, if any, as the adult population of Hungary could still very well remember from its youth. But this stance had one technical advantage over its competitors: it did not entail headaches about 'tradition'. It enjoyed the backing of the 'millennial' tradition of the Hungarian 'historical' classes.

The second answer to the question of a liberalist legitimation can be found in Bibó's 'Draft' which was *more than liberal*, because in it Bibó combined his Cartesian–liberal convictions with a non-doctrinaire socialism. As a consequence, his solution also escaped the technical problems unavoidable with any genuine liberal attempt that lacked a continuity with the existing Hungarian liberal traditions. For Bibó, 23 October saw the birth of a *new revolutionary legitimacy*, which he interpreted as a historical act putting a final end to the Hungary of both communist and conservative dictatorships; as the day of the first victorious *radical-democratic* Hungarian revolution. There is a fundamental paragraph in his 'Draft' which we consider our moral duty to quote in full in defence of our much slandered revolution:

> The compensation for all the committed economic and moral injustices, infringements of rights, and property expropriations must under no conditions be implemented on the basis of the restitution of the *status quo ante*; all compensations have to be effected whilst observing the ban on exploitative situations, and *not according to the measure* of the economic power position, but to that of destroyed homes, annihilated careers, the confiscated yield of personal fortune acquired by work.[5]

In short, then, we regard the Hungarian revolution as neither exclusively national nor exclusively liberal, but as a far more complex scenario. In the main, we subscribe to Bibó's conception: that it was the first radical–democratic revolution of Hungarian history, raising in its briefness all the major issues of a possible non-Soviet socialism, and one prepared – but not led – by an intellectual and political élite. To grasp concisely its essence, the language of Sartre's revolutionary existentialism is needed: *the social actors became free in it in that they chose themselves in their action*. And this is the only authentic point of departure towards a socialism that deserves its name.

(ii) Was the Revolution Necessary?

This question, so often asked about the Hungarian October, loses much of its sense upon closer semantic scrutiny. For such a question, if it is properly asked, is addressed to the subject *sensu stricto* of the action, and can be reformulated in the following manner: 'Was it reasonable on your part to act so?' or, alternatively, 'Were you compelled, either by internal or external, motives, drives, or "urges", to make a revolution?' And to all questions about 'making a revolution' Hannah Arendt's answer inappellably applies:

> Textbook instructions on 'how to make a revolution', in a step-by-step progression from dissent to conspiracy, from resistance to armed uprising are all based on the mistaken notion that revolutions are 'made'. In a contest of violence against violence the superiority of the government has always been absolute; but this superiority lasts only as long as the power structure of the government is intact – that is, as long

as commands are obeyed and the army or police forces are prepared to use their weapons. When this is no longer the case, the situation changes abruptly. Not only is the rebellion not put down, but the arms themselves change hands – sometimes, as in the Hungarian Revolution, within a few hours . . . Only after this has happened, when the disintegration of the government in power has permitted the rebels to arm themselves, can one speak of 'armed uprising', *which often does not take place at all or occurs when it is no longer necessary*. When commands are no longer obeyed, the means of violence are of no use; and the question of this obedience is not decided by the command–obedience relation but by opinion, and, of course, by the number of those who share it. Everything depends on the power behind the violence. The sudden dramatic breakdown of power that ushers in revolutions reveals in a flash how civil obedience – to laws, to rulers, to institutions – is but the outward manifestation of support and consent.[6]

The lines stressed by us show that Hannah Arendt not only referred to the Hungarian revolution, but in fact had it in mind when she formulated her theory. For there were only two parallel phenomena in modern revolutionary history: February 1917 in Russia (the spontaneous character of which comes very clearly to the fore from the masterly portrayal by Trotsky, who, for a moment, under the spell of history, forgets his Bolshevik predilection for a predesigned revolution as the only genuine one), and Iran 1978.[7]

A short study of the *manifest forms* of the Hungarian revolution will immediately testify to the veracity of Arendt's claim that this revolution had not been made, but had indeed 'continuously made itself'. First of all, the myth that the Hungarian revolution had been a primarily military action must be debunked. Its unstoppable momentum, augmented by *at best* only a few thousand armed insurgents,[8] made obsolete many a sterile discussion of nineteenth-century socialists (primarily of Engels, who liked the role of a revolutionary general) as to whether and to what extent armed actions are still conceivable in the era of 'modern weapons', especially heavy artillery. Arendt's statement about the armed uprising that 'often does not take place at all or occurs when it is no longer necessary' was in fact a straight translation into words of events. It was not a mythical military counter-power, but the faltering spirit of discipline of the army and the police forces, and including that of the commanding officers (systematically eroded for years by the moral and political propaganda of rebellious – and mostly, though not exclusively – communist writers and journalists against the incurable Stalinism of the regime), that made an armed uprising totally superfluous and, where it did occur, an event *ex post facto*. But another factor must be immediately added as well. *The spirit of national consensus* (which we have already analysed) suddenly appeared here and wrought a powerful effect on the social actors. Whether one believed or only pretended to believe that 'all Hungarians are brethren', armed action on the part of Hungarian military personnel (except, again, the AVH forces) became in most cases a paralysing moral impossibility.

In order to understand the 'non-made' but 'self-making' character of the revolution, it is necessary to deflate yet another legend. It had been a Hungarian joke for many years that the Hungarian people examined too diligently the Soviet films about the October revolution, and thus memorised (and then imitated) how revolutionaries took over the power centres (telegraph, railway stations, barracks, etc.) of Petrograd, paralysing the Provisionary Government. This will do for a joke but it is a false description of the events. There were hardly any public buildings taken over by particular groups of the Hungarian masses participating in the revolution. The siege of the radio building at about 9 p.m. on 23 October, which provoked the first salvos of the 'Blues' and which touched off the actual uprising, was rather an angry reaction to the stubbornness of the authorities in refusing to allow the people to broadcast their petitions. In fact the broadcasting services were simply switched off from a power-centre, and the government announcements were broadcast from that evening onwards from the parliament building: the power stations themselves, located outside the cities, were mostly guarded by Soviet units, and even when they were not there were no attempts at cutting them off. And the people were not stupid enough to believe that an *impromptu* siege of the radio building would destroy the Hungarian government's broadcasting capacity. They had an alternative method – and one that should be taken note of – by which they influenced the messages broadcast from a centre still in government hands: by the *totality* of their revolutionary strategies. Of course, certain public buildings had in fact been occupied: first of all the *prisons*, still full of political prisoners,[9] and the printing houses, in order to print and distribute all sorts of revolutionary appeals, newspapers, manifestos and documents. In a word, one can say that, while the Hungarian revolutionaries had not occupied the Winter Palace, they did lay siege to the Bastille.

What were the actual methods and manifest forms of the Hungarian revolution? First of all, the *general strike*, which later (after the second intervention and when the workers' council already had a headquarters in the form of the Budapest Workers' Council) became a *concerted* action, had in fact started – spontaneously and sporadically but always gaining momentum – immediately after the morning of 24 October. This was partly due simply to the impact of the chaos following the first intervention (it is difficult to sustain normal industrial activity when a city is full of hostile and nervous soldiers who can't understand the language but are ready to shoot at the first sign), and partly occurred as a spontaneous and angry reaction to the flood of government communiqués between 24 and 26 October, which poured slander and abuse on the working class (in whose name they supposedly ruled the country). But the unorganised nature of the general strike meant that at least some and occasionally most, of the workers still went to the workplace, and this provided an opportunity (the first in practically ten years) for workers to meet and discuss freely the state of affairs. It was from these casual meetings that the new historical institutions, the workers' councils, gradually took shape. Secondly, the unstoppable cycle of peaceful but passionate *mass demonstrations*, in Budapest and in the countryside alike, carried the slogans and the message of the revolution farther than any 'central command' could have done. In fact, the demonstrations were reminiscent of ancient choruses, in which the slogans, responding to and interacting with one another, educated the participants. And this *really was* a process of self-education. We remember quite well how surprising (and almost unbelievable) it was for us, as reformist communists, when the slogan 'Imre Nagy into the government!' had turned *within an hour* among 300,000 people demonstrating on the streets on 23 October into another, creating total *tabula rasa*: 'Free elections!' 'Self-education of the masses in the revolutionary process' – this dry slogan of party seminars had become a vivid reality, and the constant demonstrations which had as their sole function this *self-manifesting* and *educating* goal became irresistible. Thirdly, the whole country had been transformed into *one collective moment of civil disobedience*. The world soon realised this because the government broadcasts had alternately pleaded with and intimidated the population, one minute threatening them with immediate extermination via martial law, the next minute appealing to their 'better feelings'. This somewhat surprising vacillation between paternal rigour and tender maternal affection was a result of the simple reality that people no longer obeyed one single government decree, much less the political decrees, and not even the unpolitical (civilian) ones. Even the streetcars followed, whenever they could, a 'self-managed' schedule. Sometimes this stubborn disobedience seemed to be, and indeed often was, a goal in itself, and it produced enormous chaos (and the government, sending a whole nation, after a well-organised system of terror, into complete disarray with its own obdurateness and indecision, later banked on this chaos for its propaganda). This single-minded disobedience revealed the main characteristic of this rebellious subject: *its undomesticable anti-authoritarianism*. Finally, and without much ado, people had simply brought about the *freedom of the press* without waiting for any permission or encouragement. Those who earlier liked to portray in their propaganda films an unperturbed Lenin in full equanimity in the midst of total revolutionary havoc later were scandalised by the 'disorderly way' in which the Hungarian revolutionary press was produced, printed and distributed. But in actual fact it was a very encouraging sign, and a display of the general integrity of the revolutionaries, that after the Dudás group (one of the most adventurous) had taken over the printing house of the party press they did not veto the simultaneous publication of any (perhaps antagonistic) journal. There was only one publication that the printers refused to put out: the *Virradat (Dawn)*, the journal of the Arrow Cross movement, the Hungarian Nazis.

In all these manifestations the Hungarian October was a grandiose, and perhaps the only, case since February, 1917 of the spontaneous mass revolution as it appeared in the dreams of Rosa Luxemburg. Of course, had it occurred to anyone to survey the insurgents to determine whether they were truly 'Luxemburgists', in all probability it would have been found that 99 per cent would have never heard the name, let alone would credit the idea that a radical Jewess with no time for nationalism could arouse mass sympathy in them. But neither would Rosa Luxemburg have been captivated if she had listened to the spontaneous conversations of her favourite spontaneous revolutionary subjects. *And yet this was a Luxemburgist revolution which made itself and did not let anyone make it*, a revolution which exposed the ultimate *loss of legitimacy* of a dictatorship of the Central Committee just as had been predicted by Rosa in the historical moment of the creation of such a dictatorship and which *generated its own institutions of itself*, led by an irresistible *anti-authoritarian spirit*. And a radical, self-generating, institution-creating, anti-authoritarian mass movement carries the answer to its 'necessity' or 'reasonableness' in itself.

But isn't this all much too Hegelian, in the style of philosophies of history, a style that we specifically reject, and which attributes the role to a nation – or, rather, theoretically imposes it upon her – of 'exemplifying' a certain level in the mythological self-education of humankind, cost what it may? When Castoriadis writes, 'To be sure, the Hungarian Revolution was defeated. But so was the Paris Commune of 1871, yet this did not prevent revolutionaries from celebrating its example and discussing its lessons',[10] he does not seem to realise how close he remains to a tradition of which he is a self-professed critic. Equally, to be sure, a people, which consists of individuals who have *only one life* and, regardless of whether they are religious or irreligious, are most atheistic in respect of preserving this one and only life for as long as they can, *does not start revolutions in order to be subsequently celebrated and discussed in a revolutionary spirit*. And about that they are dead right. Of course, there is the criticism of the Hungarian October *because of* its revolutionary and not reformist character, to which we are hostilely opposed and will return later: this is the Trotskyite tradition as represented by Mandel and Deutscher. But even if we discount this indirect apology for Soviet expansionism there is another consideration, the voice of *Realpolitik*, the arguments of which are roughly as follows. The Hungarian nation ought to have known, both by virtue of her lengthy past experiences with great powers from the Ottoman Empire to the Empire of the Romanovs, and her experience of Soviet communism, that such a challenge by a small nation would not remain unpunished. It ought to have been realised in advance that such occurrences as thousands killed in police action, thousands afterwards executed, and tens of thousands imprisoned for many years, along with a social and cultural life the dynamics of which lie suspended for many years – that these things would very likely happen. In fact, they were rather lucky to escape the series of Katyns and mass deportations that many of the 'martyr nations' of the Soviet Union experienced. Also, luckily, they had a 'leader' imposed upon them (in an agreement between two foreign governments, the Soviet and the Yugoslav) who turned out to be a remarkably lucid Machiavellian realist instead of a persistent inquisitor in the style of Dr Gustav Husak. What they have finally achieved could have been achieved with a much more moderate movement, or the other way round: it could have *only* been achieved by a more moderate movement. This is an argument which cannot simply be dismissed. It has to be answered point by point, especially by those like us, who in those days, while admiring the daring of a nation, yet felt that 'they have gone perhaps a bit too far', but who are now convinced that the mythical–anonymous 'masses', and not ourselves, were right.

Bibó, in the first sentences of his 'Draft', also refers to the charge of a 'lack of realism', and angrily answers it: 'In so far as it [the Hungarian revolution] was declared *a posteriori* to be without a deliberated perspective from the beginning, it was made and it unfolded unaccompanied by such a perspective not because of its own insensible attitude but because of its being abandoned to its fate.'[11] But of course the moot point here is not the perfidy and shortsightedness of Western governments, more than sufficiently proven, but, rather, the attitude of the other side. Was the Soviet leadership ready, even for a *historical moment*, to consider realistically the alternatives presented by the Hungarian revolution, or had it worked always with one alternative? Molnár writes the following:

> 'Whatever the Soviet attitude was in reality, all the decisions made by Nagy between October 27th and 31st seemed to have been ratified by Moscow, *including the re-establishment of former political parties and the withdrawal of troops*. If one may believe Western observers, Khrushchev, on being questioned on October 29 at a reception at the Turkish Embassy in Moscow, even went so far as to envisage a neutral status for Hungary similar to that of Finland [which, by definition, would have included the abrogation of the Warsaw Pact membership on the part of Hungary – FF–AH]. *Pravda* announced on October 30: 'Budapest returns to normal life.' The following day the famous declaration of the Soviet Government was published, which admitted that faults and errors had been committed by Moscow with regard to the People's Democracies, in that they had reduced 'the significance of the principles of equality of rights in relations with the Socialist states'. It is a declaration of principle, but also an

announcement of a major decision, worded: '... the Soviet Government is ready to take part in negotiations with the Government of the People's Republic of Hungary, and with other signatories of the Warsaw Pact, concerning the question of the presence of Soviet troops on Hungarian territory....'.[12]

Now, everyone knows that the Soviet leaders had been thoroughly educated by Stalin in Turkish methods of government: in giving solemn pledges in total perfidy right from the start (since the pledge given to the *giaour* is not binding), and preparing traps in the meantime. Therefore, it is not impossible that every gesture made in an apparently conciliatory manner in those days was so much window-dressing. But pure dissimulation is fairly improbable, especially if we add to this the statement (discussed earlier) of the Chinese condemning – almost openly – the Soviet government. Even adherents of Turkish methods attribute a certain importance to public and printed statements, even if in no other capacity than as documents which may be used against them in a possibly victorious *coup d'état* within the party. Even if Khrushchev's remark about the possibility of Hungary's 'Finnish status' was an unashamed lie (and the First Secretary was an adroit liar), the fact remains that the type of lie that a politician can afford is not a matter of random choice. Can one imagine a Soviet politician, then or ever, who would *lie* that the Political Bureau is considering the possibility of Ukrainian independence and neutrality, or the possibility of the restoration of the multi-party system in the Soviet Union? Accordingly, it is reasonable to assume (and we do) that during the crucial days of 27 October to 1 November there were at least earnest and influential factions in the Chinese and Soviet leaderships (then in constant communication) that were not dogmatically resolved upon the second intervention.[13] This is also evidenced by the fact (already mentioned) that on 1 November Kádár made his speech in the name of the 'new' (i.e. reorganised) party declaring 23 October the day of a glorious uprising restoring Hungarian freedom and national independence. Kádár, one of the most suspicious minds ever involved in Hungarian political life, who, as a prisoner for many years, had learned the Russian lesson the hard way, was hardly the man to be lured into such a gravely incriminating statement without both prior consultations with Andropov and the belief that there was at least a chance of the

'Finlandisation' of Hungary (in which case, of course, he did not want to find himself totally out of power as a hardliner Stalinist). To our mind, all of this confirms that the Hungarian *revolution* did have a chance of lasting success, provided that three factors were simultaneously present: a collective–national Hungarian readiness for a measure of compromise (particularly in matters regarding Soviet strategic interests, and readiness in this respect has been amply proved by us); a convincing signal on the part of the Western, and in particular of the American, governments that *détente* would be initiated forthwith (and its absence has equally amply been proved by us); plus the combined pressure on the part of Chinese, Yugoslav, Italian and French communists on the Soviet government to come to terms with the Hungarian defeat. We know where we stand as far as the third prerequisite is concerned.

Bibó makes the following short statement on the *cause* of the events becoming revolutionary:

> But, anyhow, the fact that the Hungarian revolution gained momentum was not a result of its own insensibility but of the foolhardiness and bloodshed provoked by the leadership and the secret police forces; and the revolution, despite its being unprepared and unorganised, when seen as a response to bloodshed, was remarkably sober, humane and moderate.[14]

Though this much is undoubtedly correct, a full understanding requires a much longer and more complex explanation. First, the long period between June 1953 and March 1955, with its alternations between verbal renewals of the promises contained in Nagy's 'new policy speech' and their subsequent and constant miscarriage caused by a shrewd sabotage of the Rákosist leadership (including even – except for certain leftists – the decelerated release and rehabilitation of political prisoners), had made an already mistrustful population hostilely sceptical towards *any* promise coming from communist governments. The miracle was rather that the explosion came so late, not that it came. Secondly, and on the other hand, the practically open *factionist activity* between March 1953 and October 1956 of mostly, though not exlusively, communist intellectuals – put another way, the activity of a 'pressure-group', an activity which was later 'legally' declared high treason, and something which at any rate had happened for the first time in communist countries for thirty years – this activity was double-edged. In part, it undermined the moral stamina of many Stalinist or ex-Stalinist key functionaries. The classic case is that of Sándor Kopácsi (later condemned to life imprisonment), the Police Commissioner of Budapest, who was gradually convinced by the literary propaganda that shooting at his own people was a crime, and not a duty. But even those who still remained loyal to old-time Stalinist convictions had at least become uncertain about the 'best' way of acting, and reluctance in a critical situation is fatal from the standpoint of tyrannical governments.

Obviously, it is not our task to defend Gerő's 'revolutionary honour', but as interpreters of the events we simply find it both lacking and deceitful when the present party chroniclers blame everything on the 'indecision' of the 'compromised' Gerő leadership. Gerő was anything but unprepared for the role of a mini-Stalin. A communist with a long and heroic record, his behaviour under the torture of the Horthy police in 1923 was a model case of Bolshevik standards. He had been a trained Comintern functionary, learning in France how to manipulate political parties, learning in Spain how to manipulate a mass revolution; he was a colonel of the Soviet army, a perfectly cold-blooded man, and a person of remarkable intelligence (in his last years he was the Hungarian translator of Althusser, whom he must have read with sympathy, and a person whom Althusser definitely could not have accused of bourgeois humanism). A full capacity for decisive action, for cracking down on the opposition (and on a whole people, if necessary) was present in him; it could even be said to be his natural inclination. *But to act on his own was both against his convictions and the functions assigned to him by the Soviet leadership*, and the directives – which later became merely 'signals' – that he received from Moscow were contradictory, confusing, and changed by the week. It was somewhat cavalier on the part of Khruschev to call both Rákosi and Gerő 'idiots' in front of Micunovic. The constant inner struggles of an as yet unconsolidated Soviet leadership made their puppets incapable of action, and this incapacity reached its peak in the evening and during the night of 23 October – a deficiency characterised by Lukács via the cynical wisdom, 'Nothing is worse than a weak-handed tyranny!'

In fact, during this memorable afternoon, evening and night, this leadership did everything and yet nothing; they did too much and yet not enough. First they banned the mass demonstration, and then later changed their mind and gave public consent to it, which was no sign of liberalism but of indecision. During the demonstration none of the leaders was visible; nor, for that matter, were they visible *at any time* during the revolution, the sole exception being Imre Nagy, whom they implored to 'appease' the masses, but who did not receive any official capacity or bargaining power to enable him to do so. As it seemed then, the only result of this undertaking, doomed from the outset, was to kill the reputation of a rival before the masses. Gerő, in a speech broadcast by Hungarian Radio at 8 p.m., insulted the entire population in a typically arrogant manner,[15] and it was a natural reaction that a nervous – even hysterical – and ever-increasing crowd would want to enter the radio building and have their various manifestos broadcast. (Some of them obviously would have been primitive and confused documents, unacceptable to any communist leadership.) This situation can be properly dealt with by a government in two ways and *only* two ways: either its proper authorities are armed and then deployed to defend to the utmost the (symbolically crucial) radio building (which – as we shall show later – *without negotiations* is a plain 'declaration of war' on the populace), or it can attempt negotiations, having at least certain documents broadcast in the hope that next day the atmosphere will calm, and the protagonists will be more amenable to productive discussion. But the Gerő leadership invented a third answer: the numerically weak AVH unit defending the radio building was authorised to shoot salvos at the crowd, and in the intensive barricade struggle that ensued it was annihilated by a crowd that produced arms from all directions. On the lighter side, the armoured military unit sent to support did not even have ammunition; this was obviously in order to avoid serious bloodshed. The leaders immediately went into a Central Committee session, which, after an all-night debate, brought Nagy personally, as Prime Minister, into the leading body of the party (without even consulting him about this decision: he was waiting in the lobby), yet this was done without bringing any of his allies into similar central positions; all the hated names were left in the leadership. Moreover, this meeting had at least endorsed, even if in all probability it did not initiate, the first Soviet invasion. This was, indeed, everything and yet nothing. It was more than sufficient to inflame a rebellion. In actual fact, the communist leaders had left their people with no other choice but that of a total revolt against them. But, all contingencies summed up (and preserving our suspicion against all 'sociological laws'), one still has to ask: was it not so in all revolutions?

(iii)   The New Republic

In delineating the great *constructive* act of the Hungarian revolution, we have to express at the start both our gratitude and certain methodological reservations. The gratitude is due to Hannah Arendt, who coined the term 'the new republic', a term that we employ here to summarise all the constituents that in their entirety amount to what can be called *a new radical body politic* as an embryonic achievement of the Hungarian revolution. As a result of her stimulus we finally understood the originality of the positive aspect of the revolution. The methodological reservations, however, are due to our own conclusions; the chief one being that all results must be handled and regarded with the utmost caution when we talk about the outcome of *thirteen hectic days*. We should speak in terms of 'tendencies' rather than 'crystallised results', despite the fact that some of these (and precisely the most important, the workers' councils) survived the second intervention for as much as a few weeks.

We would be with the spirit of Arendt if we raise first of all the question of *legitimation*. Arendt was firmly convinced, and in our view correctly so, that without forging a new consensus and opposing it to the traditional one there is no body politic deserving to be termed radical. Without such a new consensus only a further despotism can come about. In this respect, the political leaders (if such a description fits at all the identifiable protagonists of this eminently anti-authoritarian revolution) had been confronted with a serious problem, and one that escalated as the revolution swept ahead. With some cynicism, it could be said that it was only for two extremists that the situation presented no difficulties: for Gerő and for Mindszenty. For the First Secretary, legitimation (if he was concerned with such 'bourgeois' formalities at all) began with the 1948 takeover – an event formalised into some sort of a constitution in 1949, all deviation from which was illegitimate. For the Primate, in an equally simple way, everything from 1948 – perhaps even from March 1944 – onwards (the latter being the date of the German occupation of Hungary) was illegitimate. But what could a genuinely reformist communist like Imre Nagy, or a non-communist radical representative of a nation in revolt, such as Bibó, accept as a real, democratic and radical basis of consensus? There was no easy way to answer this question. Up until 23 October, it was the intellectuals (and, of them, mostly the communists or ex-communists) who acted demonstratively in the forefront of a tacit public opinion, but this could not be accepted as a substitute for the public opinion proper.[16]

Consequently, if the new political actors intended to act honestly, and they certainly did, they could not refer to any *pre-forged* and *expressed* consensus. It was equally impossible (put in a better way, in the *process of self-making* of the revolution it became less possible) to legitimise the new and still emerging social order either by the *existing laws* or by any *tradition*: by the existing laws, for the simple reason that a pluralistic democracy (already demanded during the 23 October demonstration, a demand growing into a general slogan during the days between 24 and 30 October) was incompatible with any existing law in Hungary, however flexible the decrees of the regime; by tradition, because in Hungary history could not provide the necessary guidelines, as, for instance, it could in Czechoslovakia. If we only look back at the example of the Pilzen demonstration, during which the portraits of Masaryk and Beneš had suddenly materialised, we can at least *assume* that the tradition of the liberal–pluralistic republic was still alive in Czech political memory.[17] But in the case of Hungary even this shaky ground for a new legitimation could not be trumped up out of the depths of history. For the majority of Hungarians, we do not have the slightest doubt, the tradition of pre-war Hungary had vanished, and this was a good thing, too. To the utmost grief of Colonel Hollós and his associates, trying to present this autonomous and spontaneous turbulence of a people as a well-timed devilish plot of the CIA, they couldn't drag up a single portrait of Admiral Horthy from this period. But the laws and decrees of the coalition days (1945–8) would no longer have been adequate, either, and realistic observers of the events (some of them on the liberal side) had admitted as much.[18]

It is by way of this 'legitimation gap', and not via a lack of either courage or resolution, that we can explain the drawn-out process of a final decision on the part of many protagonists. Imre Nagy was appointed Prime Minister (or President of the Council, as the head of the cabinet was called in Hungary) in the early hours of 24 October by István Dobi, the 'President of the Presidential Council' (this is the official title of the formal Head of State in Hungary, a figurehead position without actual power but formally the repository of legitimacy). At one time Dobi had been an honest organiser of landless peasants in their fight against the landowners, but had then become an alcoholic and a political weakling; a man who begged his ex-Smallholders mates during the revolution for admittance, but who would have appointed Andropov as Hungarian Prime Minister on the spot had he been ordered to do so with sufficient firmness. The problem for Nagy, in his later attempts to extricate himself, was obviously not that of any (negative or positive) affection or obligation to this disgusting man, but the fact that he was deeply concerned with the Robespierrian question – with the problem of 'in the name of what' could he start everything anew, and what would be the generally acceptable form of this new beginning. Similarly, the procrastination of Béla Kovács concerning his joining the second Nagy government (or of coming to Budapest at all to participate in political life), or that of Bibó who, as we have seen, became a political actor only in the last two days of the revolution, was very closely connected with the problem of legitimacy – a problem that for both of them was very important, as both had been brought up in a legalistic spirit.

These different but equally representative protagonists of the revolution had obviously grappled with different problems regarding legitimation. It was after a long struggle with his Bolshevik conscience that Nagy had come finally to accept the multi-party system. But from the start it seems that he was determined *not* to enforce to any great degree his so-called 'legitimate duties'; these would inevitably have bound him to massacre many thousands of his compatriots. Here is a decisive excerpt from his trial – an act by which he knowingly tightened the rope around his neck. Nagy maintained even at the trial, when his voiced approval of this decree (of martial law decided by the Central Committee Session during the night of 23–4 October against 'counter-revolutionary elements' – in other words, against the insurgents) would have been in his favour, that he had interpreted it as a measure affecting 'only common criminals against the common law' (White Paper, p. 73). When asked in court whether he intended it to be applied to the rebels, Nagy replied: '*No, I did not want the law applied against them.*'[19] This and similar acts during the days 24–7 October, after which he set himself free and transferred his headquarters to the parliament building, were already punctures made by him in the

1949 constitution – a document the legitimacy of which was sham, and which was imposed on a people who now, in their revolutionary spirit, wanted to rid themselves of it. In so far as his 'legal' executioners state this of Nagy, they appraise his personality and convictions with relative correctness (though we shall see whether this gave any legal entitlements to try him). As time went on, Nagy must have increasingly realised that he had to choose between this sham legality and the explicit wishes of the people. And amongst these wishes there was one certainty: the people wanted a multi-party system and genuinely free elections. Upon finally deciding to side with the masses *and remain in office* (and at least *for this man* we are justified in attributing unselfish motives for this), he had to search for a new principle of legitimation that had nothing to do with Dobi and his associates. This was the principle embodied in the draft programme of his second government. As stated in Kádár's speech on 1 November, it accepted: first, 23 October as the basis of the new situation; secondly, the multi-party system, which the government in fact represented, though with the proviso that only the 1945 coalition parties could participate in it; and, thirdly, the neutrality of Hungary. In the light of this short, compact and dramatic statement, it is more than a heroic gesture that Imre Nagy, when asked about his 'civilian status' during his trial, gave his position as the 'President of the Council'. When, after the furore that this gesture caused among the 'judges' had subsided, he was corrected by the president of the tribunal ('You are the ex-President of the Council'), he answered: 'I do not think so. My appointment dates back to 24 October 1956. No legal authority has questioned this appointment.'[20] This was of course sheer bravado: Nagy must have known that Dobi had signed his demotion (and Kádár's appointment) on 4 or 5 November, and had done so without any hesitation whatsoever. But this, together with the fact that he declined to appeal for clemency, was *more* than an act of courage or staunch dignity in the face of death: it was a last act of abrogation of the legitimation of the ruling power in the name of another legitimation created by the revolution of 23 October. We have seen from Kővágó's book that Béla Kovács had reservations quite contrary in character. Similar – even though differently motivated – suspicions are manifest in the attitude of Anna Kéthly, the leader of the social democrats. First, she wanted to obtain the consent of the Second International (a body which later, in a most disgraceful way, and as a gesture of *Ostpolitik*, made a motion to expel their comrades in exile in order to mollify Suslov and company – a strategy which was, of course, not in the least successful). This was not only a moral, but also a *logical* step. The Nagy government would have been a kind of continuation of a Popular Front government, and that would no longer have been consistent with social democratic policy. Consent was therefore necessary. In his 'Draft', Bibó seems to have found the happy synthesis between these two poles, even if this remained for at least a quarter of a century a purely theoretical gesture hidden from the majority of his nation. The phrase from point 1 of the positive part of his 'Draft' – 'The government deduces its legitimacy from the Hungarian revolution of 23 October and not from the Rákosi Constitution of 1949'[21] – combined with further clauses which have already been quoted and/or analysed, produces this synthesis or reconciliation. On the one hand, these points provided constitutional guarantees of all human and civic freedoms, including free elections with the participation of non-socialist (liberal or liberal–democratic) parties. On the other hand, they provided equal constitutional guarantees for all the structural changes which had been implemented after 1945 (agrarian reform, property expropriation), though without perpetuating the then tyrannical (in other words, non-socialist) forms of the latter, but, rather, partly leaving open the door for new forms of democratic socialisation, partly legislatively ushering in self-management. This new basis of legitimation was based on a concept that we may call 'consensus in the making'.[22]

Nevertheless, after consideration, does not the new draft constitution, based on this 'consensus in the making', turn out to be a *conflict model* containing *necessarily colliding* elements between the *formal* and the *substantive* aspects of freedom? This objection has been repeatedly raised against all interpretations of the Hungarian revolution that candidly took into account two of its apparently diverging and yet fundamental aspects: the visible quest of the population for new democratic forms of *socialised* property, and the equally visible and irresistible demand of a free multi-party system. Let us also note that whilst Bibó's draft constitution seems to be a genuine synthesis of the main tendencies of the revolution, and whilst at least in the political sphere it does contain restrictions of a substantive nature (no reappropriation of the land confiscated and partitioned during the agrarian revolution, or of any other major 'force of production', such as factories and big enterprises;

and limitations on the size of privately owned land, whilst, of course, guaranteeing the freedom of all sorts of small property such as the peasant's land, the small merchant's shop and the like), it does *not* contain any limitation regarding the formal aspects of civic liberties, especially the rights of any party to enter the electoral campaign. (Obviously there was a tacit agreement, which was otherwise imposed on Hungary by the peace treaty by all victorious powers, to ban all fascist parties.) Now, are not these two tendencies conflicting ones? What happens if a party with a programme of general reappropriation of socialised property appears on the political scene? Was not Bibó's draft constitution a deeply inconsistent document revealing the inner and unresolvable contradictions of the Hungarian revolution; a document that aimed at complete freedom, and which intended to retain, *after substantial social changes*, what could appropriately be called 'socialist achievements'? We believe that it was not. In our firm view, Bibó, here again, displayed his theoretical greatness both as a statesman and a lawgiver to his nation when he simply considered that a democratic constitution is not an abstract expression of liberties, rights and duties, but *their expression based on the particular type of consensus which preceded and brought it into being*. (Hannah Arendt, for instance, argues in detail, relying on material gathered from American historians, that the Declaration of Independence, with its ensemble of human rights, with its particular form of a liberal, social and state structure, had been forged during long debates in American townships and other assemblies.) The appearance – or even the temporary electoral victory – of a party (or coalition of parties) which demands capitalist restoration is for a number of reasons a problem and a possibility that is not totally excluded (and one to which we shall come back later), yet it *does not in principle contradict the socialist character of the draft constitution*, which provides such parties with the freedom to appear on the political scene. This problem does not differ in character from that which sees the existence of communist parties with a programme of the dictatorship of the proletariat and total nationalisation operating within the framework of a liberal democracy the constitution of which specifically rejects both demands. (The classic example is the French Communist Party up until the early 1970s.) The ruling bourgeoisie reacted hysterically to the appearance of such parties, until they learned (with the exception of conservative tyrannies and military dictatorships) to handle the parties *according to their actual behaviour, and not to their programme*. All parties are allowed (in Italy, even neo-fascist ones) to include in their programme whatever they wish, as long as they abide by the rules of the game. But the rules of the game are set according to the consensus founding the body politic, and Bibó, in our view correctly, had assumed that the rules prescribed by the 'consensus in the making' were basically socialist ones in so far as they wished to retain in an *essentially modified* form the expropriated property relations and, by democratisation, even emphasise their socialist character. Therefore the substantive limitations and the unlimited formal liberties are in complete harmony in his document.

But the Hungarian masses very clearly understood one important lesson of history: that without an adequate and imposing social force all constitutions, even the best ones, are exposed to the dangers of Weimar; to being overthrown either by Stalinist or by ultra-rightist conservatives. The general slogan of the revolution, 'We do not return either land or factory' (a slogan which cannot even be denied by the official 'history' of the events, though it is called a 'shrewd trick' of the 'revisionists'), was directed against both. Departing from this and other needs, the Hungarian revolution created its own and totally original *dual system*: a model form of the 'New Republic', which consisted in *the combination of councils and traditional political parties* in a unified system. Before entering into a detailed analysis of the characteristic features and functions of this newborn invention of statesmanship, we have to distinguish it from what is called, wrongly in our view, 'dual power', in imitation of Russian political history between February and October 1917. Of the Russian situation, the following need only be briefly stated. The co-existence of Soviets and traditional political parties was *transitory, imposed on both sides* by extraordinary historical situations, and *not meant as a lasting solution* by either of them. With the exception of the Menshevik and SR parties, and, as it seemed *then* (but only then), the Bolsheviks, the traditional political parties wanted liberalism (in the form of the republic or the constitutional monarchy), but they loathed the interference of the masses in 'their business' of policy-making. The masses of soldiers, peasants and factory workers were mistrustful of professional politicians, and with good reason. The former had a socially more radical (even if vaguely formulated) programme, but since they had not then experienced the beauties of a one-party system, and had, through the dark centuries of Russian political history, undergone something less than a general democratic education, they were quite careless about constitutional guarantees of a political pluralism. Not so the Hungarian masses in 1956, after eight years of an exceptionally brutal and murderous one-party dictatorship. The thrust of constitutional guarantees – guarantees expressed by and consolidated in a free multi-party system – was irresistible.[23] But since the Hungarian masses had lived under a system of 'dictatorship over needs' two overwhelming character traits of the *subject* (not the *citizen*) of these systems, generally overlooked or only negatively treated, came equally and irresistibly to the fore in the moment of social explosion: a *general distrust* (sometimes heightened to hysteria, and often driven to its other extreme: uncritical and dangerous credulity), and indomesticable *anti-authoritariansim*. The latter is not necessarily identical with a total lack of social discipline, though it involves the acceptance of self-imposed discipline alone. It was from these two needs that *the political initiative of creating councils* (of the most varied sort) had sprung. Coming immediately to the functions and the character of these councils, it will suffice to emphasise that, in Hungary 1956, the famous 'crowd in the revolution' did want political parties. It felt stronger sympathies for certain of them, barely tolerated others, and all in all deemed their *permanent* (and not merely temporary) existence as a necessary feature of the state of affairs, *yet did not for one instant consider abandoning itself to any one or more of them*. The people knew that sooner or later they would have to return to work; that they would have to go back to their factories, enterprises and land (even if not under conditions imposed on them by the 'People State', which they were no longer ready to tolerate), and would consequently need the *relative* independence of the political class, plus its expertise. Yet they were adamant that social and political matters would not slip out of their fingers again, even though the melodies of campaign speeches might be ever so sweet, and their lyrics enticingly nationalist and freedom-loving. The *co-existence of political parties and councils* (with certain exceptions discussed below) was an express and general wish of the 'crowd in the revolution': the system was *not* identical with the Russian 'dual power'.

The political role and composition of the workers' councils was an important factor in the events of the Hungarian revolution, and a short summary of their genesis, objectives and functions is now called for. We will base this on the work of Molnár and especially

The Impact on Hungary 105

Lomax, the two historians who did the most for the objective and sympathetic portrayal of these genuinely revolutionary institutions. Molnár begins his chronicle on 26 October:

> In the space of forty-eight hours all the factories in the country had their elected councils, and at the moment of the cease-fire several central councils, representing the workers of a whole town or department, were formed, in particular at Miskolc, Győr, Magyaróvár, and in certain suburbs of Budapest.[24]

To this, Lomax adds the important example of a small but industrially all-important town, Salgótarján, in which the steel foundry and its workers' council became the centrepoint of the workers' resistance to all Stalinist manipulations and threats.[25] Molnár further characterises these councils in a manner that we do not wholly agree with.

> In short, instead of imitating the Yugoslav model, which was little known, they followed the Soviet models of 1905 and 1917, exactly as they had been taught in Marxist courses, and intended to apply them according to their own inspiration. The first concern of the councils, moreover, was not production but strikes; political strikes, which soon became general and were used to support the armed uprising and impose the people's claims on the Government.[26]

Even if Molnár emphasises the enormous political service that the councils had rendered for the revolution ('But without the councils the rebels would not have been able to impose on the Government their conditions for the cease-fire'), it is still important to turn to Lomax's analysis to see *the full implications of the statesmanship of the workers' councils*:

> Finally, on 31 October, a Parliament of Workers' Councils was convened for the whole of Budapest, at which delegates from some two dozen of the city's largest factories were present. The meeting drew up a statement of the basic rights and duties of the workers' councils, which were formulated in the following nine points: '1. *The factory belongs to the workers*. The latter should pay to the state a levy calculated on

the basis of the output and a portion of the profits. 2. The supreme controlling body of the factory is the Workers' Council, democratically elected by the workers. 3. The Workers' Council elects its own executive committee, composed of between three and nine members which acts as the executive body of the Workers' Council, carrying out the decisions and tasks laid down by it. 4. The director is employed by the factory. The director and the highest employees are to be elected by the Workers' Council. This election will take place after a public general meeting called by the executive committee. 5. The director is responsible to the Workers' Council in every matter which concerns the factory. 6. The Workers' Council itself reserves all rights to: (*a*) Approve and ratify all matters concerning the enterprise. (*b*) Decide basic wage levels and the methods by which these are to be assessed. (*c*) Decide on all matters concerning foreign contracts. 7. In the same way, *the Workers' Council resolves any conflicts concerning the hiring and firing of all workers employed in the enterprise*. 8. The Workers' Council has the right to examine the balance sheets and to decide on the use to which the profits are to be put. 9. The Workers' Council handles all social questions in the enterprise.'[27]

Whereas it is clear from this and similar documents that the working class (and generally, the 'state wage-earners') of Hungary had radically raised and equally radically solved the problem of *ownership in a socialist way* (one is inclined to say: the *only* socialist way), it is yet equally true that views had, then and after the second intervention, diverged as regards the extra-factory, *directly political* and *governmental* functions of the councils. On the one hand, Molnár quotes a very interesting (though in all probability a minor) example of an attempt at organised, universal and direct workers' (or producers') democracy - 'The delegation from the Borsod workers' council "*resolutely condemns the organisation of political parties*" '[28] - and Lomax analyses in detail how after the second intervention, under crippling political conditions in which the working class had resolutely fought for a long time against the intervening foreign army and its Hungarian agencies, the ideas of a National Workers' Council (a kind of council-government) had arisen. But, in the main, one seems to be entitled to say that the state wage-earners had clung firmly to their property, the units of production, resocialised in the form of a direct democracy, but had accepted the existence of a pluralistic political 'upper structure', the multi-party system, and free elections. And it is precisely the workers' councils as *collective proprietors* wherein we must look for both the social guarantee and the basis of the 'consensus in the making' which induced Bibó to introduce substantive restrictions into his draft constitution. And it was not mere guesswork on this theorist's part when he asserted the existence of such a 'consensus in the making'. He could, and he did, avail himself of two objective forms of evidence: of documents, and of the *manifestation of a will of all* (or nearly all).

The points we have italicised in the long quotation from Lomax raise two important problems. The first relates to the ultimate authority of ownership and reveals the single inconsistency of Bibó's theoretical masterpiece, the 'Draft of a compromise solution of the Hungarian question'. As we remember, the 31 October resolution stated that 'the factory belongs to the workers', and it is this that decides the question of property on behalf of a direct communal–collective–*unit ownership*. *Subpoints (bb)* and *(cc)* of point *(c)* in the draft constitution assume (in *bb*) 'the retaining of the *nationalisation* [the Hungarian word could actually be rather translated as 'Statisation'] of mines, banks and heavy industry', and (in point *cc*) 'the *communal ownership* of existing factories based on the workers' management, and the workers' shareholding or participation in the profit'.[29] These are undoubtedly *two distinct* programmes that in their contradiction circumscribe the first major task that this new Hungary born of a socialising revolution ought to have decided upon, had the army 'rendering internationalist support' allowed time for such deliberations.

The issue of the workers' councils' explicit wish to reserve for themselves all rights of hiring and firing the personnel of the factory is somewhat more complex. Such a proviso must sound strange to Western workers, so accustomed to the existence of trade unions and the guarantees provided precisely by them against stand-downs, firing, and the like. This is doubly strange if one first considers the fact that the only important and relatively free sections of the Hungarian working-class movement between the world wars were the so-called 'organised workers' (in other words, the trade union members), and so unionism had been an important Hungarian tradition; and, secondly, if we think of the Polish breakthrough via Solidarity. There are also important theoretical considerations against such a solution, because there is wisdom in the duplication of the individual into both *direct proprietor* (in his or her factory, enterprise, office) and member of a *direct municipal democracy* (a *citizen*) participating in a pluralism of political parties, however much these two distinct roles can, under specific circumstances, run counter to one another. And, equally, there is wisdom in tridimensionality, the third function being that of the trade union member. There are certain functions (such as sustaining the regional or branch wage-level, the level of unemployment and the like) which *cannot* be invested with a unit of production necessarily preoccupied with *its own* level of profitability and social security problems but not directly involved in similar problems of other units or the industrial branch. These functions *can*, of course, be invested with the state exclusively, but only at the price of dangerously increasing its power. Thus a really free trade union becomes a necessary addition to the new system of socialisation, and it was the single major flaw of the state wage-earners' radicalism that they practically denied the trade unions any social role. At the same time, it is also an understandable flaw. The general anti-authoritarianism, this leading feature of the Hungarian revolution, turned strongly against the parodies of workers' agencies, the trade unions as they existed under a Leninist dictatorship. And whilst the workers (most realistically) did not deny the necessity of the *relative* separation of the state agencies (this occurring, of course, under close supervision) they believed that every matter concerning the workers' lot should be dealt with as close to the shop floor as possible. In their way of thinking, the trade union organisation seemed to be too far removed, too abstract a milieu.

At this point we have clearly to consider one question. So far we have spoken of a 'dual system', a system that, whilst it allows for the competition of many parties (some of them necessarily conservative), doing so under a constitution stipulating substantive–socialist limitations but placing no restrictions on the registration of any party (except fascist parties), yet upholds the principle of direct socialist ownership by the workers. Accepting this, no realistic observer of the events could deny that nearly all the parties traditionally labelled as 'left', except the social democrats *sensu stricto*, had been seriously compromised; not only the communists, but also the so-called 'leftist' social democrats – and the same holds true of all those political representatives of the Peasant and the Smallholders' parties (with very few exceptions) who had any role during the Rákosi regime. An eminently sober observer of the events, György Lukács, in an interview given during the revolution to a Polish newspaper, placed the prospects of a *renewed* Communist Party at 10 per cent of the vote, and that was a fairly optimistic prediction. Can we, then, seriously believe and responsibly claim that, without a political electoral majority of parties with a leftist ideology, the socialist achievements could be preserved or, rather, realised in the process of a new democratic socialisation? But for a moment let us disregard the official Kádárist propagandists, whose personal interest was to answer this question in the negative, and hear from one of those who were not personally motivated. It is one of the major disgraces of Isaac Deutscher's honourable life to have acted as the indirect but resolute advocate of the Soviet suppression of the Hungarian October, and he did so because for him all regimes not led by a communist dictatorship (of course, a milder and more sensible one than that of Rákosi) necessarily meant counter-revolution and capitalism. Let us listen to his arguments:

> If in the classical revolutions the political initiative shifts rapidly from Right to Left, here it is shifted even more rapidly from Left to Right. Parties *suppressed years ago spring back into being*, among them the formidable Smallholders' Party. The Communist Party disintegrated ... Its insurgent members perished at Russian hands or at the hands of Hungarian anti-communists. [?] Its erstwhile leader, Geroe, was killed. Its powerless Premier hoped to avert the catastrophe by bowing to the storm and accepting every anti-communist demand, *until on 30th October he proclaimed the end of the single-party system* and agreed to preside over a government in which the communists did not have a majority. This spelled the end of the communist regime, and Nagy drew the only logical conclusion from the fact when, on 1 November, he proclaimed Hungary's neutrality and denounced the Warsaw Pact. He was now indeed a 'Kerensky in reverse'. [30]

Because it displays a greater intransigence and sophistication than does the usual official Soviet propaganda, the Trotskyite aggressiveness in evidence here betrays the Bolshevik secret in a more telling manner. In this view, it is not communism that exists for the world, but the other way around: it is in some mysterious way the 'duty' of nations and social classes, no matter to what extent they have suffered previously from communist rule, to submit themselves voluntarily to it. If not, then the punishment meted out to them by occupying armies and General Serov's special KGB units is well deserved. The Hungarian Communist Party engineered the miracle of a total agricultural collapse of an overwhelmingly agrarian country – a catastrophe angrily admitted by their Soviet masters. They installed a system of terror that at times saw 300,000 people in internment-camps in a nation of 10,000,000,[31] tens of thousands in prisons that were exact replicas of the worst Gestapo institutions, and many thousands executed. There is hardly any record of Hungarian communists protesting even *for their own people*, let alone for others. As Deutscher aptly put it, they had indeed *suppressed* other parties, parties that were at the worst liberal, many of them radical–anti-fascist–democrat, and some of them non-doctrinaire socialist. They had regularly ridiculed the national feeling of a much abused small nation, and made religious practice impossible. The leaders of the party stalled for time right up until the last moment. They wanted to sabotage all the reforms, even the release of political prisoners, and were ready to reverse the whole process of rehabilitation at any moment.[32] Finally, their provocative indecision pushed their nation into open revolt. But, mysteriously, people still have to accept their rule, otherwise *Weltgeschichte wird zum Weltgericht*.

But all this is perhaps just moralising and emotion. In straightforward sociological terms, one can say that Trotskyite Bolshevism, just like Bolshevism of any kind, has never understood, and most of all never accepted, that the social struggle of the masses for socialism works out its own ways, *employs and rejects its own agencies*, and it is a travesty of both history and sociological understanding to declare the existence of one agent (the Communist Party) and its most questionable – or even unquestionably unacceptable – monolithic power position as the general criterion of socialism *or* capitalism.[33] The Hungarian working class – or, rather, the state wage-earners in factories, enterprises, and offices – made their social will unambiguously clear. They were resolved not to tolerate any longer the Stalinist dictatorship (or any heir to it) over them, nor were they ready to accept any conservative authority, but rather wanted to take their fate into their own hands. These are the unforgettable words of the workers of the Győr railway-wagon factory, located in exactly that region where Deutscher mentions that anti-communism supposedly gained the upper hand: 'We do not want fascism. We've had enough of tyranny, of whatever sort . . . and we won't renounce our newly-won liberty at any price.'[34] And endless statements (also actions to that effect), either similar or identical in nature, can be recounted. Deutscher succeeded in 'localising the counterrevolution', the move towards the Right, in practically the only moment in Hungarian history when the much exalted masses made resolute measures for the self-management of their fate.

As a summary, let us once again state our arguments for and against the prospects of a *socialist* character of the 'new republic'. Undeniably, there were forces that wanted a capitalist restoration pure and simple, and some of them were far from exhibiting the sober realism of a Béla Kovács. But they ought to have acted with the brutality of the white shock-troops of Admiral Horthy in 1919, and the Hungarian population was not ready to accept such treatment from anyone, and had even made preliminary protective measures against such. It is also true that a general loss of credibility of leftist *ideologies* occurred. But, although this can be a source of danger for socialist perspectives, it is not necessarily (and in fact was not) identical with the rejection of leftist–socialist practical decisions regarding the future socio-economic structure. It is also true that the Hungarian population had very weak democratic traditions, and that its experiences with socialism of any kind had been bad. Moreover, this was at the height of the Cold War, and its peculiar form of propaganda was rife. Finally, a small nation can be exposed to economic temptations which cannot be offered even in the form of false promises to gigantic ones. But, despite all this, we state two facts. We find it a fact *beyond the slightest reasonable doubt* that the majority of the Hungarian population wished to persist in its anti-authoritarianism and did not wish to accept new (or old) masters over itself. And we find it a proposition to be equally beyond any reasonable doubt that *the beginnings of a radical democratic self-education of a nation, or socialism, is a value in itself* whatever the outcome. There is, of course, one absolute guarantee, even if it is *not* a socialist one, against a capitalist restoration: the Leninist dictatorship. But what is the guarantee against Leninist dictatorship?

The surprising radicalism in the practical arrangements of social affairs on the part of the Hungarian masses was due to two factors, one 'necessary', the other 'accidental'. The first has been described sufficiently and need not be repeated here again in detail: that the subject of the system of dictatorship over needs is distrustful and anti-authoritarian, and therefore, if it is let loose, it only accepts social solutions which guarantee maximum liberty; and, whereas it is not by necessity undisciplined, it must be a self-imposed discipline alone that this subject will accept. It is exactly the type of institution that springs from such an attitude that we have described above. On the other side the 'accidental' or, in a somewhat more accurate terminology, historically conditioned factor was the *total social vacuum* that the average Hungarian was confronted with the moment that the communist dictatorship clamorously collapsed. Pre-war Hungary had proved bankrupt and criminal. No significant party or political and social force had a legitimate claim to the task of restoring its pre-war social order. (And none made such a claim, for that matter.) Even a decrepit communist propaganda proved effective against it. But the coalition times of 1945–7 were not a tradition to return to, either. For a start, those years were not all that free. Already in 1946, as for instance became clear in the so-called 'conspiracy trial' of a Smallholders' MP (a man named Donáth, executed on the grounds of false and stupid charges), the so-called 'Military Political Section' – in other words, the Hungarian military counter-intelligence, the head of which was General Pálffy (later executed with Rajk) – reintroduced the whole horrendous system of physical torture to obtain false confessions. The freedom of the press was extensively curtailed. The non-communist or anti-communist majority parties (or their coalition in the conglomerate called the Smallholders' Party) behaved with remarkable cowardice. They either remained silent as one disobedient MP after the other disappeared as a 'conspirator', or even contributed to their self-humiliation, which eventually became their self-liquidation. Most important, they could not produce – once again with the sole exception of Bibó, who wrote an extensive and most constructive study of the 'crisis of democracy' – any counter-suggestion or alternative programme. There was no reason for either the young or the more mature to yearn for those years, even if people resurrected, in want of a better social imagination, the parties of the coalition times. Finally, and in sharp contrast to Poland, the Hungarian churches were obedient tools and suffering victims in the hands of the communist apparatus. They could not offer either a generally compelling and inspiring ethic or any social programme, and at best (and very rarely) they lashed out against violations of religious freedoms. A people who, luckily, had found themselves in the first moment of their liberation in a total social vacuum, and who did not wish to accept any conservative authority, were left to themselves to invent new social solutions. And they did.

The Hungarian system based on the councils has undergone two major interpretations, one by Hannah Arendt, the other by Cornelius Castoriadis. Though we have already referred to both, a look at further detail within them would be of benefit, partly because of the richness and originality of approach, partly because of certain moot points. Castoriadis states the following of the workers' councils: 'Rather, their importance lies in (*a*) the establishment of *direct democracy* (true *political equality*); (*b*) their being rooted in existing concrete collectivities (including, but not limited to, the factories), and (*c*) their demands concerning *self-management* and the abolition of work norms.'[35] Since we have analysed nearly all of these factors, we would only like to add a critical remark to the last words of Castoriadis' definition of the functions of the workers' councils. Beyond any doubt, the workers were weary of the 'socialist taylorism', the rigour and inhumane rhythm of which had been enforced by an omnipresent political police. In a way, one can even go a step further. There is a graphic description in Deutscher of the prophetic aftermath of the October turn: a general drunkenness followed by a collective hangover. The Hungarian revolution had a different but equally symbolic conclusion. This was the grand fête of the general strike which – apart from the serious policy objectives for which it fought – was perhaps the only realisation of 'la droit à la paresse' demanded by Lafargue; a most humane outburst of hatred against alienated labour and a festival of free political activity in its place. On the other hand, it would be a mistake to give too symbolic an interpretation of the demand of the abolition of the work-norms. This demand, in its original function, was a fight against the exploitative wage policy of a government which produced wage-levels equalled only by the most exploited working classes of the southern Balkans in Europe. It was also a deliberate move of the masses in revolt (actually, one of the stimuli between 1953 and 1956) to generate a new economic rationality and, together with it, higher standards of living.

Arendt's interpretation of the councils' role, as we may recall from her remark quoted earlier, was that their chief merit lay in the introduction of the 'federalist principle', a very important feature of her 'new republic'. For Arendt, all totally centralistic government is 'monarchic' (whatever socio-economic 'hat' it wears); the truly republican (in our vocabulary, radical democratic or socialist) is federalist in the sense that everyone is directly a citizen of the *res publica*, directly participates in decisions, even if not in all decisions to the same extent, yet everyone without exception is also party to Arendt's important proviso: one participates only if one wishes to participate. This is our ideal as well, and we believe that there existed an irresistible momentum in the Hungarian revolution in this direction. We have to mention only two objections to the relevance of this conception, both historical in nature. The first is that for centuries the more 'progressive' Hungarians were (whatever this word should mean), the less federalist and more centralist they proved to be, for the perfectly simple reason that the central county building and the local government had traditionally been in the hands of the landed gentry – a parasitic, uncultivated, brutal and immobilist social force. The second objection is just the obverse of the same situation: for precisely that reason, Hungarian liberalism, particularly its nineteenth-century version, was *centralist* (and often not even particularly patriotic, but rather pro-Habsburg) as a reaction to gentry barbarism. Of course, there was a countertendency as well: the workers' council in the revolution of 1919 played for a while a decisive historical role, very similar to that of the land and factory committees after 1945. Even so, this force was too weak to balance these centennial aversions and traditions.

For all this, Arendt's claim about the overwhelmingly federalist character of the Hungarian revolution is undeniable. Those memorable days saw the Hungarian people engaging in and endorsing Arendt's supreme value: that of political activity, carried out both for its own sake and as the highest role of the citizen. We would like to specify three particularly important manifestations of this political furore. One of them was the *free press*, published by a legion of non-professionals. The periods of genuine freedom for the Hungarian press were very short indeed, the longest of them being between November 1918 and February 1919. (At this latter date the social democratic government had already besmirched the free press of the first Hungarian republic by pushing the communist press underground.) People now wanted to make up for what they had lost for a century, and even the second intervention did not cancel their fervour. Secondly, there was a tendency towards a general armament of the people, or a people's militia –

a tendency which must naturally be handled with the utmost caution. Because of the possibility of lynchings and of provocations against Soviet diplomats and military personnel, all governments and responsible political actors were to some degree wary about the unrestricted circulation and distribution of weapons. Further, in the last moments of its existence the Nagy government made frantic efforts to create an armed force of its own, and it is questionable to what extent this would have been compatible with a people's militia. But at least this much can be said with certainty: that at that time the people had an unmistakable predilection for taking their defence into their own hands, and, in contrast to the deceitful propaganda subsequent to 4 November, they used the weapons they had, with very few exceptions, with remarkable common sense and maturity. Finally, the 'crowd in the revolution' were firmly resolved upon having a *constant and direct dialogue* with their representatives (who were not 'leaders'), and they had found in the person of Imre Nagy someone who was most ready to reciprocate.

The new republic had taken final shape (if it had at all) in the moments when it had been finally crushed. But this did not remain a forgotten episode. Drawing its lessons proved to be a very slow process. But, as we see now, its greatest historical merit was *to question the existing concept of socialism*, and at least to *suggest an alternative one*.

(iv) Imre Nagy: A 'Kerensky in Reverse', an Inconsistent Bolshevik, or a New Type of Socialist Radical?

There are martyrs of the socialist and radical movements who simply exchanged their earthly domicile for a pantheon of collective recollection in order to confirm with their honest life and courageous death the rightness of the cause they have served. It will suffice to point to the numerous victims of the white terror after the Paris Commune. And this is not meant in any pompous way but *sensu stricto*. If, as according to Weber, value rationality means maintaining and reconfirming our selected values, come what may, then those fusilladed at the wall of Père Lachaise were reconfirming the value idea of socialism as against bourgeois barbarism. On the other hand, there are others who sacrifice their lives, sometimes with admirable courage, but with whom we are at a loss when dealing with their political, moral and intellectual legacy. The Hungarian Bolshevism produced an unforgettable example of this type: Otto Korvin, the young chief of Red Security during the Hungarian Soviet revolution; a man left by Kun in Hungary, captured immediately by the white terrorists after the collapse (a hunchback, he was easy to spot), tortured and 'tried' (during which period he behaved with unique courage and extreme – and nothing short of religious – tolerance towards his weaker co-martyrs) and then hanged in December 1919. To all objective testimonies, he was a man of high morals, an enemy of indiscriminate butchery and mass intimidation who had accepted his assignments as a sacrifice of his own conscience and as a moral duty. But he was also a man of unshakeable Bolshevik–terroristic convictions: the system of terror was a frightening purgatory for him, but a purgatory that a sinful humankind *must* pass through. And it is hardly questionable that the further the left proceeds in its self-education, the less it can have in common with this mystical cult of death and self-sacrifice. Then again, there are martyrs of the socialist cause who personify in their death the promises of their life, and who pass on a great theoretical legacy that later generations constantly try to cope with, but whose martyrdom is held in respect increasingly *in spite of and not because of* their theoretical heritage. The greatest such person is Babeuf.

The Hungarian Premier, murdered 'legally' (and hardly even 'legally') as a result of Soviet–Hungarian collaboration, on 16 June 1958, almost two years after the revolution, presents an even more complex case of martyrdom and heritage for the democratic left.[36] Nagy's execution was greeted jubilantly by a part of the communist press, with silence by the other, and with indignation by socialists and non-party radicals and democrats, an indignation echoed by the propaganda of the Western world about the 'murdered great Hungarian patriot' – a world whose political representatives found him too 'red' to have negotiations with, and generated regular propaganda against him through Radio Free Europe. But after the eruption of protest, when (as Simone de Beauvoir describes) the circle of *Les Temps Modernes* was in utter despair at the news of the execution, and when Camus wrote a preface to a volume dedicated to his memory, he no longer seemed to be held in high respect, even if still regarded as a champion of the Hungarian cause, if a man of high integrity like Castoriadis was capable of writing this of him:

Or consider Imre Nagy, the politician. Where did his political cunning come into play against the treacherous lies of the Russian bureaucracy? Did he for a single moment find in himself the clarity of mind and the resolve to speak out loudly against the Russian deception with which he was so well acquainted? He muddled through, and tried to seek help... from the United Nations! History in the making; the bloody drama of power; armored tanks and guns facing the naked hands and breasts of millions of people; and Nagy the Statesman, the *Realpolitiker*, could only think of the United Nations...

And Castoriadis, for whose original philosophical position and persistent defence of the underdog we feel so much sympathy and respect, somehow finds the moral courage to add the following sentence as a footnote: 'The personal tragedy of Lukács (or of Nagy, etc.) is, in this context, irrelevant.'[37]

Against all this, it is a duty of all leftist–radical interpreters of the Hungarian revolution to reassess Nagy's most lively personality on behalf of a new self-understanding of socialism. But, to begin with, two negative remarks are necessary. First, we are not going to defend him against Deutscher's accusation of being a 'Kerensky in reverse'. Since this charge is partly the language of the 'court' that hanged him (and during the analysis of the trial we shall have the opportunity of questioning its legality), and it is partly the specific message of this study that the Hungarian revolution (of which Nagy was the most visible political manifestation) made decisive steps *forward* towards a new self-understanding of socialism as radical democracy, and *not backwards*, there would be no point in refuting in detail Deutscher's accusations. Secondly, we are not compiling a Catholic martyrology or hagiography. Our hero will not appear as a *chevalier sans reproche*.[38] He had two specific political–personal weaknesses. First, and most surprisingly for a Bolshevik of thirty-five years' standing, of all the situations he had been confronted with, it was a revolutionary explosion in which he felt most embarrassed, and at first completely paralysed. He needed to *distance* himself in time and space to consider the object and analyse the situation; and, failing this, he made only wrong moves. The monumental example of this was his *impromptu* appearance (under pressure from his friends) before a furious crowd during the evening of 23 October, without a plan for any immediate action and, in particular, without *any* official authority to say anything. The outcome was predictable and singular: the temporary self-destruction of his popularity.[39] Equally surprisingly for a veteran *apparatchik*, he was heavy-handed and unskilful in intrigues and apparatus in-fights, almost unerringly choosing the *wrong* men for allies. When politicking in a Machiavellian spirit he had always fallen prey to the genuine Machiavellians.[40] But, strangely enough, both weaknesses, preventing the Prime Minister from acting at times as efficiently as was needed, but *never decisively influencing the outcome of events*, already suggested a *new type* of socialist radical. In a way, we can say that the Hungarian crisis between 1953 and 1956 became a *representative drama of the inner disintegration of Bolshevism*, and that it produced, with many transitory types, *three representative figures*. The first was Kádár, the model type of the *Khrushchevite*, with his 'Khrushchevite Hungary' of the 1960s. The second was Lukács, the *inconsistent Bolshevik*; the man with the sincere conviction of being 'the authentic Bolshevik', and who, precisely because of this inconsistency, could become the defender of the revolution of 1956 – an indefensible cause when viewed from strictly Bolshevik premises. Moreover, Lukács was a constant critic of the half-heartedness of Khrushchevite promises to take a self-critical look at socialism – a half-heartedness which he himself shared in many respects, philosophical as well as political. The third figure was Nagy. This man, through his inner torments, through that struggle between anxieties that is indeed dependent upon great moral qualities, had transcended Bolshevism. He merits a great place in the history of radical movements.

The first dimension of Nagy's historical role has already been discussed: he was *the first Eurocommunist*. In fact, he was *anti-Khrushchevism personified*. Instead of employing grandiose and bombastic phrases in the service of a paternalistic consolidation of Stalin's decaying work, Nagy had taken self-criticism – the moral and political responsibility of Bolshevised socialism for the degeneration of an originally emancipatory cause – so seriously that it had literally become for him a matter of life and death. His presence at the head of a government that sanctified the (social and national) emancipatory deed of a nation was the symbolic act of returning the power usurped by Bolshevism to those who alone could be both its source and its daily implementers; the 'masses', often respectfully alluded to in myth, always mishandled and oppressed in practice. Let us add, in direct rejection of Lukács' remark quoted above, that all of this happened without 'liberal illusions' – at least, in the case of the Prime Minister, who himself had very specific provisos for his remaining in office, provisos that amounted basically to the exclusion from the cabinet of all parties that had not been registered in the immediate post-war situation, when the general trend pointed not to communism, but at least towards the left. But, one could remark, honourable as such a role of being a proto-Eurocommunist is, it is also a closed chapter in socialist history, and is generally so in radical leftist history. All those who wanted to, have learned the lessons. And even if Imre Nagy was indeed, as we assume, the first Eurocommunist or, rather, *Eurosocialist*, this is at best a historical question of an honest self-criticism, one which is obligatory for the *now* Eurocommunist parties which *then* slandered his life and celebrated his murder, or at least remained silent about it.

And, indeed, the features that make Imre Nagy's honest life and stoic demise more than a tragic and sublime chapter of revolutionary history, and which resurrect him as a protagonist of the present, can only be gained by a sketchy reconstruction and a reinterpretation of the stages of this development. In doing this, we rely mostly on the book by Miklós Molnár and László Nagy.

To begin, it is important to know that (after the formative experience of his arrest and court sentence in the 1920s, during which trial he behaved in a courageous way that foreshadowed much of what was to come more than thirty years later) he became a '*deviationist in the agrarian question*', an advocate of the democratic land reform and partitioning – not nationalising – of the huge estates. This is important not only because he constantly preserved his heretic views in agrarian problems, making him the obvious choice of the Soviet leaders, and not only because he became acquainted and intimately worked together with Bukharin, but also because there was, right from the start, an element – and a visible element – in all his agricultural heresies which grew into a central factor in his later political strategy. This was the demand for a political strategy *based on confidence*, and without which a reasonable agricultural strategy is not conceivable.[41] This is the first appearance of the principle of consensus in his strategy.

We have mentioned (to the extent necessary within this framework) Nagy's 1953 'new policy speech', and also (very briefly) his fight with the Rákosist apparatus, which he finally lost, with the result that in March 1955 he was ousted from the leading body of the party, and later from the party itself. Here we only have to list the features that indicate this gradual transition. On the surface, Imre Nagy appears to be nothing more than the most resolute Khrushchevite politician in a period when Khrushchevism had not yet existed.[42] *Substantively speaking* – that is to say, taking a sociological inventory of the elements contained in it – his speech could easily be published in Kádárist Hungary (minus the name of the author); it would even appear *démodé*. In itself, not even his insistence on the rehabilitations is wholly his invention. Nagy himself remarks in his *Memoranda* that Khrushchev, in a conversation with him on 1 January 1954, urged the accelerated process of rehabilitations and blamed its slowness on Rákosi.[43] At that time there was a fair chance that he might have become what Kádár had in fact become: the model Khrushchevite. Even so, three elements discernible in his attitude in this period do in retrospect suggest something *above and beyond* a model Khrushchevite. The first is his persistence *in a consistent policy objective of grasping the whole of social life in a given period*. The incoherence of Khrushchev's and his mates' speeches was not only – and not even primarily – the result of an incapacity for clear thinking. Kádár, for instance, according to all fair reports, is a remarkably lucid and coherent man. But, first, no Khrushchevite speech should contain the condemnation of the *entire* preceding period, since even then, even amidst the most horrible crimes, the 'construction of socialism' went on without disruptions: continuity is emphasised through all minor discontinuities. Secondly, the more incoherent a speech is, the greater the room it provides for totallly opportunistic tactical manoeuvring. Kádár is a master of these deliberate incoherences.[44] Nagy put an end to these tactically useful ambiguities, and his main ambition was (and the theoretical success of it is irrelevant here) to work out as consistent a theory of a new phase of socialism (or a new approach to the problems of socialism) as possible. Further, he tacitly shifted the locus of decisions affecting a nation's life to the nation itself, instead of waiting for decisions from Moscow. Undoubtedly, he tried to keep as good a contact with Moscow as was possible (and lost in that competition against Rákosi). But we have suggested that his 'new policy speech' was something more than just a smooth tactical change in line with directions from Moscow; and in March 1955 he resolutely brushed away all attempts at mediation on the part of

Suslov, even though he must have known from the Moscow confrontation that deliberalisation was, at least for the time being, the prevailing opinion in Moscow. This was in fact the first time that he had questioned Moscow's authority. Finally, in harmony with this, a tone appeared in his speeches that was regarded by the average (and sometimes even by the oppositional) communist as nationalistic, but which was simply a language comprehensible to those brought up via a Hungarian – religious and lay – literature, instead of being a shabby replica of party reports from the Soviet Union.

In the period between March 1955 and 23 October 1956, Nagy was to question much more. He started with the prerogative of the dictatorship *to initiate and suppress all social movements from above.* In other words, his attitude contained the demand of at least a degree of *political pluralism.* Obviously, we are speaking about the existence and activity of the so-called Imre Nagy group, later an important factor in his 'legal murder. Here we have to follow closely the valuable analyses of Miklós Molnár and László Nagy, who established to begin with that it would be superficial to consider Nagy as the 'Hungarian Gomulka'. The Polish politician intrigued and won in the upper reaches of the party alone, whilst the Hungarian opposition centred around Nagy 'attacked the established power from the outside, as it were; at its basis', and not only in 1956 but earlier on, in 1955.[45] Further, these two authors meticulously characterise the composition of the Imre Nagy group, which consisted of the following subgroups: (*a*) his immediate entourage, personal friends, and collaborators; (*b*) a representative group of writers and scholars that spoke for at least the higher-level communist intelligentsia, and which gave voice increasingly, and more and more irresistibly, to the general popular dissatisfaction; (*c*) a group made up of a certain type of party functionary – in part, economists, and particularly experts of agrarian questions, and, in part, the dissatisfied elements of the ideological apparatus; (*d*) the so-called 'Rajkists', some of whom were accused along with ex-Minister of the Interior, László Rajk, executed in 1949, and some of whom were members of the International Brigades, and were exposed more than others to the barrage of the Abakumov apparatus.[46] But the term 'attacked the established power from the outside' needs some further qualification, especially taking into consideration what purposes it later served in court. Miklós Molnár and László Nagy made it clear that this term has to be understood between two extremes. On the one hand, the Nagy group had never been a secret conspiratorial centre (no amount of effort on Colonel Sumilin's part could conjure up *any* evidence to that effect); nor was it, on the other hand, 'His Majesty's opposition', a kind of clamorous busybodying of offended or neglected functionaries vying for what was up for grabs. Least in question is the Kádárist characterisation: it was of course no longer a Bolshevik type of action. The authors mention an internal division in the group regarding the objectives (whether to reduce the goal to a reform within the party or organise something broader and not only communist in character), but basically they give a correct description of the Nagy circle when they call it a *pressure-group*. The pressure-group moves within two borderlines. On the one hand, it proceeds towards creating a public sphere broader and freer than that officially allowed, and takes certain risks by doing so. On the other hand, it is not at all the aim of the pressure-group to overthrow the existing power. It does not declare the authority of this power to be non-binding, for it wants to exert pressure *on* it, not *against* it. That the latter was characteristic of the Nagy group and of Nagy himself is detectable from the fact that he simply sent his *Memoranda* both to the Central Committee and even to Andropov himself. This gesture was sometimes regarded as naïve, even though it was most consistent with the method of functioning of a pressure-group. It is important to emphasise here that any secret conspiratorial activity is in flagrant contradiction to the very essence of a pressure-group.[47]

What was the *content* of these famous *Memoranda*, which the author sent only to official authorities but which, as the main document of the pressure-group, were circulating in Budapest, certainly not on the initiative of Nagy but equally certainly not against his will? Here he went a significant step farther than in the question of organisation, which is a typical inner contradiction with committed Bolsheviks. Very characteristically, in his conception the initial step should be – and here we must closely follow the highly unusual terminology – the liquidation of the 'Bonapartist dictatorship' of the Stalinists 'which had crushed with one blow both reaction and the young Hungarian democracy . . . by destroying the democratic allies of socialism'.[48] The term 'Bonapartist' needs some explanation here, given that the Hungarian Stalinists to whom it was directly applied did not (and could not) have any military aspirations. In all probability, this was a substitute for the

'Thermidorian' characterisation of the Stalinist regime, well known for its Trotskyite connotations to everyone with a party schooling, but it basically meant that overnight the Khrushchevite Prime Minister proceeded to elaborate a theory of the universal degeneration of a power which called itself socialist.

The next step would certainly be ridiculed by sophisticated Althusserians for its simplistic and 'ideological' humanism and 'moralising' character, but we do not quote it simply because in this lurid atmosphere created by Serov it provided a minimum of hope for humanity. There are other generally important features of the position, for example, the following:

> The members of the party and the Hungarian people as a whole do not desire a return to capitalism. They desire a regime of popular democracy which would be the incarnation of the socialist theory, a regime which would take account of working-class ideals, *in which public life would rest on ethical foundations*, which would not be governed by a degenerate Bonapartist power *and dictatorship*, but by the working people itself in respect of law and order. The people would be master of the country, and would control their own destiny in a native land in which the life of the state and of society would develop under the emblem of love and humanism.[49]

Our italics here serve two purposes. First, we want to show that, whether wittingly or unwittingly, Nagy had introduced a *language* (for instance, rejecting the dictatorship *tout court*) which made him and his way of thinking no longer compatible with any kind of Bolshevism, including a reformist one. Secondly, though we shall return to the problem of what he here called 'ethical foundations', it should be noted that whilst we are convinced (and we have argued for this elsewhere) that politics should not (and cannot) be moral-led it is still the case that political activity, especially radical democratic or socialist political activity, must have some moral principles, otherwise it will degenerate into a system of tyranny. Nagy could be naïve and innocent (as indeed he was in the theoretical questions of morality) but the fact that he had sensed the need for such moral maxims spoke for the breadth of his perspectives.

In all probability, Molnár is right in stating: 'Nagy's comments do not imply that he had any intention of re-establishing the former coalition parties in reparation for the wrong done to them by the installation of a communist dictatorship. Until the revolution Nagy wanted the Popular Front to be the medium for his ideas.'[50] But his Stalinist adversaries showed themselves to be better judges of tendencies than he was when they sensed the threat in his 'Four Principles' elaborated in 1955, which are as follows: (1) the separation of state and party powers; (2) the reorganisation of state administration so that the communities and the departments would not be under the authority of the Ministry of Interior; (3) the reinforcement of the role of the parliament and of the government (to the disadvantage of the party's power, as the cult of the party survived the cult of Stalin); and (4) the reorganisation of the Popular Front.[51] Obviously, this was an inconsistent programme or, rather, one that had not been thought through, for if all these changes had been seriously intended, as they were in Nagy's case, they would have turned out, sooner rather than later, to be incompatible with the prerogatives of any single ruling party. (Naturally, the Stalinists were not preoccupied with inconsistency but with any degree of effective meddling with their *absolute* prerogatives.) But even in these half-hearted and internally contradictory suggestions the dominant question had been touched upon: *the source of legitimation*. If there can be such a thing as a 'cult of the party', if it is not a concession but a *right* (of the parliament, the government, the Popular Front) to be at least relatively independent, then the party as the sole and absolute source of legitimation is shaken in its position. This is clearly no longer identical with any theory of the 'dictatorship of the proletariat'.

Finally, the passages dealing with foreign-policy principles are most telling, and foreshadow the drama of the revolution. The relevant quotation is the following: '*Our country must avoid participating actively in the conflict of the blocs*, must avoid allowing itself to be dragged into a war or used as the field for battles and manoeuvres. In all these questions one must allow a nation the right to decide for herself, beyond any possibility of argument'.[52] The comment on the possible shade of meaning is correct as well: 'He demanded a new federation of Danubian states strong enough to handle its own destiny' – here appears in a concrete form what we have called the 'norm of synchronisation of East European history' – 'which would maintain close relations with the USSR, but would be able to set up its own socialist society in conformity with the requirements of its own situation, and would remain in every way outside the power blocs.'[53] After all this, the later abrogation of the Warsaw Pact should no longer greatly surprise the reader.

The next phase of Nagy's political activity (the second last one) was that between 24 and 28 (or perhaps 30) October – one of the most criticised (and slandered), from several directions. On the one hand, there was (to begin with, quite a strong) disillusionment on the part of many of the 'men in the street' who had earlier lionised Nagy. He did put his name to the appeal to the Soviet army, and he did let a speech be broadcast that, even if it was in marked contrast to the aggressive threats of Gerő, and later the hardly less threatening talk by Kádár, the new First Secretary, was still one in which he called the tragic events 'counter-revolutionary' in character. It took a great amount of determination and the convincing talent of a genuine statesman on the part of the Prime Minister to regain his fading popularity. Nor should we believe that the first and confused gestures were all camouflage. Even if he had already transcended the boundaries of Bolshevism, there remained in Imre Nagy (as in all reformist communists) vestiges of the old instinct first to condemn (or at least distrust) the people for seizing arms, and then to think afterwards. The second type of criticism is straightforward, but, as Miklós Molnár correctly puts it, romantic: that when it turned out that his name was put to the appeal to the Soviet army Nagy should have left the Central Committee building on 24 October and identified publicly with the insurgents. But here we are again dealing with scenes from nineteenth-century patriotic frescoes rather than with political realities. Such an act would have resulted in a butchery ten times the size of that which finally took place, and would have put an end to any chance of the revolution articulating its demands. The third 'criticism' is the chapter written on these days in *The History of the Hungarian Revolutionary Working-Class Movement*: a chapter which displays Serovian moral principles and a logic unfit for a grammar-school essay, but which, precisely because of its undisguised hatred and bias, contains certain important admissions of his enemies.

In actual fact, after having committed the double mistake of allowing himself to be pushed into a politically suicidal speech before the Parliament late in the evening of 23 October, and then accepting next day the position of Prime Minister, without having a strong group of his own in power positions (which left him isolated between hysterical or resolute political enemies), Nagy had only three courses open. The first would have been Kádár's future option: putting down the uprising and the general strike with false promises of a future 'democratisation', and then increasing the rule of terror. That would have been a straightforward course, but it is a source of certain types of greatness in history (for which nations feel long-lasting gratitude) that some people do not readily admit that the shortest distance between two points is a straight line. The second course would have been resignation, and leaving the political scene for good. In all probability such a gesture would have saved his life, but equally certainly it would have left a nation exposed to its enemies, alone and without any leadership (since no other of his group had anywhere near his degree of authority). It would also have meant the betrayal of his earlier policy urging action. The third course, and that actually taken by Nagy (in our view, with ever-increasing deliberation and premeditation), was the politics of paralysing the Stalinist action, which, with a strange reference to the Biblical quotation that 'all they that take the sword shall perish with the sword', simply wished to crush the uprising – and all types of resistance, if need be – through carnage. He relayed the popular demands to the members of the central apparatus who were ready to understand the democratic and radical meaning of the message, and led constant talks with the Soviet leaders (from the 25th onwards, Andropov's political authority was supplemented by the presence of Mikoyan and Suslov, who carried the weight of the Presidium with them) in order to attain evacuation. This was the *only* political course that could save the short-lived Hungarian revolution, provide it with the possibility of self-expression, and pass on its message and political legacy to a posterity which can squander or fulfil its heritage as it sees fit. We can only be grateful to the 'chroniclers' who in their blind hatred have erected a statue of the Prime Minister in the education of future generations by confirming his role of paralysing the impatient executioners of the Hungarian revolution.[54]

This reconstruction of the phases of Nagy's oppositional career (except the last) provides some features for us to begin to sketch the portrait of *a new radical political militant*. First of all, he was one of the most remarkable specimens of a novel type in political activity: the *post-Machiavellian* politician. This century has seen various sorts of 'politics of ultimate ends' at their most horrendous: a fanatical zeal filling the world with terror apparatuses and annihilation-camps, losing in the process all their fanaticism and principles, and leaving behind them the sheer brutality of power alone. The reaction was predictable: an enormous increase, both on the left and on the right, of a self-conscious and even conceited pragmatism (with a Machiavellian twist) as an alleged safeguard against the horrors of ideological and moralising politics. But, for a number of reasons (which we cannot even begin to touch upon here), in this world of superpowers and nuclear stalemates – a world which survives only with the greatest difficulty – a post-Machiavellian politics is needed: a politics which would not deduce its legitimation from Rousseau's 'general will' (neglecting and violating the 'merely empirical' will of all), which would not combine in virtue and terror a neo-Jacobinism, and which would not pompously believe in the omniscience of those purely pragmatic and short-term moves that would inevitably lead the world to the brink of self-destruction, and perhaps even push it into the abyss. In a long process of self-education in which he had been stripped of both the vestiges of Bolshevik zeal and the religious belief in the mystical 'general will' (whose representative is the party) but during which he had never become a liberal or a social liberal but had remained radical, in a development the result of which was not a new political doctrine deduced from moral principles but an absolute and unconditional belief that only a politics having moral maxims at the forefront of its activity deserves the name of 'socialist', Imre Nagy stands before History as one of the first great representatives of the post-Machiavellian politician.

Secondly, Nagy had also become *a statesman of the craft of forging consensus*. We have mentioned the part that confidence played in his early considerations about the correct communist agrarian policy, and we could witness how this partial principle of his had grown into the demand for a new consensus. But this statement needs further qualification. First, one could remark that the world certainly did not have to wait for a disillusioned communist (or for a new type of radical, if you wish) in order to discover the principle of consensus – an old maxim in liberal politics. Even so, in analysing the 'consensus in the making' of the 'new republic', we did point out what *specific* attributes this *novel* principle of consensus presupposed and obtained. It was a consensus with *substantive restrictions* and with *unrestricted formal liberties*. The underlying idea (which had never become theoretically clear in Nagy, who was a philosophical dilettante) was a revolt against the system of dictatorship over needs and *a demand of the recognition of all needs except the ones which presuppose the use of others as mere means and which are identical with a system of exploitation.* This is a principle of consensus which is not only a tautological repetition of well-known liberal maxims, but which is also thoroughly incompatible with any kind of liberalism.

Nevertheless – and this objection is being put from a quite opposite direction – is *the principle of consensus compatible* with any kind of *socialist* politics at all? Is it not necessary, even if a socialist politics has not degenerated into a system of 'Bonapartist dictatorship' but remains, true to its promises, the domination (not the dictatorship) of one class, or a combination of social classes and groups, over the others, that such a rule should entail the exact opposite of any kind of consensual politics? We think that Nagy's remark in his *Memoranda* that not even the interests of the working class should be counterposed to the national interest testifies to his being at least partly aware of this dilemma. We cannot deal here in depth with the problem, but two factors can be pointed out. First, the substantive restrictions in the new consensus undoubtedly exclude certain ways of life (leading to exploitative needs) and, in so far as they do so, they presuppose a system of *hegemony* (a cultural hegemony in the Gramscian sense). But such a system of hegemony is not only based on substantive restrictions, but equally upon unrestricted formal liberties; consequently, socialist politics and consensus can be reconciled. Secondly, no one has suggested that the schema of the 'new republic' was *a model without conflicts*. Even if we disregard the possibility of an attempt at a capitalist restoration in the event of an eventual electoral victory of parties having such an aim (which is strongly – even overwhelmingly – counteracted but not absolutely excluded by the council system), the fact remains that the 'new consensus' is not a final settlement. Its rebargaining anew and anew belongs to the specifically radical–democratic character of the 'new republic'. And it was in this particular sense, in the sense of recognising all needs except the alienative–exploitative ones, that Imre Nagy became a statesman forging a consensus of a *novel* type.

In addition to this, Nagy exhibited a further quality: he was the type of political personality the *anti-authoritarian revolution needed and will always need*, whenever and wherever it occurs. That he had temporarily lost his popularity is more often emphasised than the obverse: the incomparably more surprising fact that the crowd clung to him, despite false appearances and certain wrong (but never treacherous) moves. He emanated an air of confidence, and as a post-Machiavellian politician could be trusted by the top of the political caste (as the case of Béla Kovács described by Kővágó demonstrates), even though mutual trust is not habitual in this stratum; and equally trusted, after he had made certain decisive gestures, by the simplest man. But it was far more than personal confidence that underlay his political appeal; that made him indispensable to this anti-authoritarian revolution. In contrast to popular misconceptions, such a revolution neither needs – nor does it tolerate – charismatic leaders. This is so for the perfectly simple reason that charisma by definition means the transfer of legitimation into the leader's will and personality, and this contradicts the principle of a democratically created consensus. Nor would a commanding man of conservative authority, such as the Cardinal Mindszenty, have been acceptable to the rebellious subject on the streets of Budapest, even if we now disregard the exact and easily predictable content of his programme. But Nagy was neither charismatic nor conservative–authoritarian. He behaved as a democratically appointed (and daily reappointed) *arbiter* who gladly took on his shoulders (for he felt it to be a moral duty) the nuisances of this 'chaos' and daily reappointment; who incessantly negotiated with often-colliding interest-groups; who tried to forge, make and remake the new consensus. In this he was inexhaustible, imperturbable and determined. From the impact of events and the advice of his friends, he was always ready to learn; but people who regard him as a political pushover, a man receptive to each and every demand of any random group, either belong to his slanderers or simply misread the *gradual* maturation of his ideas.

Finally, but not at all of least importance, Nagy restored the *national dimension* of radical socialist politics. This century has, on the one hand, prostituted the idea of internationalism, has perverted it into an expansionism of secret travelling envoys and emissaries who have introduced to various countries Stalin's Turkish methods of government, often without even bothering to learn the language; and has, on the other hand – and as a reaction – given rebirth to the most vulgar 'socialist' chauvinism: a politics incompatible with any kind of democracy, let alone the radical type. Nagy's plan of a Danubian Confederation was a polemic against both these political styles. He rejected the transfer of national legitimacy from one nation into the other, the 'fatherland of all workers', and had abrogated thereby a basic *Leninist* (and not only Stalinist) principle.

If it is true (and we believe in Jorge Semprun's maxim) that everyone should die his or her own death, then Stalin succeeded in robbing a generation of revolutionaries not only of their life, the meaning of their life, but also of their death. But the Nagy 'trial' was a reversal of this truly infernal trend; this attempt to debase the humaneness and dignity of even a dying man. This was solely due to the just as wise as unassailable heroism of the Prime Minister of the Hungarian revolution, conscious of his duties to the very last moment, when he went to the gallows with the programmatic words: 'Long live the socialist and independent Hungary!' Not only did he die with simple grandeur and in full awareness of the burdens that both dignity and his self-professed moral–political maxims imposed on him, but also his death, just as he did the last phase of his life, transcended the bounds of the purely individual. With a measure of Hegelianism, we could say that Hungary needed some good examples to be set on the part of the leaders of her systematically fallen revolutions – men who constantly provoked destiny but then abandoned their followers to their fate.[55]

In Hungary's long and mostly tragic history, the leaders of fallen revolutions and wars of independence behaved after defeat with an at least questionable sublimity. The best of these were the aristocrats. There was the Prince Rákoczy, who after a long anti-Habsburg war of independence in the early eighteenth century, became, first at the French Court, later in the Ottoman Empire, a recluse from politics and a mystical semi-Jansenist. There was the Count Károlyi, the great Hungarian democrat who left Hungary after the fall of the first short-lived democratic republic, doing this as a sign of separation from the communist rule but, even more emphatically, as a pre-warning against the restoration of the conservative forces of the past that he predicted and feared. He later became a fellow-traveller, and one with many illusions, but he never became a tool in the hands of the Stalinist masters, and when the show-trials started he broke off, with a symbolic gesture, relations with the 'socialist' Hungary. And there was Kossuth, who, after 1849, after a republican adventure which many sceptics predicted (and correctly so) would be short-lived, had a problematic career as an emigrant that provoked time and time again the outright contempt of Marx: an émigré career ennobled only by his last long years in Turin exile, where he actually formulated (in the self-criticism of an aggressive and foolhardy nationalism) the idea of the Danubian Confederation which stimulated Imre Nagy. The worst and most self-humiliating example of behaviour after defeat was the communist retreat in 1919, a retreat that took place after a short, unnecessarily violent, and inconsiderately administered rule in which this internally weak but provocative dictatorship succeeded in betraying the earlier hopes of the Hungarian workers for a rule by councils. In his abdication speech Kun declared the Hungarian working class unworthy of being ruled by the communists but he suggested that under the whiphand of the white terror they would learn the proper lessons. Moreover, he not only left behind him in Budapest certain of his political enemies from the party (to name them, Lukács and Korvin, with the cynical dictum – as communicated to us by Lukács – that they should try to become martyrs if they had such an irresistible inclination for it), but he then also evicted Szamuelly from the train carrying the escaping government (Szamuelly, his former ally, the man of terror, and a person not at all acceptable to the Austrian social democrats). He did not, however, forget to take with him a good portion (and perhaps the whole) of the Hungarian national gold reserve, which he and his emissaries (according to Zoltán Szántó's unpublished memoirs, which we have read) later used to corrupt members of the Landler faction, a group with which he was in constant internecine strife.

And after such a history as this, Hungary needed a person who would ultimately live up to his promise. So did, after the Moscow trials, radical socialism in general. Budapest proved – contrary to Sartre's article on 1956 – that this creed was no longer the property of the communist parties. In a tortuous process of legal murder, Imre Nagy lived up to the promises he had made to his nation and to his socialist cause. But since we have often used here the term 'legal murder' we owe some explanation in order to prove that this is more than a *Kraftausdruck*. The problem also has a theoretical relevance.[56]

In the main, the document presented by the public prosecutor (as we can see from the Hungarian Government White Book, from Kopácsi's book, and from the various official descriptions of the 'Nagy case') contained three elements, each in itself amounting to high treason: conspiracy in the period prior to the 'counter-revolution' (actively preparing the way for an armed uprising); the premeditated disorganisation of the power-centres, and thereby complicity in 'counter-revolutionary crimes'; and the abrogation of the Warsaw Pact, *lèse-majesté*. All else is either verbal pyrotechnics or additional character defamation (such as the allusions in the 'scientific literature' that it was someone from the Nagy group who had singled out for the counter-revolutionaries the Budapest Party committee building in the Kőztársaság-tér as a possible target of butchery). It is plain from the above that Nagy had chosen for himself (and in our view correctly) a *double* technique of defence.[57] On the one hand, he used the technique that Trotsky had employed in his trial after the 1905 revolution, when the latter constantly referred to the fact that it was not he but the Tsarist government who had acted unconstitutionally. As a result, all leaders of the Petrograd Soviet fought for the *restoration* of an *infringed* legality and legitimacy. This was very clearly the case with regard to the third point of the charge, the abrogation of the Warsaw Pact. Disregarding now the issue of to what extent such an act can be declared at all a criminal offence, and even if we allow that Nagy could not have acted without the consent of the Hungarian parliament and the previous consultation with other Warsaw Pact countries (both are debatable points but neither would justify the death penalty), it is still undeniable that the Soviet government broke the promises *formally confirmed* by the declaration of 30 October about the inviolability of national territories of 'the socialist countries', and it was only *after* the unmistakable signs of a new invasion and a warning note to Andropov that the Hungarian government nullified the pact.

Of the three points above, the theoretically more important are the first two, in respect of which Trotsky's technique could not be used. The dilemma boils down to simply this: can or cannot the activity of a pressure-group (and we have seen that the Nagy group was a pressure-group and nothing else, and no Serovian technique could produce evidence to the contrary) be declared conspiratorial? And further: can or cannot a political activity occurring *within* a leading political body, and aimed at changing the policy of this body (and this in fact was what the 'Nagy–Losonczy group' did) without using violence or threats against it, be declared destructive of the power-centres? All citizens of a liberal–legal state will unhesitatingly answer in the negative. (One should strongly bear in mind that in the case of this being answered in the affirmative, then it follows that General de Gaulle ought to have been executed for his deliberately organised transformation of the 4th Republic into the 5th, and Nagy did considerably *less* than this.) But all

Leninists (Khrushchevite or non-Khrushchevite), for whom the supreme value, the guarantor of the desired state of affairs, and the exclusive and inappellable source of all 'rights' (or rather concessions) is the political power, the executive, the judiciary, and the legislator in one person, will answer it thus: that if such an activity leads even indirectly to the weakening of the 'socialist state', let alone a questioning of its authority from below, it *is* counter-revolutionary activity and has to be dealt with accordingly. And it is here that we can see why all the Khrushchevite propaganda about the 'restoration of the Leninist norms of socialist legality' was only ideological window-dressing serving to cover and uphold a *reduced* and *somewhat rationalised* system of terror; a system which can be – and actually is – incomparably more tolerable than the Stalinist (or even the Leninist) system was, but which still has nothing whatsoever to do with *legal order*. Any legal system deserving its name presupposes: (*a*) some sort of preliminary consensus (in whatever form it may be expressed) regarding its general principles; (*b*) a certain number of individual and collective rights that are *not* dependent on *any policy objectives* of any given executive power; and (*c*) certain formal and theoretical guarantees of such rights, and at least the formal possibility of renegotiating the basic principles of the legal system in question. Khrushchevism, in the rare moments when it spoke frankly, specifically denied all three preconditions. Consequently, its 'restored socialist legality' had only one means of dealing with people like Nagy and his group: murdering them under somewhat formalised conditions.[58]

In a way, the entire Nagy affair – the negotiations made with him (obviously involving duress) in Romania, the final decision to finish him off, and the trial – had increasingly become a test of the Khrushchevite claim to the 'restoration of the norms of socialist legality', a test which revealed that the claim was false from the start or, rather, an ideological concomitant of a *considerably rationalised system of terror*. That it is such a rationalised system, and no longer simply the cumulation of uncontrollable Stalinist purges (which hit the society like natural catastrophes, sometimes threatening the demographic equilibrium itself), is beyond doubt. But it had remained a system of formalised terror, and not a legalistic structure, the latter not being identifiable with any random principles committed to paper, because if it were identifiable the Nuremberg laws could equally claim the authority of legality. Nothing shows this more clearly than the fact that Nagy was *offered*

– publicly by Kádár, and privately by various confidential emissaries – not only impunity but also the possibility of participation in the Kádár government, an act which in itself is incompatible with any kind of legality. Either Nagy was guilty of counter-revolutionary crimes, in which case he had to face trial (and not ministerial promotion), or he was not. For the law, there is no third alternative. And this allegedly 'higher principle of socialist law', which is nothing else but an arbitrary and tyrannical principle of terror, has the effect that it can relapse at any time into plain and unsophisticated 'Leninist' terror. In his *Memoirs* of the Soviet abduction of the Czech Party Presidium, Smrkovsky relates that in the first hours he and his companions were briskly told by a Soviet major that the whole group would soon be tried by a 'revolutionary tribunal', presided over by Comrade Indra, their colleague in the secretariat of yesterday; in other words, by a modified version of the Chekist 'troika' from Lenin–Stalin times. (That events did in fact take a different turn is another matter.) Nagy's 'Trotskyite' technique of being prepared to engage in a dialogue with the adjudicating terrorists served just that purpose of *unmasking* the Khrushchevite lie about restoring any kind of legality deserving the name, and exposing it as a somewhat upgraded form of terror.[59]

But what was the *function* of the trial, particularly at such a belated date, when Hungary had long been 'consolidated' (in other words, forced into a general state of silence and fear)? The 'Yugoslav explanation', that is to say, the reference to the fact that in 1958 Soviet-Yugoslav relations were again at a low, explains at best the choice of date of the trial. It does not explain its course, and even less its intended function. They could have murdered the members of the group without a legal rigmarole (just as they did in Losonczy's case), and 'informed' the population some ten to fifteen years later that they had died in the process of investigation; they could have deported them to the Soviet Union without any explanation; they could even have tried and either executed or pardoned them without any official statement. But they went out of their way to make the legal murder known, to publicise it as an act of 'higher justice', and to make a whole nation their accomplice via a forced silence. Our belief is that this was a trial of *communist disobedience*, inside and outside the Warsaw bloc. One should not forget that *all* the executed members of the group (or those murdered without formality) were known either in Hungary or abroad as communists: Nagy in particular, and also Losonczy, and Szilágyi and Gimes only in Hungary; and it was known even of Maléter, a soldier appearing on the Hungarian political scene only during the days of the revolution, a Soviet partisan and a sentimental communist (which he remained until his last moment). There is a particularly interesting and convincing documentation to the effect that the trial was designed as a warning to the adherents of a too determined national communism, or to those carrying the seeds of what has later been called 'Eurocommunism'. Kopácsi describes a significant moment of the trial, during which Nagy's lawyer, who in a spirit most contrary to the 'higher socialist legality' decided to be a counsellor for the defendant and not an aid to the prosecution, referred, in defence of certain of Nagy's statements, to opinions expressed by representative communists.

> He keeps quoting certain opinions expressed by leading personalities of the international communist movement on the events of 1956 in Hungary. He quotes Togliatti, the first secretary of the Italian Communist Party, and Ernst Fischer, the member of the Political Bureau of the Austrian Communist Party. The presiding judge interrupts him, yelling obsessively: 'You are not quoting the "international communist movement" but shrewd revisionists who deviate from the correct line!'[60]

From this episode it is very clear as to who were regarded as Nagy's accomplices in his 'counter-revolutionary crimes'; people who, because of technical obstacles, could not be put in the dock with the accused.

However, the second aspect of Nagy's stance during his trial is of more importance than the 'Trotsky argument' about the legitimacy of his acts. This second aspect was the categorical rejection of the Kádár legitimacy. We have already pointed to the meaning of the symbolic gesture of giving his civilian status as the President of the Council, and we have mentioned that he did not apply for clemency; and these two acts, one very positive, one very negative, constituted a clear challenge to the legal and moral grounds on which it was being pretended to try him. But it is paramount that we quote here his last words, pronounced in that rare moment when a person becomes a symbol; his words that spoke for a murdered revolution, that comprised the last statement on its behalf for a long, long time:

I have attempted twice to save the honour of the word 'socialism' in the basin of the Danube: in 1953 and in 1956. The first time I was obstructed by Rákosi, the second time by the Soviet Army. In this trial, in this tissue of hate and lies, I have to sacrifice my life for my ideas. I willingly sacrifice it. After what you have done to these ideas, my life has no value any longer. I am certain that history will condemn my murderers. One thing alone would repulse me: to be rehabilitated by those who will murder me.[61]

In these words *the self-imposed spell of the Bolshevik religious creed, by which courageous people were driven into humiliation, were robbed of life's meaning (and not only by torture and blackmail), had been broken for good.* Bukharin, in an apocryphal letter, allegedly appealed to the *imaginary continuation of the same authority* that had sent him to a debasing death: to a future Central Committee. Nagy, not only in his life, but also in his way of dying, radically swept away this false and usurping authority. But let us emphasise again: these words, words uttered in an intimate closeness to a posterity already awaiting him, expressed more than a *querelle de famille* within communism. These were the last acts of a nation's revolution, and they were performed in dignity, and in unblemished greatness. This prime minister, who believed himself to be a minister in the literal sense, who believed that he was empowered by his nation, carried out his final duty, discharged his final obligation. His death – and we say this with him: his death stripped – and stripped before History – his murderers of the legitimacy that is invested in, exists for, is constituted by, *the people and the people alone*; a nation that these murderers oppress, *never represent.*

(v) Violence in the Revolution

Grotesque photos of savagely lynched people appeared in the newspapers even during the revolution, and were later reprinted several times by the Kádár government to help justify its defence of a 'law and order' threatened by 'fascists and criminals'. This visual bludgeoning created the semblance of a continuous *Krystallnacht*, a gigantic and uninterrupted chain of pogroms which, together with a Cold War propaganda on the part of those abandoning Hungary to her destiny, raised doubts even in people who had neither been brainwashed by any leftist ideology nor had ever been fellow-travellers. And since of late the Hungarian government (as already mentioned) has found a strange supporter in the person of David Irving, an admirer of Hitler, who in his book entitled *Uprising!* (London: Hodder & Stoughton, 1981) emphasises the mob and the *anti-Semitic* character of 1956, it is about time to re-examine the role of violence in the uprising. But before this we must make three remarks. The first is the simple statement of our abhorrence, after having lived nearly all our lives in a continuous atmosphere of violence, of man persecuting, torturing and killing man – an abhorrence that applies even to cases where we cannot deny the limited relevance of coercion. The second is an equally simple statement of the fact that in those days we signed all *impromptu* documents drawn up by intellectuals in protest against these manhunts and lynchings, actions which of course saved nothing except the calm of our conscience. But the third is that we do not believe that those who teach in schools the sublimity of the September massacres of the French revolution, who have remained systematically silent about the popular furore in the Spanish Civil War on the left and, what is incomparably worse, remain silent about the terror of Lenin's government, would be especially qualified to lecture about justice and humanity when a part of a nation's population resorts to violent acts only after having been treated for years by methods not a bit better than those of the Gestapo; by a government with which Kádár's regime admits a continuity, even if with certain reservations.

This being said, we should obtain information about the *exact number* of the victims of mob terror and, secondly, about the immediate events that led to such acts. We shall sum up the first with the words of Lomax:

> But the extent of such incidents should not be exaggerated, for although the Hungarian authorities have no hesitation in speaking of 'a murderous manhunt to which hundreds and thousands of communists and democratically minded people fell victim', the only figure they have ever produced for these victims is one of 234 deaths adduced in the judgment at the end of the Imre Nagy trial in 1958. In the White Books themselves, further particulars are given of 220 of these victims, of whom 164, or over three-quarters, were members

> of the armed forces of the state (85 AVH, 40 army soldiers, 27 police and 12 frontier guards). These figures are not only for Budapest but for the whole country, and include those who died in the armed defence of party and AVH strongholds, and even several who themselves fell victim to AVH bullets. Even compared to the figure of 2,700 deaths, which is the Hungarian authorities' own estimate of Hungarian fatalities during the revolution (Western estimates suggest much higher figures), the number of 234 representatives of the forces of oppression to fall victim of popular vengeance represents a relatively small proportion. Indeed, it would seem to establish the Hungarian Revolution as one of the most bloodless revolutions of all time.[62]

Accepting that we are in general agreement with Lomax's conclusion, the question still needs further examination. If we disregard the strictly humanitarian approach to the problem of violence, according to which no blood whatsoever must be spilt (to which we would gladly subscribe as a leading maxim of social action), there are *two* ways of viewing and interpreting what happened. The first is the Hungarian government's (and all Leninist systems') firm conviction that the death of one single representative of its power, whether this person is armed or unarmed, innocent or guilty, is such a crime that it authorises them to respond with any amount of retributions, executions and imprisonments. It is also an act which in itself, and irrespective of the number of victims, decides on the counter-revolutionary character of certain events. The necessary obverse of this dogmatic conviction is for those same governments to practice a terror against their subjects which is deemed legitimate irrespective of the number of its victims, and to which the only objection allowable is that made upon pragmatic grounds ('it was superfluous' or 'it was counter-productive'). Accordingly, it was a display of consistency on the part of the Kádár government that its courts hanged soldiers and officers (certainly by the hundreds, but perhaps even in far greater numbers) whose only 'crime' was that they had fought against Soviet army units following the 4 November intervention, and had done so in the firm belief that they were defending the only legitimate Hungarian government. (And this was done after the solemn promise not to punish anyone for participating in the armed struggle.) Yet this conception can never be anything but *extra-legal* and *terroristic*, for in it the very concept of murder is defined ideologically (certain acts of manslaughter qualify for murder, certain others – in infinitely greater number – do not). This perspective accepts only *one legal agent*, the party-state, as the *source*, the *implementer*, and the *sole protégé* of the 'law'; all others are a conglomerate of (potentially proscribed) subjects, not citizenry. Within this framework it is consistent that *in principle* all representatives of power are by definition innocent (and are punished for certain deeds only in an arbitrary way, either as a result of personal revenge, or because – once again a pragmatic consideration – they became counter-productive), whereas any form of insubordination on a part of the people makes them all hostage, as it were, of retributive actions, and makes an infinitely greater degree of violence on the part of government agencies 'legitimate'.

The other way of viewing what happened can be termed the *legal–liberal* approach – a manner of handling social tensions whereby, together with the legal punishment of lynching and popular justice, there is at least the *theoretical* possibility of an equally legal punishment (and not only farcical disciplinary measures) of those representatives of the executive powers who overstep the bounds of their authority, who cause a public outcry, or even uprising, with their inconsiderate behaviour, etc. More important, in all such cases there is more than one legal actor; for, at least in principle, the sovereignty is invested with the citizenry and, again in principle, the executive organs are only derivative from the former, and therefore the abstract possibility of re-negotiating the general consensus without bloodshed remains open. We are fully aware, and no Leninist–Stalinist dictatorship will make us forget, that this is only the *ideal form* of events in capitalist liberal states, where the natural impulse of government is to cover up anything done by its agencies, to preserve everything in an unchanged state. But the reality does not alter the validity of the ideal type. It is obvious that we do not accept the first conception described above, and it is equally obvious that the principles inherent in this second approach were not active in the case of Hungary. Consequently, all allusion to 'legality' is only camouflage.

What actually happened was that, during the night of 23–4 October and the following three days, the Hungarian government – through the AVH salvos before Parliament on 25 October, and in the cities of Miskolc, Győr, Magyaróvár, and in their attacks upon peaceful demonstrators who, representing an obvious majority of the nation, were demanding a renegotiation of the fundamental social issues – *declared war on the population. Thus the state of civil war set in, to which only the principles of a revolutionary natural law apply.*[63] Here two remarks are appropriate. The first is that the act of a 'government declaring war on its population' – a major principle of this 'natural law' – stems from an old revolutionary tradition. The Winter Palace salvo of January 1905 upon equally peaceful demonstrators – an attack that (according to the Bolshevik version of history) destroyed all confidence in Nicholas, and which later, and rightly so, counted amongst the grave crimes that justified *his* (of course, not his family's) summary execution; an attack that did away with the need of renegotiating then and there the 'social contract', and which was identical to the salvos before the Budapest Parliament, and in Győr, Miskolc and Magyaróvár – this act, for all radical chronicles of Russian story, was an out-and-out declaration of war on the population. We are simply following the well-established revolutionary tradition when using this language and terminology, and if one does not apply double standards, which is precisely the methodological secret of the Leninist 'class approach' to fundamental human values, one has to use this terminology in the appropriate case.[64] The second remark is that the Kádárist leadership, according to the testimony of all its official documents, has remained until now implacable in its conviction of the correctness of this declaration of war on the population. The Government White Books bitterly complain that 'On October 27th . . . resolute military action would have been sufficient to *annihilate completely the counterrevolution*',[65] and the whole chapter (frequently quoted here) on the 'counter-revolution' is one continuous jeremiad about the lack of the iron fist that would have crushed without mercy the overwhelmingly peaceful and exclusively democratic movement of their own nation, no matter what the cost in human life. Neither then (up until the moment when Imre Nagy had freedom of movement) nor ever since has the idea entered these minds that a renegotiation of the basic issues, a creation of a consensus with – instead of imposing a dictatorship upon – the masses in whose name they allegedly govern, but whom they in fact rule, would be a better idea than crushing their 'counter-revolution'. And at this point, the strange feature so surprising for Western visitors, and seemingly so sterile (out of which, in fact, many valuable intellectual exercises in Marxism–

Leninism afterwards grew) – namely the verbal duel between a government calling the demonstrators 'counter-revolutionaries' and the stubborn reply of the demonstrators (otherwise either totally unideological or, *on the purely ideological level*, not necessarily leftist) that they were 'revolutionaries' – becomes understandable as far as the function of the term is concerned. The crowd correctly felt that it was the government that had declared war on them, *and not vice-versa*; that it was the authorities who wanted to keep everything unchanged and, if need be, would employ the most brutal methods to that end. Thus they, the masses, represented the change, the innovation, the 'revolution', which also meant that they had accepted the state of war imposed on them; and they acted accordingly.

In fact, the mass violence had two distinct forms. And according to the conception of a revolutionary natural law, applicable to a situation of revolution alone, they should be judged in two totally different ways. One of them was the *manhunt of the mob* after officers, soldiers and plain-clothes employees of the hated AVH, the most spectacular and the most horrible example of which was the carnage before the Budapest party centre on the Kőztársaság-tér. A manhunt is a fascist action because its purpose is the *indiscriminate* and *collective* extermination of *a group of people* without entering at all on the question of guilt or innocence. It remains a fascist activity even if committed against fascists or such organisations as the AVH, the members of which, in significant numbers, behaved no better than fascists did. Therefore, if any (consolidated, even though not legitimate) authority later hanged the participants – *but only the participants* – of such horrors, as happened on the Kőztársaság-tér, it was only doing a service to civilised humanity.[66]

The second distinct form – and in our view a totally different case – is represented by the public execution of the AVH soldiers and officers in Magyaróvár and in Miskolc: persons executed in the first instance not because they were soldiers and officers of this organisation but because they had acted in a certain way. Here is Lomax's description of the event: '[On 26th October: Győr] News came of a massacre at the nearby village of Magyaróvár, where the AVH *turned their machine guns on an unarmed demonstration* in the village square. The crowd had included many women and children, and almost a hundred people had been killed, some two hundred more wounded.'[67] This event, which resulted in an armed uprising, led to the subsequent execution of three or four officers by the crowd. It cannot be emphasised enough that these machine-guns were directed against *peaceful demonstrators*. Now, there are only two possibilities here. Either the Hungarian government, in office until 30 October or 1 November, gave confidential orders to its secret police forces to shoot at any gathering of people *irrespective* of its peaceful or armed character (in which case the insurgents were pathologically magnanimous in turning their fury only against AVH officers) or, what is more likely, the AVH acted on their own, according to the long and successful training that all such organs of oppression with unlimited powers get. *In either case* we cannot find any difference between these and other popular acts of justice which, for instance, were experienced by *identified perpetrators of war crimes* in the concentration-camps during the aftermath of the liberation. Lamentable as it is, this is how even the most generous and kind-hearted crowd behaves in a state of war imposed on them in which no legitimate authority other than their insurrected selves exists.

Leninism began its historical career by turning war into civil war; but on the streets of Budapest, by returning with a foreign army as its sole remaining trump, the Hungarian Bolsheviks completed a full circle: they had transformed civil war into a war against their own population. This element, always present in the events from the early hours of 24 October onwards, contributed to the fury of the masses and their inclination to violence. They not only felt themselves being driven into a state of war by a just as foolhardy as inconsistent, just as hysterically cruel as irresolute, authority; they also felt offended in their national feelings. As a result, the *slogans* were vehemently anti-*Russian* (not only anti-Stalinist) but, strangely enough – and this is said in great praise of the Hungarian revolution – the actual behaviour of the population was not at all racist. Naturally, not much love was lost between the Hungarian population and the Soviet soldiers (even though there were some sporadic elements of fraternisation). But there were no traces, with the exception of one horrendous killing of a wounded Soviet soldier by a woman doctor (!) (later justly executed for this monstrosity by the Kádár government), of the methods that the Spanish *guerilla* had employed in practically every village against isolated members of Napoleon's army. And when, in the phase subsequent to 4 November, people restrained themselves from employing such gruesome methods of ambush upon Soviet soldiers and their Hungarian police forces (a method which generally concludes in a decimation of the population and a moral self-debasement of the militants themselves) this desperate and betrayed revolution made a great and manifest display of soberness and humanity. As is well known (though this is already beyond our story), they resorted instead to the weapon preferred by the epic battle of a general strike against foreign invasion: a quite unprecedented and unique example of collective action and consensual discipline.

Two particular aspects of the violence in the revolution – or, rather, of its salutary absence – should be mentioned here. The first is the question of *anti-Semitism* raised by Irving's book about the Hungarian revolution. In this matter we can perhaps be objective witnesses along with the many dozens of our next of kin who perished in various Nazi concentration-camps. It was certainly a painful experience for us that, after many a year of coercively effected silence which, together with all political manifestations, included the Jewish question as well, we could hear again in those fateful days anti-Semitic statements from passers-by on the streets. We always knew that Hungarian anti-Semitism could not disappear in a mere ten years (and how could it have disappeared in what Beria described as a 'Jewish kingdom', with the emphatic presence of Jews in the Political Bureau and at the top of the AVH?). Nevertheless it stung when we heard the well-known words of abuse again; and, even though they were only sporadic, they went unpunished and without public rebuttal. (One of the few comforts of the Rákosi era for Jews, which made many of them fanatical apologists of the most horrendous acts of the regime, was that as Jews they were protected against the public manifestations of anti-Semitism.) On the other hand, there is a simple and objective criterion of the anti-Semitic or non-anti-Semitic character of a revolution: the presence or absence of violence, of *pogroms*, against Jews. And here the following statement of fact will suffice. Whereas in the short history of Hungary's more or less (rather less than more) free period of parliamentary regime between 1945 and 1948 there are two pogroms (in the full and visible presence of a police force with many Jewish officers), no pogrom or even attempt at a pogrom occurred during the days when the people had full access to weapons. Equally important is the fact that, despite a clamorous official propaganda which is ready to identify all insurgents with the criminal elements of the underworld, and in a situation when in fact all prison gates were forced and all prisoners released, there were still hardly any acts of criminal intent (looting of shops and the like). The Kádár government has made declamatory speeches about such crimes rather than proven them. Of course, no romantic enthusiasm helps in understanding hard social facts; and if there had lacked some sort of a reorganised police force, either at a municipal or a central level, or at both, the Hungarian revolution in the long run would have faced serious problems of public order. What we simply deny here is the claim of a city dominated by manhunters and hoodlums, a vision that existed only in the imagination of the Stalinist enemies of the Hungarian people.

In view of this, can we state with a clear conscience that there was no threat of coming retribution? Even if we here disregard the Kádárist statements in the party version of the events, with their usual credibility (they 'knew' that a 'big pogrom' was being organised for 5 November), we cannot with absolute certainty answer the question in the negative. The first source of danger was the generally unstable attitude of the subject of this dictatorship over needs. Having been brutally manipulated, and not only misused but daily cheated by all authorities, this subject was not only deeply distrustful, but also unstable enough – as mishandled people usually are – to be receptive to that transformation that sees absolute incredulity become hysterically excitable and childishly naïve credulity. Practically all gossip (about secret Stalinist plots, newly uncovered torture-chambers of the AVH, and the like) was given immediate credit, and since the collapsed regime had, indeed, done nearly everything of which only a pathological mind is capable this was not particularly surprising. The second source of danger was presented by the appearance of conservative authority on the political scene: Cardinal Mindszenty. Strangely enough, it was a priest who had given voice with the greatest emphasis and with the widest publicity to the spirit of popular vengeance, even though he did not visibly display this spirit when referring to the necessary trial of the 'guilty men of the regime'. Apart from the fact that all Hungarians over thirty years of age may have had some knowledge of the 'impartial and independent' courts that this archbishop and advocate of 'historical continuity' must have had in mind, there is also an important theoretical–moral question implied in his attitude – a question recently put on the political agenda and resolved in an exemplary way by the Portuguese, equally raised and resolved in a horrifying way by the Iranian revolution. Both these countries have a long history of conservative semi-fascist tyrannies, and had two equally hated and dreaded omnipotent political police organisations, the Portuguese PIDE and the Iranian SAVAK. In the first case, because of circumstances with which we are partly acquainted, partly unacquainted, in Portugal (to our knowledge) no member of this murderous organisation was either condemned to death or executed, whilst on the other hand the Iranian revolution began with exemplary executions of their own home-made Kaltenbrunners and Serovs. This latter process had initially been accompanied by certain admissions on the part of 'progressives' that regretfully this odious work had to be done. But even these people must have soon realised that the cycle of retribution was moving beyond the punishment of mass murderers to include the sickening and inexcusable butchery of homosexuals, adultresses, and members of national minorities. This development, of course, was not a 'closed circuit', a self-feeding process, but was conditioned by broader social factors and considerations; the moral balance is, however, menacing and instructive. On the whole, one can say that it 'pays better morally', to use an expression only apparently utilitarian, if some of the guilty men (except Nazis – but not *only* Nazis) escape punishment for their crimes against humanity, rather than letting the process of justice degenerate into a triumphal march and carnival of vengeance. And, whilst in speaking about these hours of struggle we took sides unhesitatingly with the people in their cruel and unenviable duty as the dispensers of swift and artless justice for the bloody acts committed against them, we utterly oppose any *principle* of mass retributions after a victory.

This is why we consider Bibó's *constitutional* guarantees, which represent a spirit exactly opposite that of the revengeful act of the Cardinal, to be so crucially important. Point 3, subpoint (*a*) of his draft constitution prescribes the following initial act of clemency: 'Amnesty must be given to all denominations of political crimes and to *all crimes of which it can be stated that they have originated from honest convictions*; the abolition of the death penalty.' And subpoint (*b*) prescribes the reorganisation of state and factory personnel on the basis of qualitative selection but with institutional guarantees that such reorganistion will not be prejudicial to people who had the benefit of 'accelerated courses'.[68]

But it is also important to understand something of the dimensions of the retribution subsequent to the revolution. The Kádár government was careful *never* to release *any* documentation which would have shown how mercifully they punished the 'cruel counter-revolution', which according to their official documentation, the White Books, resulted in the death of 230 of their representatives. Let us assume that the casualties of the 'events' include the 230 victims given by them, the majority of whom have fallen in action. In that case, the remaining 2,400 indicated by the White Books had either fallen in action on the revolutionary side or were simply killed, and can be regarded as *their* victims. This would give a relation in *favour* of the 'cruel counter-revolution', though we do not yet know anything of the executed. But these simply cannot be the true numbers. In this area few facts are known, but still the following can be stated with certainty. First, they have hanged (and in larger numbers imprisoned) people of the type to whom the government solemnly promised impunity: soldiers and armed insurgents whose only 'crime' was that of fighting a foreign army.[69] In the case of non-military insurgents it was the simple Turkish technique of giving non-binding pledges to the *giaour*; in the case of the military men it was a somewhat more sophisticated bending of the rules: they had committed treason against a government whose leader was executed by the Kádárist government as a traitor. Secondly, Béla Biszku, the man of terror in his capacity as Minister of the Interior in the worst years, and an eminent disciple of the Serov academy, mentioned in a somewhat inconsiderate speech in Parliament that there were 60,000 imprisoned men in Hungary in 1958. Now, if we take again the official numbers from the pre-revolutionary October 1956 (3,000 political and 10,000 common criminal prisoners), and double the number of common criminals (there is no reason at all for doing this except that it makes our point absolutely clear), then we are left with 40,000 political prisoners in a country of 10 million, and this is *without* counting those executed, and in particular not counting those other tens of thousands who were in internment-camps without any kind of court sentence for periods ranging from three months to three years, a fate that could be prolonged on the basis of a simple administrative order, formally issued by the public prosecutor's office, and practically at the 'request' of the political police. Thirdly, among the people that we have asked and who have spent many years in various prisons, there was *unanimous* agreement about *daily* executions in the horrible period of 1957–8. But it is an official fact that nine members (!) of the Ujpest Workers' Council (!) were *executed* in 1959, three years after the 'counter-revolution'. After all this, we are fully entitled to ask plainly and simply: who were the real perpetrators of massive violence, and against whom?

(vi)   Kádárist Hungary: The Product of a Crushed Revolution

Nations, these anonymous–collective entities (or, less mystically, the subjects who constitute them) are utilitarian in the sense that they constantly measure gains against losses. In terms of such a calculation, was the Hungarian revolution a gain or, rather, a loss for the nation? The answer to this will not be simple. If we only think of the many thousands of lives (any realistic assessment will produce no lesser a number) extinguished in the years of terror (1957–9), if we operate with this absolute yardstick, the balance cannot but be negative. We have to add to this not only the tens of thousands who had spent many years in prisons, but all those who have constantly had to – *and to this very hour still do* – live under unceasing police surveillance, who have silently suffered social disfavour, who are forcibly underemployed (unless they perform 'favours' for the regime). To be a '56-er' is still a very heavy burden in Hungary. Recently, in 1977, an additionally (and this time irrationally) brutal reprisal *a posteriori* – a decree depriving the once-imprisoned of a considerable part of their state-guaranteed superannuation (because of the years spent in prison on the 'expenses of the state') – has abandoned many of them to endure their final days in poverty. Their political life ineffaceable, politics still haunts them, and will haunt them to their death. This is an indicator which surely shows a *negative* balance.

But, then, on one occasion we heard an old peasant saying: 'Things have become more tolerable since the revolution has triumphed.' (And this was not a single case.) What could this phrase mean in the mouth of an old peasant, a man who was obviously not communist, and of whom it was clear that, if he had subscribed to any kind of 'ism', he was an 'anti'? It meant, very simply, that in order for a nation to be crushed it also *had to be bribed*. Since this section does not claim to be the story of Kádárism, but simply its characterisation as the product of a crushed revolution, we shall not go into the many methods, devices and social channels through which this collective bribery of a nation is being effected. The statement of the very fact of an ongoing bribing will suffice here: a policy which, for instance, in the case of our old peasant, meant a much more realistic agrarian policy, with more concessions, than that before the revolution. If he did not attribute this change to any generosity of the ruling apparatus, but to the salutary fear put into them by being expelled from power for a few days, he was absolutely right.

But, deeper still, Kádárism has wrought a change the importance of which transcends the bounds of simple bribery via an expanded range of consumer goods: it has *redirected Hungary back to the traditional national course of her distorted development*. This may sound cynical, but if we know to what this change should be compared we shall immediately see that this is not a value-free statement, but to some extent, tragic as it is, is positively value-laden. The Rákosi period was totally *outside* Hungarian national development, crippled as it has always been, and it can only be measured with the yardstick of life that obtains in territories that have been under direct Turkish administration for 150 years. Very simply, it was a period of *direct Russian rule*. Should we sum up the extremities of this Orwellian era, we could say with the brevity of a maxim that it ranged from the extermination of vineyards (wine was the number one agricultural product of Hungary) to the proscription of a considerable part of the national literature. And even though brutality has always belonged to Hungarian life, in the form of the oppression of peasant masses by an aristocracy and the landed gentry, this was still not identical with the life of the Russian serf, which borrowed many of its features from the *masters* of Russia; from the rule under the Tartar yoke the vestiges of which enlightened Russians – for instance, Pushkin – so vehemently hated in their own nation. Now, it was precisely this Tartar character of Russian brutality which the 'first and last Jewish king of Hungary' had successfully imported, and this was a rule that not even the cynicism of the gentry could have dampened. Kádárism has effected here, too, an upgrading and streamlining of the system of oppression. The regime, with its executions and mass imprisonments after 1956, is now not less brutal, but it implements its policy in ways and through channels which are more adequate to a *national*, even if *deeply distorted*, history. (In order to prevent any misunderstanding here, it should be stated that for us the measure of normality is the development of nations with democratic or at least consistently liberal traditions.) It has been particularly successful in producing a reversion to two traditional character features: to the *cynicism* which is now *bon ton* in all bargainings with the authorities and, in a strange combination with the former, to an increase in the *respect for authority*, a traditional feature in a nation – especially of its *older* generations – that has practically always existed in submission to forces which have decided its fate. (Even though the 'masters' would make a mistake if they overestimated this tendency in the overwhelmingly anti-authoritarian subject of the dictatorship over needs, it could still be said generally to hold true.) Ever since the time when this authority has existed in part as a repressive *pater familias*, and not only as a brutal and commanding voice in a foreign uniform, it has contributed far more effectively to this rule.

But there is at least one aspect in which we can speak of gains, and do so without irony. Since the Hungarian masses were resolute enough to fight out their social and national cause against a tyrannical state power that had declared war on them; since they stood firm and did not collapse immediately in the face of an overpowering military superiority; since they 'called the bluff' of those Western powers promising them guarantees and giving them nothing – because of these things, *for the first time since the national war of independence in 1848–9* (which was a social revolution as well) *it is the world that has a debit against Hungary, and not the other way round*. Of course, the question of Hungarian responsibility in the First World War is a debatable point but, whatever the actual measure of this responsibility may have been, it was not in proportion to the 'punishment' that the victorious powers meted out to Hungary in terms of bereft territories. But it is beyond doubt that the Hungarian ruling classes (in this respect often supported by chauvinistic masses of the poorer population) were senior partners in an intricate system of a national oppression of several minorities, and shared thereby a part of the Habsburg responsibility. Even more lamentable is the balance in the Second World War. Hungary remained, in fact, Hitler's last ally. Its lower classes did not have the strength and the organisation, its upper classes the resolution, to make at least a final bid to escape this entanglement, dangerous as such a move may have been. The Hungarian military, and not only the organs of repression such as the *gendarmerie* and military *gendarmerie*, behaved miserably in the Ukraine, and parts of them committed blatant war crimes in Yugoslavia. What is more shameful, the Hungarian authorities pushed 600,000 Jews into railway wagons destined for Auschwitz, and thereby became partners in producing the *third largest* quota of the Holocaust. Though it is true that they did this on German orders, the Hungarian people stood by in silence, and did not make the slightest gesture of support. Such things do not make a pleasant record, but to all indications, if we can go by the writings of leading Hungarian non-Marxist intellectuals (once again, with the sole exception of István Bibó), the nation rejected even the idea of admitting at least partial responsibility for what happened. The reason is obvious. Hungary felt in its defeat immoderately and unjustly penalised (as compared to neighbouring nations who were hardly more morally exonerable) in being subjected to foreign occupation. The latter fact in particular changed the efforts of those communist theorists trying to convince the nation about the necessity of inner reform, turning them into either vain (even if sincere) attempts (in the case of Lukács) or, on the part of those on the payroll of the occupying authorities, into arrogant lecturing (in the case of Révai). And because this 're-education', though it took place in the name of a very sporadic and weak Hungarian *democratic* tradition (a constant point of reference in Lukács' and Révai's essays), very soon became nothing more than what the communist *practice* of democracy means it is small wonder that these people found an unsympathetic, though of course silent, audience, and one that was sometimes even bullied into feigning jubilation.

Perhaps we are not being too optimistic if we say that *potentially*, though up until now *only* potentially, this situation has changed as a result of the first democratic and radical mass revolution of Hungarian history; a revolution that brought its cause, even if only for a few days, to the point where its ultimate contours could become visible. In a world where superpowers cynically collaborated, in which radical causes betrayed so often their original aims, where movements with an emancipatory message degenerated into various sorts of conservative and fundamentalist tyrannies, the Hungarian October, with the outlines of its socialist (because radically democratic and self-created) 'new republic', emerges unspoiled and promising; a cause capable of instilling moral and social self-confidence into a nation desperately needing it. *This is a gain, even if it is still only a potential one.*

But the present state of affairs, with its many everyday ups and downs, is disconsolate. Of course, Kádárist Hungary became the pet of the Western liberal press, partly for reasons such as there being 'nice, ordinary discos like at home', but also for the obviously more substantial reason that it has the best organised, least irrational – moreover, instrumentally rational – and therefore *to some extent* tolerable system of oppression. And if one went to the trouble of making some comparative studies (and these would hardly need to be in-depth examinations) this statement would undoubtedly be verified. But there is one basic lie about Hungary: the lie about an *allegedly existing compromise between the government and the people*. There is no such compromise and, under the present conditions, one could not even exist.

There are two criteria in the absence of which we cannot speak of any real compromise. The first is the *autonomous* (even if sometimes restricted and only *relatively* autonomous) existence of various social factors which possess a measure of social power, though this might not necessarily take the form of an armed force. These more or less autonomous forces may be wholly institutionalised on both poles (this is the situation between entrepreneur, state, and trade unions in the most liberal of the capitalist countries), they may be only semi-institutionalised, or perhaps even tolerated without formal institutionalisation, but their relative autonomy and separation from one another is an absolute precondition of any genuine compromise, which comes about as a result of collisions between them. The second precondition, which appears to be less 'solid' but which is in fact a very substantial factor, is *the ultimate readiness on both sides to come to terms*: in other words, the recognition of the limits set by the rules of the game as binding, and the equal recognition of certain authorities within them. (Of course, the particular limits recognised as binding change over time, but within any given period there *must be* some (both overtly and tacitly) accepted limits, otherwise we are in a situation of revolution.) These authorities must carry at least a degree of legitimation created either by a public or by at least a tacit consent, otherwise they cannot become arbiters in situations of social conflict.

Now, a compromise in Kádárism is just as impossible as it is in the most brutal Stalinist dictatorships (say, in North Korea or Albania) because within it *there is no autonomy of any social force* (except for the 'autonomy' of the apparatus from all of social life – in other words, its domination over it). This situation exists for two reasons. First, because the apparatus *does not want to come to terms with the population*: it only wants to give orders to it and, at best, to make concessions to it. Secondly, because although this apparatus possesses a *consolidated* authority it has no *legitimised* authority, and hence can never function as an arbiter without oppressing this population.

Let us start with the last factor. What are the circumstances by which the Kádár government is consolidated (in fact perhaps the most consolidated of all governments of the Warsaw countries), even though not legitimised? First of all, there is the brutal but *goal-rational* oppression of the revolution. One would make a serious mistake in supposing that the mass reprisals following the revolution were an irrational raging of vengeance. Undoubtedly, there were many elements of (even personal) revenge in it, the more so the more that matters were in the hands of the local security commanders, men who were mostly cowards during the storm and bloodthirsty bullies when restored to power by the Soviet tanks. But the whole procedure presented a much more cold-blooded and ruthless scenario. There had to be *a large enough number of executions (and long-term imprisonments)*, otherwise they could not attain the necessary level of salutary terror, especially within the working class, in whose name they ruled. But terror could not be allowed to become excessive, otherwise it would turn into its opposite: if people do not have anything to lose, they resort to the means of Spanish *guerilla*. In certain cases, people could be simply finished off (as with the Losonczy murder), but generally everything had to happen *'legally' and without physical torture*. And this latter stipulation was not invoked primarily for the benefit of the Western press. They had such a bad reputation in those years that they didn't give a damn what was written about them anyway. (Some of them built this reputation upon a brutal inner indifference, others upon a desperate cynicism, fully aware of what they were doing.) 'Legality' was necessary so as to convince people that they would be afflicted only for certain types of 'deeds' – in other words, for *disobedience*, and not irrationally, in a random manner, such as had occurred under Rákosi. For, in punishing disobedience, one teaches *obedience*. Going by this 'logic', one substantive implication, for example, was that confessions obtained under duress became worthless. Finally, it was all-important that as many militants as possible *should deny, if not the whole cause, then at least their role in the revolution*. The organs of persecution did not need a crash course in Max Weber to know that for value rationality to remain valid *people are needed who uphold the value under duress*.

So the resistant ones had to be broken, and the authorities were ready to do this: *admission* not of facts, but of *guilt*, meant life – as, for instance, in the spectacular case of Kopácsi, who, being the Police Commissioner of Budapest, and having opened the police arsenals for the insurgents, in Kádárist terms would have deserved the death penalty to a far greater extent than the journalist Gimes, who did not bow and was hanged. The second factor of an unlegitimised but firm consolidation was the *covert but constant hints at the isolation of the cause of the revolution by the Western powers*. These occurred almost publicly in the first months, when every means were allowed, and later in a more restrained form, but still with unmistakable glee. Such reminders have never ceased to be part of Hungarian politics. Thirdly, and briefly (we repeat that we are writing here a history of the revolution and not of Kádárism), it is important to note that the Kádárist apparatus has never regained the arrogant self-confidence that 'brother' apparatuses constantly testify to (and which has, for instance, brought the Polish leadership to catastrophe three times in one decade). They have never wholly forgotten the revolution that begot them, and with a Machiavellian sophistication (mainly due to the capacities of their leader) have designed a system of oppression as goal-rational as possible under the given conditions. Finally, the fact mentioned above, that they have reverted to a *national pattern of oppression*, has helped them to find, even though remaining in the position of masters, a language that is to some extent in common with their people. All this adds up to the consolidation of *government*, not the legitimation of a *system*; and the latter, *as it stands*, having never been accepted by this nation, is illegitimate precisely in this sense.

The Kádárist apparatus also made sure that the factors that could lead to the other basic condition of a genuine compromise, *the relative autonomy of any social force from the apparatus*, should be completely effaced. The general conditions for the elimination of autonomous social factors and their dynamics were supplied by the restoration of the dictatorship: the oppression and formal outlawing of all forms of opposition and pluralism (including pressure-groups), the scrutinising of all social life by one centre, and the like. But there were also special Kádárist techniques which, increasingly from the early 1960s onwards, guaranteed the semblance of a situation in which a compromise apparently existed, when in fact no compromise existed at all. The turning-point in this play was the ingeniously designed and totally unexpected gesture of ever widening the decrees of personal amnesty, a strategy that concluded in the general amnesty of 1963, a move that evidenced both the consolidation and the self-confidence of the regime, but which also eased the tension of a long period of persecution, thus augmenting this consolidation. Yet the methods of affecting a compromise (instead of introducing a real one) had been forged during the worst period of reprisals: the strategy of repression being *selective*, striking not the obedient tools of the regime but the truly disobedient elements, and crushing even the mildest form of opposition (strengthening simultaneously the disposition to servility); the strategy of *rewarding*, for all acts of recantation, and especially for the recanting of personal principles; and the strategy of *prevention*, of having all social life riddled with informers so as to warn *prior* to the act rather than punishing afterwards.

All this created an appearance of calm and the cheap illusion of greater legality, though in reality it merely meant that the apparatus of oppression worked more effectively than before. Furthermore, a certain amount of criticism not affecting the vital questions of social life had to be, on the one hand, *sincerely encouraged* (without people being trapped by such encouragement, as was usual in the Rákosi period) but, on the other, totally *atomised*. The usual form of this is an invitation to 'have a conversation with the party', which means a sometimes fairly outspoken and cynical encounter with a highly placed official: an encounter that usually remains without consequences but which will not incur persecution (though it is often tape-recorded) as long as it remains private and never assumes the form of any *collective petition*, which can be punished very severely by the law. This wise policy of not increasing the level of terror was supplemented by a consistent policy of small concessions, but always under two conditions. The concession must not be institutionalised, otherwise it would become a *right* autonomous of the executive–legislative–judiciary, and it must *preclude* any pressure, *never following and yielding to it*. Not even demands admitted as just are accepted by the regime, if such pressure precedes them. In the former sense, Kádárism, with all its 'liberalism', remained a police state; in the latter, a tyrannical, even though rational, paternalism. The leaders persist in the policy of group and individual corruption. It is not a clandestine practice as in all 'socialist countries', especially with regard to the leading *apparatchiks* and the intelligentsia: it is a more or less *overt ethics*. 'The party likes those who can ask favours of it', said Aczél, the then secretary of the Central Committee, himself a puritanical man with a deep contempt for those being corrupted by him. And, of course, as far as their main interest is concerned – the creation of an *ostensible* compromise – they are right. They were especially successful regarding the officially accepted ideological intelligentsia, whom they could corrupt and transform into a talented agency of the main Kádárist lie and technique of domination: maintaining the myth of a compromise. To that end the state licence of anti-socialist cynicism is issued to the propagandists of 'real socialism' as well. The Hungarian intellectual, arriving at a conference on state finance and, as a representative of the state, telling everyone 'confidentially' that he or she is 'of course not taking any of this seriously' – this person is an important pillar of the regime, suggesting that there is everywhere real freedom in it, a freedom which is totally and extensively supervised from the buildings in which so many were executed and who knows how many murdered.[70]

If we disregard the two general sociological preconditions of a genuine compromise, the *historically* given preconditions of a genuine compromise between Kádárism and the Hungarian population would be the following. The first is the *institutionalisation of at least certain rights* creating a measure of autonomy *for at least some social forces*. This may happen in the Yugoslav form, as a 'gift from above', in the Polish form, fought out on barricades and strike campaigns, or in many other ways. One cannot simply confront history with scenarios elaborate in *minutiae* in advance. The second precondition is the transfer of at least a part of the *national sovereignty* from the 'fatherland of all workers' to where it properly belongs: to the hands of the Hungarian government, even if the latter is only a consolidated and not a legitimate government. This could be effected through refraining in the future from any military action against *any* ally of Hungary within the Warsaw bloc, as the deeply despised Romania did in the case of Czechoslovakia – by far the most courageous and most honest act of the Ceasescu leadership. If need be, this risk should be taken, even though it may have significant cost. And it would be very indicative of a free and democratic (preferably socialist) Hungarian future if such radicalism characterised not only treatises written in security but also the behaviour of both responsible social actors and the man in the street – people exposed to very genuine dangers. The third precondition would perhaps be the most difficult one to attain: that

Kádár return (without following the recipes suggested there) to his speech of 1 November 1956, which admitted that a new Hungarian history had begun on 23 October of that year, the day of social freedom and national independence. Let us avoid all misunderstanding: we are not counsellors to the Hungarian government and, even if we were, we would not advise this government, which owes its life to the death of a revolution, to take up exactly the same intentions that it annihilated a quarter of a century ago. This would be an impossibility. We simply state that, without actually admitting what in fact happened at that time, without admitting that the events constituted a national and social revolution and not the uprising of a reactionary mob, and especially without admitting just who the real victims were, a government based on a true compromise, and not its fraudulent substitute, will never come about. Indeed, perhaps such a government never will. Then so much the worse for the strategies and plays which in their entirety constitute its system of domination.

Miklós Molnár, a loyal chronicler and defender of 1956, declared the revolution to be a 'monumental mistake'. Precisely because we know that Molnár – and so many other non-utilitarian defenders of 1956 – does not have *gains through, but meanings and patterns in, social action* in mind, we have to object to his argument with the following: if they wish to state that Hungary 1956 has become *obsolete*, has become discarded by historical 'progress', then their statements are simply misleading. We are fully aware of how problematic the concept 'progress' is, even in its most limited meaning. For instance, this is how Carlos Semprun Maura, in his *Révolution et contre-révolution en Catalogne*, sums up the outcome of a classic counter-revolutionary period:

> Irony, which exists in everything, appears in a striking manner in the modern history of Spain, since it is 'francoism' which has realized the communist programme – that is 'the bourgeois revolution'. Certainly, like the ailing daughter of old syphilitics, this bourgeois revolution, born late, has not had from its sisters, the gift of a cultural and social renewal, the increase of democratic liberties, or the disappearance of ancestral prejudices . . . But, to use the language of modern Marxists, the economic basis of the bourgeois revolution has been created – even though Spanish Marxists deny it.[71]

This certainly is a debatable (and in fact a much debated) sentence, and it is one that was committed to paper with knowledge and honest conviction. But we doubt that anyone motivated by similar feelings could write anything like this about the crushed Hungarian revolution. *For the first time in Hungarian history*, a revolution was so radical that none of its main objectives has been discarded by a subsequent, even if 'syphilitic', development, as was the case with at least a good portion of the demands of 1848 during the period of the 1867 *Ausgleich*. And what were the radical demands of the Hungarian revolution which have never even come close to being realised? First, the restitution of total national sovereignty. Secondly, the democratisation of the work of socialisation by a system of direct management, which would have put an end to the dictatorship over needs and which, at the same time, could have prevented a capitalist restoration. Thirdly, people have learned from the early naïveté of attempts at creating a system of councils. Such a social experiment, if unaided by reliable political agents in the political sphere – a sphere in which the people, despite a supplementary system of direct democracy, can have only indirect representation (at least, for the time being) – may easily be betrayed, misused, and made totally empty; fit only for throwing away. Because of this, the crowd in the Hungarian revolution not only demanded a full restoration of general civic liberties (of religious confession, of a free press, and the like), but also specifically demanded a system of political pluralism – though, of course, one that would be closely watched by an attentive populace instructed by earlier experiences. A final addition to this is a document of the utmost importance, Bibó's 'Draft of a compromise solution of the Hungarian question' (in our view, a plan of action that would have become highly popular) – a combination of substantive restrictions and a formally unrestricted system of liberties. In their entirety, these features reveal a new experience in the modern history of political revolutions, with *direct mass action at the pinnacle*, irrespective of the ideologies actually expressed and manifested by those crowds. One cannot say that *any* of these radical demands has even partially been realised. Consequently, the Hungarian revolution and its programme remain on the *general East European* agenda, even if only as a *regulative idea*.

In his last words, which reached us after a very long delay, Imre Nagy, forger, arbiter, martyr and symbol of a murdered revolution, outwardly rejected the lamentable and comical offer of being rehabilitated by those who were going to murder him, and did murder him. His will must be honoured by all those who have respect for humanity, and especially by those who understand both his work and the greatness of the Hungarian revolution.

But in the end, after all of this, who will predict with certainty that there will be no public funeral for Imre Nagy in Budapest? And if there is, and this prime minister finally retires to his pantheon, then in looking at the popular posters that accompany him it may not be so uncertain as to what slogans will be written on them.

Notes: Chapter 2

1 It is proved beyond any reasonable doubt by F. A. Váli, in *Rift and Revolt in Hungary* (Cambridge, Mass.: Harvard University Press, 1961), and particularly by Miklós Molnár, in *Budapest, 1956: A History of the Hungarian Revolution* (London: Allen & Unwin, 1971), that the Soviet armoured divisions were deployed at about 2 a.m. on 24 October, at a time when the Hungarian Central Committee was still having its stormy meeting and when Imre Nagy was still waiting in the lobby for his comrades to make a decision. But the decision did not come from the Hungarian authorities; they could only give their *a posteriori* sanction to it.
2 We have a most interesting documentation of the fact that such a conclusion had been drawn up, not only by an outstanding theorist such as Bibó, but also by others, and people who were not at all necessarily on the left. The evidence is in J. Kővágó, *You Are All Alone* (New York: Praeger, 1959), a document of inhumanity, suffering and exceptional courage, and which contains a more than acceptable amount of naïve and narrow-minded confidence in the Western democracies. Kővágó was one of the very few resistance fighters against the Nazis in Hungary. After 1945, as a young hero of the liberal–conservative Smallholders' Party, and by virtue of his immaculate anti-fascist record, he was elected mayor of Budapest – a very young person to be in such a job. It was easily predictable that he would be arrested after the communist takeover. He spent five terrible years in prisons no better than those of the Gestapo, run by men with unmistakable Gestapo-like mentalities. During this period he stuck to two fundamental principles: his passionate anti-communism and his unshakeable belief that the Western democracies, at the first available historical opportunity, would liberate Eastern Europe. He at least has the self-irony to describe in detail the foolish assessment of the actual situation to which his doctrinaire belief in the Western redeemers has led him. The *pointe* and the only elegantly written part of a weak book (but a very valuable document) is its conclusion. Kővágó, as the representative in exile of Hungary, spoke on behalf of his 'enslaved nation' in the United Nations. He was so excited during the first sentences (full of nineteenth-century pathos) that he did not realise what was going on in the hall. When, regaining calm and self-presence, he looked around, he realised that the hall was empty: the delegates had left to watch the arrival of an Oriental celebrity. The sentence which became the title of the book, 'Oh, my country! You are all alone!', burst out of him at precisely this moment. This is the feeling which we call the general, even if *a posteriori*, realisation of the fact that the Hungarian revolution fought against the *whole* of the Yalta–Potsdam edifice.
3 Isaac Deutscher, *Russia, China, and the West: 1953–1966* (Harmondsworth: Penguin, 1970), pp. 88–9.
4 It is a strange position indeed for us, as Hungarian Marxists and radical socialists, to defend Mindszenty (of all people). But ever since David Irving, who has 'scientifically proved' that Hitler was unaware of the 'final solution', and who has lately turned full circle, and has written a pamphlet against Hungary 1956, characterising it as an anti-Semitic mob uprising, and in which he accuses Cardinal Mindszenty of complicity in fascist politics – after all of this we have to say very clearly that Mr Irving simply and uncritically echoes versions of 'political realities' which are in fact clichés of Soviet propaganda. Mindszenty was undoubtedly a political advocate of a capitalist restoration. But his 'crimes against the people', the basis of his so-called trial, consisted in precisely this and nothing else: in a rightist *conviction*, occasionally a rightist propaganda, and in no conspiracy against a government whose legality was, to say the very least, itself questionable.
5 István Bibó, 'Draft of a compromise solution of the Hungarian question', *Magyar Füzetek*, no. 4 (Paris, 1979), p. 140 (our italics). In our view, this is sufficient proof that this project went *beyond* liberalism. There is one point at which Bibó (who clearly wished to avoid confrontation with the Primate) explicitly rejects Mindszenty's position. There is no need, his 'Draft' further states, for any kind of United Nations army

or police force to ensure the order or freedom of future elections. The latter is guaranteed by the fact of the revolution; the former by the unprecedented moral discipline of the nation. There is, however, one implicit limitation of liberal principles in all realistic attempts at formulating the future framework of parliamentary democracy in Hungary. It is not mentioned in Bibó's 'Draft', but the problem repeatedly appears in Kővágó's book mentioned above, in the chapters describing the wild conjectures and the somewhat more down-to-earth negotiations in the circles recognising the Smallholders' Party. The problem consists in the following: Can any number of parties, without limitations, be legally registered, and therefore allowed to compete in the electoral campaign, or would there be certain limitations? The position of Nagy – a man who had, after the honest self-laceration of a Bolshevik career lasting more than thirty years, accepted the multi-party system and the pluralist principle that were both so alien to him, but did so consistently and without tactical considerations – was that he could only co-operate with the coalition parties legalised after 1945. (Tildy, the ex-President of Hungary and himself a member of the Smallholders' Party and a state minister without portfolio, mentioned this to Kővágó in the last days of the revolution.) This was not a tactically motivated decision, either, but simply the result of the conviction that these parties, and they alone, remained intact from being compromised by an alliance with either Hitler or an internal, home-made Hungarian fascism. The Smallholders' leaders had come, after much reluctance, to the same conclusion; they were, however, led by the tactical consideration that perhaps the Soviet leaders would be ready to accept the 1945 situation enjoying their endorsement, but certainly not anything beyond that. In rough outline this is in harmony with the 'Finlandisation' of Hungary, and it means a (not constitutionally stipulated) restriction.

6 Hannah Arendt, *Crises of the Republic* (Harmondsworth: Penguin, 1973), pp. 116–17 (our italics).
7 The tragedy of the Iranian revolution, which almost immediately debased all its emancipatory promises as well as its mission, can be spotted in the fact that a conservative authority had been prepared to, and in fact did, take over after the victory.
8 Miklós Molnár's estimate (in *Budapest, 1956*, p. 134) of the number of armed insurgents (of course, *before* the second intervention) is as follows:

> According to the Hungarian Government white paper, the Buda groups on the right bank totalled 1,200; a figure which included groups like that of Dudás, whose activities were political rather than military. At Pest, the Corvin Passage, Tűzoltó Street, and Kilián Barracks groups, during the early part of the uprising, numbered 600–1,000, including the sub-groups and advance posts. In all there were 1,200–1,800 people in the central organised groups, who were later to form themselves into the revolutionary council of the armed forces. There were, however, many others whom we cannot include in this analysis owing to the lack of data and their extreme mobility.

After the second and final intervention the number of those putting up armed resistance seems to have been considerably larger for a short time, but it is fanciful to describe the Hungarian story as a *war* of independence. On the part of the Soviet army, it was rather a swift and brutal police action, and Khrushchev mentioned with satisfaction to Micunovic within a few days that the results 'were far better and much quicker than they had expected'.
9 *The History of the Hungarian Revolutionary Working-Class Movement*, the official party version of the history of the working-class movements, claims that 3,000 (!) political prisoners were released by the 'counter-revolutionaries'. If we consider that the authors' data must be a diminution of the actual numbers, and that this alleged 3,000 comprised the number of political prisoners after a series of amnesties, this is a figure which in itself characterises the prevailing situation under a 'Gerő liberalism'. *A Magyar Forradalmi Munkásmozgalom Története*, ed. the Institute of the Party History

The Impact on Hungary 161

of the Hungarian Socialist Workers' Party (Budapest: Kossuth, 1979), p. 578.)
10   C. Castoriadis, 'The Hungarian Source', *Telos*, no. 29 (St Louis, Miss., 1979), pp. 4–5.
11   Bibó, 'Draft', p. 143. This is the argument about the attitude of the West analysed in detail by us in another version above.
12   Molnár, *Budapest, 1956*, pp. 159–60 (our italics).
13   The autobiography *Khrushchev Remembers*, provides unexpected and, on the whole, irrefutable proof of the fact that such a historical moment did exist, although it is not entirely clear during which days. (In all probability, it was between 25 and 31 October.) Of course, there are only indirect indications to that effect in the text. Soviet deliberation, Khrushchev wrote, took place when they pulled their troops out of Budapest. In the meantime – and this is brand-new information – Mikoyan and Suslov remained on the field of operations as emissaries or plenipotentiaries. They did not return home, as was generally assumed by both participants in the events and later chroniclers, but rather remained at Vecsés military airport, near Budapest, which was under exclusive Soviet administration and which became the improvised headquarters of all Soviet operations in Hungary. This gives us as the latest possible days of decision 30 October–1 November, as we know now that, on 2 November, Khrushchev and Malenkov were already in Yugoslavia for secret negotiations with Tito during which they informed the Yugoslav leaders about certain decisions – we shall describe them in what follows – that had been made in the previous days. We are simply going to quote the narrative of the crucial negotiations between the Soviet and the Chinese communist parties with a few abbreviations. Even if we have to take Khrushchev's statements with a grain of salt – particularly so at this point, where other information (for instance, that coming from Yugoslav sources and reaching the State Department) stated a much greater reluctance on the part of the Chinese than portrayed by Khrushchev – two features of the events stand out quite poignantly. The first is that, although the stronger Soviet option was undeniably intervention by force, the options of the leaders were, up to a certain point, far from being closed, and in principle they could have been convinced against taking the fatal step. Secondly, whatever the Chinese boasting *a posteriori* about their 'major corrective role' was in regard to 'revisionist' Soviet policies, the Chinese were apparently inadmissibly subservient and irresolute – only, we repeat, less enthusiastic as the Russians would have them – at a moment when they in fact could have influenced Soviet development at a crucial juncture.

> This was a historic moment. We were faced with a crucial choice . . . To make sure that all countries understood us correctly on this point, we decided to consult with the other Socialist countries – first and foremost with the fraternal Communist Party of China. We asked Mao Tse-tung to send a representative to consult with us about the events in Hungary. The Chinese responded quickly. A delegation led by Liu Shao-chi flew in. Liu was a man of great experience and prestige, much respected by us . . . We stayed up the whole night, weighing the pros and cons of whether or not we should apply armed force to Hungary. First Liu Shao-chi said it wasn't necessary: we should get out of Hungary, he said, and let the working class build itself up and deal with the counterrevolution on its own. We agreed. But then, after reaching this agreement, we started discussing the situation again, and someone warned of the danger that *the working class might take a fancy to the counterrevolution. The youth in Hungary was especially susceptible.* I don't know how many times we changed our minds back and forth. Every time we thought we'd made up our minds about what to do, Liu Shao-chi would consult with Mao Tse-tung... Mao always approved whatever Liu recommended. *We finally finished this all-night session with a decision not to apply military force in Hungary* . . . Later in the morning the Presidium of the Central Committee met to hear my report on how our discussions with the Chinese delegation had gone. I

told them how we had changed our position a number of times and how we had finally reached a decision not to apply military force in Hungary ... After long deliberation, the Presidium decided that it would be unforgivable, simply unforgivable, if we stood by and refused to assist our Hungarian comrades ... So it was decided. But Liu Shao-chi ... still thought that we had agreed not to apply military force in Hungary. We thought we should inform him that we had reconsidered our position ... Liu agreed that our revised decision to go ahead and send in troops was right. (*Khrushchev Remembers* (Boston, Mass./Toronto: Little, Brown, 1971), pp. 417–19; our italics)

Perhaps the time which elapsed between Liu Shao-chi's belief that the decision was *not* to intervene and his being informed later that the Russians would in fact intervene accounts for the difference between the Chinese communiqués which Molnár records but cannot explain.

14   Bibó, 'Draft', p. 143.
15   We believe that he was simply obeying his own natural inclinations, rather than devilishly plotting with the Soviet army to nip the revolt in the bud, as many conspiracy theorists believe. But we have here no evidence either for or against this view.
16   One example will suffice to demonstrate to what extent even the feelings, let alone the opinions, of a silent majority prove to be inscrutable in these societies of dictatorship over needs. *A week before* the revolt broke out, *The Literary Journal*, mouthpiece of the rebellious writers, published a reader's letter from a certain Mr Horn, a factory technician, who expressed his doubts regarding the social relevance of the clamorous debates of intellectuals in the so-called Petőfi Circle. 'What's the use of all this?' he asked. 'The working class is, and will remain, politically passive for good, and uninterested in such hair-splitting ... and without them what good can we do?' And this inscrutability, let us emphasise for the Western leftist's sake, is *not* identical with the well-known problematic inherent in tacit consent. Arendt correctly argues that movements of disobedience, should they meet resistance on the part of the 'silent majority', immediately prove by the fact of resistance that tacit consent is not a totally negative principle, and is at least predictable – *to some extent*. Political inscrutability in the dictatorship over needs is, however, agnosticism pure and simple of the political observer, imposed on him or her by the atomising oppressive character of the dictatorship.
17   Naturally, such assumptions and estimates have to be handled with the utmost care because they are literally anybody's guess. For instance, Walter Lippmann, in the 1960s, during an interview with *Der Spiegel* journalists, expressed his view that in a free election in East Germany the slogan forged in the late 1950s – 'Ohne Ulbricht, ohne Adenauer' – would prevail, and East Germany would vote social democrat. The *Der Spiegel* interviewers strongly doubted his view. Who can say who was right?
18   Kővágó mentions the greatest example of this: Béla Kovács, the abducted general secretary of the Smallholders' Party, who had recently returned from the GULAG. We do not question the credibility of Kővágó's account, despite the scornful description of 'career-seekers' given in 1959 by Béla Kovács to the Hungarian press – a category in which he obviously included Kővágó. The gesture was not necessarily noble, but Kovács' position is understandable. First of all, he was suspicious of his ex-colleagues, who had sold him out to the communists back in 1947 but who were now full of cheap enthusiasm without being aware of Soviet resourcefulness. Secondly, they had a real political disagreement. Kővágó and others had simply wanted to return to the 1930 programme; Kovács, however (and this is very important to note when assessing the chances of success for Bibó's 'Draft' and its socialist provisos), was more realistic, and emphasised that the historical clock could not be simply turned back (Bill Lomax, *Hungary, 1956* (London: Allison & Busby, 1976), p. 133). The description of Kovács' views by Kővágó, on the basis of a conversation between them in the late hours of 1 November, reads as follows:

He knew, as I did, that the whole Hungarian nation wanted to be rid of Communism forever. There was no doubt whatsoever that this included national Communism also. But his main argument was that he knew the Russians better than I or anybody else . . . The Soviets would never permit a small nation under their domination to regain her freedom . . . His view was that the revolution must forge its own new order with bloody sacrifices. In his eyes it seemed that *this new order would not resemble a clean Western type of democracy. It would be something new in which, despite our opposition, institutions and customs established by the Communists would still remain part of the social and economic life of the country.* He was convinced that even the new order of state which was created in relative freedom in the years of 1945–46–47, belonged to the past . . . The Revolution forged the whole nation into a sacred unity against Soviet domination. *It would not be so easy to find the same unity when searching for a synthesis of the free enterprise system and socialism.* (Kővágó, *You Are All Alone*, p. 209; our italics)

We do not question the credibility of this passage for the simple reason that it is a testimony *against Kővágó and for* Kovács' political realism. Kovács' *motives* are clear: a predilection for a capitalist and liberal regime; a hatred and an unceasing distrust of *all* types of communist, including the reformists. But his political realism teaches him – and this is the crucial part of his creed – that there is no return to a Hungarian past, for this would be a return to oblivion. He attributes this *mostly*, even if not *exclusively*, to the Soviet presence in the area, whilst we overwhelmingly attribute it to inner factors, but the result amounts to the same: to the acceptance of a situation in which liberal freedoms and a socialist organisation of the socio-economic order must co-exist. And even if the just claim is made that Kovács was not representing the whole of the Smallholders' Party it would have to be equally admitted that he was most influential within it.

19   Molnár, *Budapest, 1956*, p. 124.
20   The description of this and other scenes from the prison period and the trial stem from Sándor Kopácsi, *Il nome della classe operaia* (Rome: Edizione e/o, 1979), p. 238.
21   Bibó, 'Draft', p. 140.
22   Obviously, 'consensus in the making' always contains elements of wishful thinking, and it has remained so particularly in Hungary, where it has never come to free elections. But the following results of an attempt at a representative survey may at least suggest something of the relevance of the design of such a draft constitution. Miklós Molnár and L. Nagy describe, in their *Imre Nagy: Réformateur ou Révolutionnaire?* (Geneva/Paris: Librairie E. Droz/Librairie Minard, 1959), the following surveys among Hungarian refugees of the revolution. One of these, comprising 343 refugees then recently arrived in Austria, produced the following response to the question 'Who would have been in your opinion the most desirable Prime Minister in Hungary in the year preceding the revolution?': I. Nagy, 31 per cent; G. Losonczy, 9 per cent; J. Kádár, 4 per cent; T. Déry (oppositional writer), 2 per cent; G. Lukács, 2 per cent; various and without opinion, 52 per cent. The second question was 'Who in your estimation was the worthiest of being appointed Prime Minister?' The answers: B. Kovács, 31 per cent; I. Nagy, 30 per cent; J. Mindszenty, 10 per cent; I. Bibó, 9 per cent; P. Maléter, 6 per cent; Z. Tildy, 4 per cent; others or no answers, 10 per cent. In another survey, made by the Free Europe Press in 1957, the unspecified results gave I. Nagy the priority with 35 per cent of the vote. University Marquette (Milwaukee, Wis.), in a survey published in January–February 1959 (but still made *before* the execution of Nagy and his colleagues) of 129 young Hungarians studying then at various American universities produced the following response to the question 'Whom do you consider to be the three most remarkable Hungarians of our century?': I. Nagy, 34 per cent; Cardinal Mindszenty, 31 per cent; P. Maléter, 26 per cent; B. Bartók, 21 per cent; Z. Kodály, 16 per cent; E. Ady, 12 per cent; A. József, 8 per cent (the last two are leading radical national poets). We do not wish either to exaggerate the

importance of such surveys, which can be methodologically criticised, or pretend that we are very satisfied with all their results (for instance, the surprisingly high percentage that Mindszenty scored and the total absence of the greatest Hungarian democrat, Count Károlyi, President of the first Hungarian Republic from the last survey). Least of all would we say that under *normal circumstances* (or under any circumstances, for that matter) such surveys can be substitutions for free elections. They show only so much: that the people who accepted for a historical moment the 'consensus in the making', and particularly the great personality of Nagy, who died for it and in its name, had at least a relative and short-term justification for believing that they were entitled to introduce the new and final period of Hungarian and socialist legitimacy deriving from the revolution of 23 October.

23 And we should like to express our firm view, in irreconcilable contrast to theorists like A. Hegedűs, I. Szelényi and others, that it has remained so – only people for the time being learned the 'Hungarian lessons'. Of course, we cannot deny that such a representative workers' leader as Walesa expressed, together with a contempt for intellectuals, his dislike of political parties and predilection for church authority; but, even if this was a genuine expression of a political will, it is *more conservative* (since fundamentalist) than *any* demand for pluralistic political life. We also hope that this is a minority opinion among East European workers and their political representatives, even if it is now necessarily hidden because of the obvious implications.

24 Molnár, *Budapest, 1956*, pp. 174–5.
25 Lomax, *Hungary, 1956*, pp. 100–1.
26 Molnár, *Budapest, 1956*, p. 175. Molnár himself contradicts this statement a few pages later: 'The council programmes up to November 4th were a mixture of democratic and socialist, anti-bureaucratic demands, but lacking the unanimous slogan of the Soviets of 1905 and 1917: "All Power to the Soviets"' (pp. 177–8). This is true – and this is why his *earlier statement* is not entirely appropriate. We only have to add that, according to our whole conception, we do not find this to be a weakness but an organic part of a new (dual) conception of power.
27 Lomax, *Hungary, 1956*, pp. 140–1. The passage here italicised by us raises two distinct problems which we are going to discuss later.
28 Molnár, *Budapest, 1956*, p. 179 (our italics).
29 Bibó, 'Draft', p. 141 (our italics).
30 Deutscher, *Russia, China, and the West*, p. 89. We shall shortly discuss the merits of this continuous denigration of the greatest European social post-war upheaval – the only one which deserves the name of 'proletarian revolution' in the way Trotsky described February 1917 (a description and term which we find inadequate) – but prior to this a remark is necessary. A significant historian *may* (not necessarily should) make silly mistakes too close to obscure events, such as claiming that Gerő had been murdered (which never happened – in contrast to murders ordered or assisted by him), but it is not absolutely necessary to reprint them ten years after.
31 This figure was once published in Hungary in Tibor Déry's autobiography, *Ítélet nincs* (Budapest: Magrető, 1967), and no one tried to refute it.
32 This is fact, not conjecture. Marosán, in the same unpublished part of his memoirs that we have discussed earlier, mentions the following fantastic event. In September 1956, when Rákosi was no longer in power and Rajk had been officially rehabilitated (as well as Marosán himself who had been appointed Deputy Prime Minister), the AVH circulated a 'confidential' document stating that – despite every public statement to the contrary – Rajk was indeed a spy and an agent. When he indignantly showed this document to Hegedűs, then Prime Minister, the latter promised quick action, but of course nothing happened. People do not have to be aware of such facts to gauge the general credibility of a leadership.
33 Here, for the sake of argument, we simply leave out of consideration that we simply do not accept the Soviet societies as socialist ones. Together with G. Márkus, we have written a lengthy book, *Dictatorship over Needs: A Study of*

34 Lomax, *Hungary, 1956*, p. 90.
35 Castoriadis, 'The Hungarian source', p. 14.
36 We shall come back to the 'trial' of Nagy and his group. Here only the following facts need be stated, which, according to the testimony of Sándor Kopácsi (and many others), are beyond any reasonable doubt. The 'Nagy case' had not for one moment been entrusted to the Hungarian–Kádárist leadership alone; it had been directly supervised by the Khrushchevite head of the KGB, General Serov, and his emissary, Colonel Sumilin, who *instructed* the Hungarian Political Bureau rather than counselled them. On the other hand, the Hungarian political leadership had to be – in fact *was* – implicated in these representative political murders. We know from those who participated in or contributed to the session that a Central Committee meeting in Budapest discussed and decided the sentences for the Imre Nagy group. In this case, Kádár, otherwise a champion of a miserable 'legality' whose principle is an inconsistently formalised 'sic volo, sic jubeo' rather than any penal code, tolerated a flagrant deviation from any legal formalities. Losonczy, the second man of the group, according to Kopácsi's testimony, was simply murdered in December 1957 (Kopácsi, *Il nome della classe operaia*, p. 230). The explanation is logical. Losonczy, an able wartime underground communist organiser, was first imprisoned in 1950 as an 'imperialist agent' and, through torture and humiliation, went mad and also became tubercular. When released in 1955, he regained his health, and in 1956 he was the most active (and the most hated) member of the Nagy group. When imprisoned again, he relapsed into his paranoia and made confessions like: 'I confess to being a spy on the payroll of Josip Broz Tito and Eisenhower; I admit that I incited a fascist counter-revolution against my nation and against the army of the glorious Soviet Union, the fatherland of all workers.' In 1958 such confessions were not only no longer *de dernier cri*, they were simply unpresentable in court. So Serov, obviously indignant over the bad taste of his star prisoner, simply had him eliminated. Another 'minor blemish' on the legality of these trials was that Jozsef Szilágyi, candidate for the role of Minister of the Interior, a man of irrepressible courage and whom they could not handle, was quickly 'tried' and hanged three months *before* the Nagy trial, but his execution was reported by the Hungarian press *together* with the others.
37 Castoriadis, 'The Hungarian source', p. 8.
38 But we do not subscribe to the method Hegel called 'die Geschichtschreibung des Kammerdieners', either. Yes, Nagy was a vain man. So what? In a political–theoretical analysis only the personality traits count which promote or hinder the exercise of public–political functions.
39 Marosán, in the true spirit of an ethics of *vae victis*, remarked to us with utter contempt: 'Had he remained at home, next morning he would have had all of Hungary in his pocket.' But perhaps Nagy did not want 'all of Hungary in his pocket'.
40 In this respect, Lukács had a very negative opinion of the Prime Minister. After his first fall in March 1955, when Ferenc Fehér tried to mediate between him and Nagy in order to unify the socialist opposition to Rákosi, he firmly answered: 'I am an old factionalist myself [he was referring to the 1920s]. I know how to make factions. One does not organise factions with *litterati* but with *apparatchiks*. This is dilettantish politics.' General relations between the two were fairly hostile. When Ferenc Fehér tried, during the spring of 1956, to bring the two together with the mediation of Gábor Tánczos, the secretary of the Petőfi Circle, after a week he returned with the answer that Nagy was not interested. Nagy found Lukács unreliable, believing that in the 1930s in Moscow he had not defended even his friends (which was untrue, and in all probability this negative opinion had its roots in Nagy's ineradicable and consistent hostility towards Lukács' friend in the 1920s, Révai, the first inquisitor of Nagy's agrarian policy), a theorist who did not even speak up for the writers he was friendly with and had a respect for, like Déry during the Rákosi period (which was a half-truth but, then, Nagy tended to forget that he himself was Minister of Natural Taxation, a

ministry whose only policy objective during those years was the brutal exploitation of the countryside). He made, however, a correct negative remark about Lukács which was most characteristic of his political personality. 'And the final touch was', Nagy said to Tánczos, 'the Madách article.' Imre Madách, a representative and pessimistic post-Romantic writer of the second half of the nineteenth century and the celebrated author of *The Tragedy of Man*, a lyric-poetic tragedy in the style of *Faust*, had his play outlawed and banned from the stage during the Rákosi period because of its early criticism of (mostly utopian) socialism. It was readmitted to the stage, as a symbolic act of national reconciliation, in the last month of Nagy's premiership. Immediately after his fall, Márton Horváth, the arch-Stalinist editor-in-chief of the central party newspaper, trapped Lukács into criticising the drama – an article which expressed fifty-year-old convictions but which served as an ideological rationale for banning the drama again. Of course, Lukács was innocent in this infantile act of censorship, but equally, as an old Bolshevik, he ought to have known better. Nagy initially evaluated this act on the part of Lukács as joining his Stalinist enemies, which was again untrue, but he also viewed it, *very correctly*, as a blatant disregard of an old-time Bolshevik for the *national feelings* of the population, and in this respect, and at precisely that time, he *was* radically changing his position. Lukács himself behaved in a noble way towards the persecuted. In Romania, during the months of internment and 'persuasion', he rejected any criticism of Nagy, with whom he did disagree on many points. 'Let us wait until he walks at large in the streets of Budapest, *then* I shall come up with my critical remarks.' The news of Nagy's execution drove him into a frenzy and he wanted to make some spectacular act of protest, and it took hard work on his wife's part to convince him not to do it. When now in the book *Lukács György élete képekben és dokumentumokban (The Life of György Lukács in Photos and Documents)*, (Budapest: Corvina, 1980) a sentence of his has been quoted condemning 'the liberal illusions of the Nagy group' – a sentence quoted from a manuscript which specifically defends 1956 against the charge of being a 'counter-revolution' – then the editors show themselves to be apt disciples of a Russian literary school: the Serov trend of realism.

41 This early period is to be found in Molnár and Nagy, *Imre Nagy*, pp. 18–27.
42 Just a few months before he suggested to Tito that 'perhaps' Nagy was an agent of the Western secret services, Khrushchev was complaining bitterly to Micunovic about Rákosi's stupidity and aggressiveness in ousting Nagy from the leadership.
43 Quoted in Váli, *Rift and Revolt in Hungary*, p. 148.
44 Two examples of this will suffice. In 1958, despite all previous promises to the contrary, the question of whether collectivisation should be imposed upon the peasantry was raised. There were two policy proposals on the table of the Hungarian Central Committee: the hardliners demanded forced collectivisation pure and simple, and the technocrats advocated collectivisation only up to the level where the economic resources of the country could still support it (with machines, credits, etc.). The Kádárist resolution was a combination of both, which is a logical impossibility but a very comfortable basis for the position (like God's) of taking sides with the stronger battalion. A similar example: in 1967 his *confidant*, then ideological secretary of the Central Committee, G. Aczél, coined the slogan 'Not the monopoly, but the hegemony of Marxism'. That would have meant a measure of *institutionalised* freedom. Frightened by this, the apparatus obviously put Kádár under pressure, and a few weeks later he 'explained' in a speech that the slogan was correct and remains valid but does not entail that anti-Marxist or non-Marxist views may be published.
45 Molnár and Nagy, *Imre Nagy*, p. 132.
46 ibid., p. 133.
47 ibid., pp. 145–8.
48 Quoted from Molnár, *Budapest, 1956*, p. 96.
49 We wish to emphasise Nagy's turn towards the *members*, not the apparatus, of a political party. In his renewed conception, sovereignty belonged, in a political party, too, to the 'masses'.

50 Molnár, *Budapest, 1956*, p. 97.
51 Molnár, and Nagy, *Imre Nagy*, p. 49.
52 Molnár, *Budapest, 1956*, p. 97 (our italics).
53 ibid., p. 98.
54 *History of the Hungarian Working-Class Movements*, pp. 571–8. This time we can believe them: they speak against their better interests.
55 In order to avoid the charge of idealisation (which we shall not be able to prevent anyway), we have to state here again what is generally known: that, of all the ministers of the Nagy government, Bibó alone remained in the Parliament in the early hours of November; all others, including the Prime Minister himself, looked for shelter, he at the Yugoslav embassy. This gesture could have been the result of his habitually wrong impulses, or it could have been – as Molnár suggests – guided by the feeling that in the Yugoslav embassy he would preserve his freedom of bargaining with the Soviet leaders; and, if it had happened once already, it was not *in principle* excluded from happening again. Whatever the reasons, *we positively know* (from Kopácsi, *Il nome della classe operaia*, p. 288, and from the personal communications of Lukács, Zoltán Szántó, Gábor Tánczos and others sharing his fate in the Romanian deportation, and, on the other hand, via Marosán, from those who sent him to his death) that he had rejected all offers of a compromise based on a 'self-criticism' and the denigration of the revolution. In other words, he had not simply been 'thrown to his fate'; he had *chosen* his death. The only basis of negotiations that he was ready to accept was the legitimacy created by the revolution.
56 There can be no doubt that the trial was stage-managed by mass murderers. Here is a short biography of the man in charge, this Khrushchevite Kaltenbrunner, this implementer of the 'restored norms of socialist legality'. Ivan Alekssandrovich Serov, born 1905, was already in the 1930s in Stalin's personal secretariat, in that innermost sanctum of super-political police. In 1939–40 he commanded the campaigns for the Sovietisation of Baltic countries and the liquidation of 'politically undesirable elements' there. In 1940 he was in charge of NKVD organs in the Ukraine, and in 1943–4 in charge of deporting Chechens, Ingushes, Kalmyks and Crimean Tartars from Northern Caucasus. In 1945 he was the Deputy Chief of 'Smersh' in the Soviet Zone of Germany, and in 1954–8 (the time of our story) Chairman of the Committee of State Security (KGB). (*Who's Who in the USSR, 1961/1962*, ed. H. E. Schulz and S. S. Taylor (New York: Scarecrow, 1962), pp. 669–70.) Definitely the man for the job – a worthy successor to Jagoda, Yeshov, Beria and Abakumov.
57 Of course, he could have simply remained silent as the second charged in the trial of the 'Four-member leadership', or – what amounts to the same thing – he could simply have stated provocative slogans as, according to all testimonies, Szilágyi did. But Nagy knew that in that case he would simply be murdered, and he needed even that minimum degree of self-expression granted by a mock trial in order to bring into play a posterity to which alone he wished to relay his message. It is also true that such behaviour suited his personality better.
58 As it seems from Kopácsi's book and from the general tendency of Kádárism, in contrast to an indignant Serov, who found this whole legal rigmarole just so much wasted time, the Kádár leadership timidly insisted on a kind of formalisation of the procedure.
59 If we accept the characterisation of the Khrushchevite 'restoration of socialist legality' as a *rationalised* form of terror, we shall immediately understand that Khrushchev's cynical argument against Stalin (that the Bukharin trial was 'superfluous') and Micunovic's equally cynical argument against Khrushchev (that the Nagy trial was 'superfluous') betrayed the very spirit of this *rationalisation* of terror, which boasted of being legal and humane.
60 Kopácsi, *Il nome della classe operaia*, pp. 265–6. In order to avoid misunderstandings, we do not wish to state any numerical prevalence of communists among those sentenced after the revolution. We simply do not know a thing

about the general proportions. Our statement is restricted to the Nagy trial alone.
61 ibid., p. 266.
62 Lomax, *Hungary, 1956*, pp. 127-8.
63 It is very important to emphasise that with the sole exception of the siege of the radio building mentioned earlier – a siege which almost certainly could have been avoided by a more prudent attitude on the part of the authorities – and despite the fact that from that night on more and more weapons were available, the main character of the movement of general disobedience had, from approximately that point in time onwards, consisted of *strikes* and *demonstrations*. The uprising did *not* proceed towards a general armed seizure of the symbols and tools of the executive power, which is proved by the fact (mentioned above) that the insurgents had not seized the public buildings. Let us, once again, remind the readers of Molnár's realistic assessment of the ridiculously *small* number of *armed* insurgents.
64 The event which can be regarded as the exact replica of the January 1905 salvo was that which occurred when salvos were fired from the top of the Ministry of Agriculture (a building opposite the parliament building) at thousands of peaceful demonstrators protesting against the lies (broadcast by the relocated government radio) calling the movement a counter-revolution. The number of (unarmed) victims was between 100 and 200. Later, the Kádár government, with very good reason, tried to remove this too-incriminating evidence of this act of declaring a civil war, and invented the clumsy lie that the bloodbath was the work of 'counter-revolutionary provocators'. Miklós Molnár, in his *Budapest, 1956*, pp. 144-6, with a quite scrupulous and over-objectivist documentation, proves (what the whole of Budapest took for a certainty at the time) how utterly impossible it was in this well-guarded area for 'counter-revolutionaries' to devise and implement an action like this, let alone to predict the outbreak of a new demonstration exactly where it happened.
65 Quoted in ibid., p. 137.
66 And our opinion will not be changed by the fact that, according to all indications, and also to the explicit formulation of the party history of the events, something sinister was going on in the Budapest centre of the Communist Party: the organisation of an armed force, which, given its clandestine nature, could only have been used forcibly to put down the revolution. The people murdered there were either totally innocent in all conspiracies or behaved as soldiers surrendering after a siege: in both cases they can be put to death only in the spirit of Kaltenbrunner's or Serov's ethics.
67 Lomax, *Hungary, 1956*, pp. 84-5 (our italics). David Irving's bitterly hostile book on the Hungarian revolution describes the whole event in exactly the same way, but gives the number of victims as fifty-nine, and the number of those subsequently lynched by the people as three soldiers or officers.
68 Bibó, 'Draft', p. 140 (our italics). It is very important to consider – and we shortly shall – what this exact and discerning mind meant by separating 'political crimes' from crimes 'originating from honest convictions'. The first is unambiguous: it abolishes *all* political sentences pronounced after 1948 on the simple and convincing basis that these were acts of terror, not justice, including cases in which the accused had an undeniably conservative position but was no spy or conspirator against valid Hungarian laws (of course, not in the sense that the AVH 'interpreted' this category). The second type of amnesty specifically protects men like Kádár and specifically excludes from such protection people like Mihály Farkas, former secretary of the Central Committee, member of the 'four-member leadership', head of the secret police organisation, and also his son, a colonel of the AVH, the personal torturer of Kádár during his arrest. There can be no doubt that, after the archives had been opened, material proving his role in destroying people's careers, robbing them of their freedom, perhaps their life, could have easily been found implicating Rákosi's Minister of the Interior, János Kádár. But as far as is generally known none of these acts stemmed from motives of personal sadism or personal gain: they were the acts of a man with *ruthless convictions*. The two Farkas, however, were common fascists, who personally murdered political prisoners,

and even some of their ex-colleagues who had become rivals or burdensome, swiftly moving into their luxury villas. The most repulsive case – the murder of Colonel Szűcs, another executioner, by the younger Farkas and his accomplices, and the subsequent 'expropriation' of his earthly belongings, possibly acquired in a similar way – was widely known. The latter type was, of course, not protected by Bibó's constitution. This distinction, displaying great magnanimity, ought to have been (but of course was not) imitated by the Kádár government.

69 Kopácsi mentions at least one example – the executed colonel, Mecseri, hanged together with his 20-year-old soldiers with whom he had fought against Soviet tanks – but we know of many similar events in 1957–8.

70 Let us emphasise again that we are speaking here about the *power techniques* of Kádárism in abolishing genuine social compromise and introducing its phony appearance. The whole of its socio-economic structure has already been briefly analysed by us, and this is not the place to reiterate the story. Only the following has to be stated here: whereas we simply do not have the right – when we look, for instance, at the appalling economic situation of the Polish population thirty-five years after the war – to underestimate the relative rationality of the Kádárist socio-economic strategy, we have to stress that these economic strategies did not result in overcoming the oppressive system that we call the 'dictatorship over needs' in a broader socio-economic sense, either.

71 Quoted in Hugh Thomas, *The Spanish Civil War* (Harmondsworth: Penguin, 1979), p. 917.

Index

Abakumov 39, 53, 121, 166
Aczel 155, 166
Adenauer 162
Albania x, 2, 40, 60, 151
allies 3, 4, 18
Althusser, L. 95, 123
Andropov, Y. 10, 39, 76, 93, 99, 122, 126, 132
Antonescu, Marshal 50
Aragon, L. 72
Arendt, H. 48, 86–7, 97, 102, 113–14
Arrow Cross 90
Asia, impact of Hungarian Revolution on 64ff
Asian Communism 2
Auschwitz 150
Austria 21, 23
Austrian Social Democrats 131
AVH (Allamvédelmi Hatóság) – Secret Police xvii, xviii, 65, 88, 96, 138, 139, 141–4, 168

Babeuf 16
Balkan Confederation 63
Barbusse 47
Barrot 48
Beauvoir, de, S. 116
Bebler 63
Beneš 26, 98
Beria 26, 30, 32, 37, 38, 53, 70, 71, 166
Berlin, East workers' rising 9, 25
Bibó, I. 8, 10, 11, 13, 14, 15, 16, 17, 22, 49, 52, 62, 67, 68, 80, 81, 86, 94, 98, 99, 103, 107, 112, 150, 159, 167
  Draft Constitution 101–2, 107, 145, 168–9
  Draft on Hungarian Question 12–13, 14, 67, 84, 85–6, 92, 94, 101, 107, 157, 159–60, 162–3
Bierut 53, 71
Biszku, B. 146
Bjelkin 36, 39
Bohlen 69
Brezhnev, L. xii
Britain, attitudes to Hungarian Revolution 15, 18–19, 20
  relations with Soviet Union 5ff
British Labour Party 3

Budapest Workers' Council 89
Bukharin 27, 74, 119, 136, 167
Bulganin 66, 69
Bulgaria x, 19, 40, 60

Camus, A. 116
Carter J. 23
Castoriadis, C. 31, 48, 67, 72, 91, 113, 116–17
Ceasescu 41, 155
Chesnokov 53, 54
Chiang Kai-Shek 20
China 2, 40
  attitude to Hungarian Revolution 64ff, 161–2
  New China Agency 64
Churchill, W. 3, 4, 5, 6, 7, 18, 20, 67
Clay A. S. 68, 69
Cold War xiii, 1, 3, 24, 111, 136
Comecon 41
cominform 53, 58, 71
Communist Party of France 102
Communist Party of Hungary see also Hungarian Socialist Workers' Party 12, 56, 110
  Central Committee xiv, xv, xvii, 25, 27, 72, 96, 99, 122, 165, 166
  Political Bureau 25, 143, 165
  record of 110
  support for 109
Communist Party of Romania – Political Bureau 59
Communist Party of the Soviet Union 13, 70
  Central Committee 27, 43
  Political Bureau xix, 26, 30, 37, 39, 54, 69, 71
  Twentieth Congress 13, 29, 43, 44, 52, 53, 60
Communist Systems 2, 3
  East European xii–xiv, 2
  Asian 2
Czechoslovakia x, 19, 39, 40, 50, 53, 59, 61, 98, 155
  Prague Spring xii, xiii, 42
  reaction to Hungarian Revolution 60ff

Danish Communist Party 42

Index   171

Davies 19
Dekanozov 36, 39
Democratic Socialism 13, 14, 15, 19, 44, 72
Der Spiegel 66
Déry, T. xv, 164, 165
De-Stalinization 4, 13, 25ff, 38, 43, 44
détente 23, 24, 60, 71, 94
Deutscher, I. 30–2, 72, 82, 91, 109, 110, 111, 113, 117, 159
Djilas, M. 58
Dobi I. xiv, 25, 98–9, 100
Donáth, F. xv, xviii, 112
Dubcek xii
Dudás, J. 160
Dulles, J. F. 23, 68, 69

Eastern Europe 2
  impact of Hungarian Revolution 8, 49ff, 157
  liberal parties 9
  press 50
Eden, Sir Anthony 15
Eisenhower 23, 68, 69, 165
Eurocommunism 19, 42, 44, 46, 118–19, 135
Eurosocialism 119

Farkas, M. iv, x, 25, 168
Fehér, F. 165
Fehér, L. 55
Finland 10
Fischer, E. 135
Fontaine, A. 71

'Gang of Four' 66, 167
German Democratic Republic (GDR) x, 40, 61, 70–1
Germany 21
Gerö, E. xiv, xvi, xvii, 25, 29, 38, 52, 56, 70, 95, 96, 97, 125, 161, 164
Geroe, E. 109
Gheorghiu-Dej 41, 53, 59
Gimes, M. xv, xix, 65, 135, 153
Gomulka, W. xvi, 41, 52, 55, 61, 64
Gottwald 39

Hammarskjöld 15
Harich, W. 59–60
Hartwig, M. 60
Háy, G. xv
Hegedüs, A. 164
hegemony 46, 128
Hitler 6, 20, 50
Hollós, E., Colonel 98
Honecker xviii

Horthy, M. Admiral 39, 95, 98, 111
Horváth, M. 166
Hoxha, E. 53, 54, 55
Humanité, L' 72
Hungarian
  Central Workers' Council 33, 65
  Church 112
  Democratic Independence Movement 65
  de-Stalinization 27, *see also* Kádárism
  liberalism 79–80, 83, 85, 86, 114
  liberalization 13–14, 27, 28, 32–3
  neutrality 10, 14, 15, 92, 100
  Peace Treaty (Paris) 8
  Smallholders' Party xix, 4, 84, 108, 109, 112, 159, 160, 162, 163
  social democrats xix, 4, 45, 100, 108
  Socialist Workers' Party xviii, 12; *see also* Communist Party of Hungary
Hungarian Revolution
  and anti-Semitism 137, 143–4
  and Bolshevism 118, 123–4, 142
  attitude to West 8, 24, 76
  civil disobedience 89–90, 168
  criticisms of 91–2
  democratic nature of 87ff
  'dual system' of power 103–4, 108–9
  effects on Hungary 103ff, 157
  free press 114
  general strike 89
  Hungarian attitudes to 75ff, 106–7, 110–11
  Hungarian Army attitude to 76
  as liberal revolution 79–86
  Military Political Section 112
  multi-party system xviii, 99–101, 103–4
  national consensus xviii, 77–80, 88, 97–8, 101, 127–8, 163–4
  nationalism 77–81, 82–3, 86
  occupations xvii, 88–9
  options facing leadership 30ff
  people's militia 114–15
  political direction of 103–4, 108ff, 162–3
  possibility of success 94
  significance of 5, 149–50, 157
  and socialism 106ff, 117
  violence in xviii, 137ff, 168
Hungary
  'Finlandisation' of 10, 14, 32, 37, 92, 93, 94, 160
  possible militarization of 31
  religion 81–2
  Soviet Republic of (1919) 61
Husak, G. 40, 92

Indra 134

intellectuals ix, 46, 47, 49, 53, 59, 84, 98, 121, 137, 150, 155, 162
  Revolutionary Council of 65
International Brigades 121
Iran 87, 144–5
Irving, David 10, 23, 137, 143, 159, 167–8
Italian Communist Party 43, 71
Italian Socialist Party 43

Jagielski 78
Jagoda 167
Jen Min Jibao 64
jews 7, 81, 143, 149–50

Kádár, J. xi, xii, xiii, xvi, xviii, xix, 12, 15, 39, 41–2, 44, 54, 56, 70, 72, 78–94, 100, 109, 118, 120, 125, 134–5, 136, 137, 138, 142, 144, 145, 147ff, 166, 167–8
Kádárism 41, 67, 72, 147ff, 167, 169
Kaganovich 26, 34
Kaltenbrunner 145, 167, 168
Kardelj 55, 63
Károlyi, M. Count 47, 130, 164
Katyn massacres 4
Kennedy 19
Kethly, Anna 45, 100
Khrushchev N. xii, 7, 25, 26, 30, 33, 35, 36, 37, 38, 41, 44, 55, 56, 57, 59, 61, 69, 71, 73, 78, 92, 93, 120, 160, 161, 166, 167
  'secret speech' xvi, 7, 29, 35, 59, 73–4
Khrushchevism xii, 118, 120, 133
Kissinger 17
Kopácsi, S. 95, 131, 153, 165, 167, 169
Korea 22
Korea, North 151
Korean War 3, 9
Korvin, O. 116, 131
Kossuth, L. 62, 130
Kovács, B. xviii, 4, 99, 100, 111, 129, 162–3
Kövágó, J. 100, 129, 159, 160, 162–3
Kún, B. 116, 131
Kuomintang 2

Lafargue 113
Landler, J. 131
Larsen 42
Lázár, G. 59
Lefort, C. 48
'Legal Murder' 131ff
Lenin 26, 137
Leninism 36, 71, 129, 138, 142
Les Temps Modernes 47

Levesque, J. 64
Lippmann, W. 162
Liu Shao-chi 161–2
Lodge H. C. 69
Lomax, B. xix, 64, 105, 137–8, 141
Losonczy, G. xv, 132, 134, 135, 152, 165
Lublin Committee 4
Lukács, G. xviii, 19, 59, 60, 70, 72, 95, 109, 118, 119, 131, 150, 165–6, 167
Luxemburg, R. 90

MacArthur, 3
Madách, I. 166
Malenkov 27–8, 30, 32–3, 55, 56, 70, 71, 78, 161
Maléter, P. xix, 135
Mandel E. 72, 91
Mao 36, 161
Márkus, G. 164
Marosáni, G. 37, 45, 59, 70, 164, 165, 167
Masaryk 26, 98
Maura C. S. 156
M.D.P. 12
Mecseri 169
Menon, K. P. S. 65
Méray, T. xv, xix, 68–9, 70
Michnik, A. 52, 62
Micunovic, U. 55, 56, 57, 61, 73–4, 95, 160, 166, 167
Mikoyan xvii, 126, 161
Mindszenty, J. Cardinal xix, 75, 81, 82, 84, 85, 97, 129, 144, 145, 159, 160, 163–4
Mitterand, F. 46
Mlynár, Z. xii
Molnár, M. xix, 15, 64, 66, 67, 70, 74, 76, 105, 119, 121, 123–4, 125, 156, 159–60, 162, 163, 164, 168
Molotov 26–7, 33, 34, 71
Münnich, F. 56
Murphy R. D. 69
MVD 32, 36, 39

Nagy, I. xiv, xv, xvi, xvii, xviii, xix, 4, 10, 15, 24–8, 32, 44, 52, 55–7, 59, 62–6, 70, 72, 73, 76, 81, 92, 94, 96–101, 109, 115–36, 157–8, 159, 160, 165–6, 167
  appeal to Soviet Army 78
  Draft Proposal for Second Government 65, 100
  election as Prime Minister 96, 98
  as first Eurocommunist 44, 118–19
  execution of xix, 57, 130
  foreign policy 124
  'Four Principles' 124
  as 'Hungarian Gomulka' 121

Index   173

last Government 8, 10
and 'legal murder' 131ff
'Malenkovism' of 26, 28
'Memoranda' 26, 120, 128
and multi-party system 99–100
and 'national communism' 27, 73
'New Government' Policy Speech xiv, 25–7, 94, 119–20
political beliefs of 119ff
as model of new radicalism 126ff
second Government 4, 10, 45, 100
Soviet attitudes to 25ff
trial of 99–100, 131ff
Nagy, L. 70, 119, 121, 163
'National Communism' 37ff, 135, 163
Nationalism (Hungarian) ix; *see also* Hungarian Revolution
Nehru 65, 66
Nekrich, A. 7
Németh, L. 79
Népszabság 54
New Left 46
NKVD 167
Novotny 60
nuclear weapons 8, 9, 20, 21, 22

Ochab, A. 52
Ostpolitik 100

Pálffy, Gy, General 112
Pálóczi-Horváth, G. 35, 43, 61, 70
Paris Commune 91, 115
Pázmány 82
peasants 26, 27, 52
Petőfi Circle xv, xvi, 51, 60, 162, 165
Petőfi Party (National Peasant Party) xix, 12, 108
Philby 47
Pilzen Riots 26, 98
Poland x, 4, 7, 9, 39, 40, 41, 50, 64
effect of Hungarian Revolution 52
Solidarity 107
Polish Government-in-exile 4
Polish leadership 4
Polish October 9
Popular Front ix, 22, 44, 45, 46, 101, 124
Potzdam Agreement ix, 5, 6, 7, 8, 9, 15, 16, 17, 49, 76, 159
Poznan Revolt xvi, 9, 29
Pravda 63, 92
Preobrashensky, D. 34
Pushkin, A. 148

Radio Free Europe 23, 24, 116
Rajk, J. xv

Rajk, L. xv, 60, 71, 112, 121, 164
Rakóczy, Prince 130
Rákosi, M. xiv, xv, xvi, 12, 14, 25–6, 27, 29, 32, 38, 39, 43, 44, 45, 53, 54, 56, 70, 71, 95, 101, 120, 136, 143, 148, 152, 164, 165–6, 168
Rankovich 71
real socialism *see* Communist Systems, Eastern Europe
Révai, J. xiv, 150, 165
Revolutionary Workers' and Peasants' Government xix
Rokossowski, M. 61
Rolland, R. 47
Romania x, 4, 19, 40, 41, 50, 53, 57, 133, 155
attitude to Hungarian Revolution 59ff
Rousseau, J. J. 61

Sartre, J. P. 47, 48, 86, 131
Secchia, P. 71
Semprun, J. 130
Seniga, G. 71
Serov, A. General xix, 110, 123, 125, 132, 145, 165, 166, 167, 168
Slansky 39
Smrkovsky 134
Sobieski, J. 49
Socialisme ou Barbarie 48
Soviet Union 4, 7
attitudes to Hungarian Revolution 121
Hungarian proxies 5
impact of Hungarian Revolution on, 24–42
invasions of Hungary xix, 10, 56, 76, 92–3, 96
K.G.B. xix, 23, 110, 165, 167
military and secret police 4, 39
occupation of Hungarian Parliament 10
Presidium 26, 76
post-Stalinist directions and options 30ff
press 50
relations with Hungary 10
Soviet Marxism 46
Stalin, J. xiv, xvi, 1, 2, 4, 5, 7, 9, 21, 29, 30, 32, 33, 35, 36, 38, 39, 48, 51, 53, 56, 65, 69, 71, 73, 74, 124, 167
Stalinism 22, 25, 30–1, 33, 34, 36, 41
Steele J. 70
Sumilin, Colonel 122, 165
Superpower politics 1ff, 6, 9, 16, 63, 127, 150
Suslov, M. xvii, 101, 121, 126, 161
Szalai, B. xiv, 25
Szamuelly, T. 131

Szántó, Z. xviii, 131, 167
Szelényi, I. 164
Szilágyi, J. 135, 165, 167

Talleyrand, Ch. M. de 57
Tánczos, G. 165–6, 167
Tardos, T. xv
Thomas, H. 169
Thorez, M. 43
Tildy, Z. xviii
Tito, J. xi, xvi, 2, 9, 37, 38, 53, 54, 55, 57, 62, 71, 165, 166
Togliatti, P. 43, 72, 135
totalitarianism 3
Trotsky, L. 29, 43, 87, 132, 164
Trotskyism 72

Ujpest Workers' Council 146
Ulbricht, W. 22, 25, 59, 61, 70, 71, 162
United Nations 11, 15, 16, 21, 55, 117, 159
USA 4, 6, 20, 24
   attitudes to Hungarian Revolution 15, 19–20, 21ff, 68–70
   CIA 23
   possible options for, 21ff
   press 2, 23
   relations with Soviet Union 7, 15, 17, 18, 19–21, 24
   State Department 3, 68

Váli, F. A. 28, 63, 68, 70, 71, 159
Vietnam 40
Virradat 90

Vyshinsky, A. 4

Walesa, L. 164
Warsaw Pact 10, 14, 38, 39, 41, 54, 55, 58, 61, 69, 92, 125, 132
Weber, M: 115, 152
West, the 8
   attitudes to Eastern Europe 8, 9, 15–16, 71, 152
   attitudes to Hungarian Revolution 8, 14–18, 22–4, 37, 60, 116, 150–1, 152
   attitudes to Kádár xiiff, 12–14, 150, 152, 153
Western Left 1, 3, 67
   attitudes to Hungarian Revolution 3, 42ff, 67
Wilson, W. 8
Workers' Councils xviii, 4, 48, 89, 97, 103–4, 104ff, 164
   and trade unions 107–8
   and political parties 106
writers xv, 4, 49, 72, 121
Writers' Association xv

Yalta Agreement ix, 5, 6, 7, 8, 9, 15, 16, 17, 49, 52, 76, 159
Yeshov, N. 32, 167
Yugoslavia 2, 9, 14, 37, 40, 41, 51, 53, 54, 55, 57, 58, 63, 71
   attitudes to Hungarian Revolution 53ff
Yugoslavian Independence 21

Zaisser 70
Zhukov, G. Marshal 30, 69

For Product Safety Concerns and Information please contact our EU
representative GPSR@taylorandfrancis.com
Taylor & Francis Verlag GmbH, Kaufingerstraße 24, 80331 München, Germany

www.ingramcontent.com/pod-product-compliance
Lightning Source LLC
Chambersburg PA
CBHW070612300426
44113CB00010B/1502